WOMEN, POWER, AND POLITICAL REPRESENTATION

Canadian and Comparative Perspectives

Edited by Roosmarijn de Geus, Erin Tolley, Elizabeth Goodyear-Grant, and Peter John Loewen

T0341439

Delving into the pressing topic of gender and politics, this volume provides fresh comparative perspectives on what works to promote women in politics today. Inspiring and informative, *Women, Power, and Political Representation* offers a comprehensive overview of the role women play in contemporary politics and pinpoints the reasons behind their underrepresentation.

Discussing the challenges and opportunities women face when running for office, as well as women's experiences as political leaders, this book offers a broad and thoughtful overview of the pitfalls women encounter, from gender biases to sexual harassment, in the notoriously male-dominated political arena. Featuring a range of voices that articulate a path towards women's political advancement and equality, *Women, Power, and Political Representation* is an important and timely resource for scholars, students, and women working professionally in Canadian and international politics.

ROOSMARIJN DE GEUS is a postdoctoral fellow with the Nuffield Politics Research Centre at the University of Oxford.

ERIN TOLLEY is an associate professor and Canada Research Chair in Gender, Race, and Inclusive Politics in the Department of Political Science at Carleton University.

ELIZABETH GOODYEAR-GRANT is an associate professor in the Department of Political Studies at Queen's University and director of the Canadian Opinion Research Archive.

PETER JOHN LOEWEN is a professor in the Department of Political Science and the Munk School of Global Affairs and Public Policy at the University of Toronto.

Women, Power, and Political Representation

Canadian and Comparative Perspectives

EDITED BY ROOSMARIJN DE GEUS,
ERIN TOLLEY, ELIZABETH GOODYEAR-GRANT,
AND PETER JOHN LOEWEN

UNIVERSITY OF TORONTO PRESS
Toronto Buffalo London

ISBN 978-1-4875-0754-1 (cloth)   ISBN 978-1-4875-3646-6 (EPUB)
ISBN 978-1-4875-2520-0 (paper)   ISBN 978-1-4875-3645-9 (PDF)

Library and Archives Canada Cataloguing in Publication

Title: Women, power, and political representation : Canadian and
    comparative perspectives / edited by Roosmarijn de Geus, Erin Tolley,
    Elizabeth Goodyear-Grant, and Peter John Loewen.
Names: Geus, Roosmarijn Adriënne de, 1988–, editor. | Tolley, Erin, editor. |
    Goodyear-Grant, Elizabeth, 1976–, editor. | Loewen, Peter John, 1979–, editor.
Description: Includes bibliographical references.
Identifiers: Canadiana (print) 20210183284 | Canadiana (ebook) 20210183292 |
    ISBN 9781487525200 (paper) | ISBN 9781487507541 (cloth) |
    ISBN 9781487536459 (PDF) | ISBN 9781487536466 (EPUB)
Subjects: LCSH: Women – Political activity. | LCSH: Women – Political
    activity – Canada. | LCSH: Sex discrimination against women. |
    LCSH: Sex discrimination against women – Canada.
Classification: LCC HQ1236 .W6443 2021 | DDC 320.082 – dc23

University of Toronto Press acknowledges the financial assistance to its
publishing program of the Canada Council for the Arts and the Ontario Arts
Council, an agency of the Government of Ontario.

Canada Council   Conseil des Arts
for the Arts   du Canada

ONTARIO ARTS COUNCIL
CONSEIL DES ARTS DE L'ONTARIO

an Ontario government agency
un organisme du gouvernement de l'Ontario

Funded by the   Financé par le
Government   gouvernement
of Canada   du Canada   Canadä

Contents

Part Three: Responses to Women's Electoral Under-Representation

Part Four: New Research Directions

Illustrations

WOMEN, POWER, AND POLITICAL REPRESENTATION

Canadian and Comparative Perspectives

Introduction

ROOSMARIJN DE GEUS, ERIN TOLLEY, ELIZABETH
GOODYEAR-GRANT, AND PETER JOHN LOEWEN

The number of women in legislative and executive offices has increased over the past decades. The proportion of women in legislatures worldwide has almost doubled from 14 per cent in 1999 to 25 per cent in 2019,[1] but progress remains slow. An average of 25 per cent still means women remain vastly under-represented in the majority of legislatures across the world. Women's access to executive power has seen even slower progress, with the proportion of women in ministerial positions worldwide increasing only marginally in a ten-year time span, from 14 per cent in 2005 to 18 per cent in 2016.[2] Such incremental changes suggest that the progression of women in politics cannot be taken for granted. Plateaus, losses, and backlash are just as likely as progress.

Other indicators are equally worrying. Despite more women entering politics, women remain under-represented in the most powerful political offices, resulting in a gendered division of political power across most countries. For instance, as of June 2019, women make up only 5 per cent of heads of governments and 6.6 per cent of heads of state. What is more, the division of ministerial positions is highly gendered in most countries, which means when women exercise political power, they do so primarily in "pink collar" policy fields.[3] Such patterns have important implications for women's substantive representation, with women legislators largely confined to the least powerful and prestigious offices. Nor is it clear that the increased but curtailed participation of women in politics has had downstream effects, either in the sets of policies that countries implement or in change to the way that politics is done.

This volume presents new and accessible scholarship on the state of women's participation in politics, in Canada and elsewhere. In doing so, it sheds light on when and how women can make gains in legislatures and leadership positions and on the challenges that women continue to face when they participate in politics. Contributors also explore potential solutions, most importantly various types of gender quotas, that may increase women's access to political power.

The volume is divided into four parts. We begin with a Canadian perspective, in part to understand why women's representation in politics has stalled, followed in the next section by a comparative lens that examines institutions, processes, and behaviour in other settings. Section 3 examines policy remedies for women's under-representation, focusing on quotas. Section 4 concludes the volume by providing new perspectives on the study of women's participation in politics.

In the opening section, contributors ask: where are the women in Canadian politics, and what should we understand about their under-representation? Following the 2019 federal election, women Members of Parliament made up 29 per cent of the House of Commons, thus placing Canada 58th out of 190 countries in a global ranking of women's presence in national legislatures.[4] This middle-ground ranking may be surprising in a country that is often perceived to be progressive when it comes to women's rights and participation. Yet Canada's history of women's participation is mixed. Canada has had just one woman prime minister, Kim Campbell, who occupied the country's highest political office for a brief period in the early 1990s. In 2014 half of Canada's provincial premiers were women, but since April 2019 this has dropped back to zero.

This non-linear pattern of women's access to political power in Canada is the subject of the volume's first chapter, by de Geus and Loewen, who explore the history of women's appointments to federal cabinet positions. They show that over time descriptive representation of women in cabinets has increased, in particular with the gender parity cabinets in 2015 and 2019. Yet in assessing the various cabinet portfolios held by women over time, the authors show that descriptive representation has not necessarily resulted in either substantive or symbolic representation of women in Canadian politics. What is more, their exploration indicates that women's participation in the executive realm is non-linear and fragile, suggesting that advances made can easily be lost.

In addition to political appointments, a second hurdle for women's advancement in politics may lie with voters' support for women candidates. This is the focus of the second chapter, by Sevi, Blais, and Arel-Bundock, who explore women's electoral success in the Canadian province of Ontario (the country's largest) over the course of the twentieth century. The authors find no present evidence of voter discrimination against women, suggesting that once women run for office they are elected at the same rates as men. It appears that voters, then, are not the main obstacle when it comes to women's access to political power.

A third hurdle for women may come from media reporting, since most citizens learn about political candidates through the news media. This challenge is covered by Trimble's chapter on the gendered mediation of Canadian political leaders. Trimble documents research on the *Globe and Mail*'s coverage of thirteen leadership contests in the period 1975–2012, revealing that gendered perceptions of visibility, competitiveness, suitability, and capability are pervasive in Canadian news reporting on women candidates. The gendered nature of reporting does not necessarily disappear once women achieve leadership positions, but Trimble finds evidence that once more women enter these positions their novelty status diminishes, and the news media may play an important role in shifting and challenging accepted cultural norms and stereotypes.

Finally, Bourgeois explores the intersection of Indigeneity and gender, highlighting an often-overlooked facet of political representation in Canada. Using the case of Jody Wilson-Raybould, the first Indigenous person to serve as minister of justice and attorney general of Canada, Bourgeois highlights how structures of the Canadian state, shaped by the country's colonial history, have constrained the ability of Indigenous women to participate and advance within the Canadian political system.

The next section turns to a comparative perspective on women's participation in politics. The first chapter continues the theme of challenges faced by women: Dolan, Shah, and Stripp document the experiences of fifty-five women who ran, but lost, in the 2018 United States congressional election. Using rich and in-depth interview data, the authors show that structural challenges such as family responsibilities, a lack of access to personal or donor money, lack of access to campaign staff, and lack of party support shape women's candidacies. Yet the interview data question commonly held assumptions about women's lower levels of confidence and political ambition, suggesting that many women have the ambition and confidence to (re)run for office, but they have their qualifications questioned by others and encounter structural barriers along the way. Alongside Sevi, Blais, and Arel-Bundock's conclusion that voters are not biased against women candidates, this chapter reinforces the need to look beyond voters and political aspirants as the architects of women's under-representation.

Echoing themes presented in Bourgeois's chapter on Indigenous women's experience in Canadian politics, the second chapter in this section highlights the analytical leverage that is gained by differentiating the broad category of "woman." Brown explores the dynamics of race, gender, and physical presentation encountered by Black women political elites in the United States. Situating her analysis in the example of

Black women's hairstyles, Brown uses interview data to provide an in-depth account of the negotiation of norms of respectability within both the Black community and the broader electorate. The chapter draws attention to the constraints Black women face on account of intersecting race and gender norms in politics.

The final three chapters in this section focus on women who have accessed political power but operate in male-dominated environments. Barnes and Beall look at women's legislative behaviour in the Argentine Chamber of Deputies. Using data on plenary discussions, the authors hypothesize that women could circumvent the existing power deficit by increasing their contributions to plenary speech, but do not find evidence of this. Rather, women in the Argentine Chamber of Deputies speak less frequently and use fewer sentences and words than their male counterparts. This finding suggests that existing power deficits (namely, lower levels of women's representation) reinforce other gendered power dynamics, such as the ability to participate in political debate.

O'Brien focuses her attention on party leaders, often the most powerful actors in politics. Unsurprisingly, women remain under-represented in these positions across countries and party families, with the exception of green/environmentalist parties. Across parties, when women *do* obtain the position of party leader, O'Brien shows that their policy platforms are no different from those of male party leaders, despite common perceptions that women politicians will implement more left-leaning and women-friendly policies. However, as O'Brien discusses, women's access to these positions – and their ability to maintain them – is shaped by the need to adhere to party and political norms, which remain predominantly male oriented.

Continuing the theme of gendered power dynamics in politics, Raney and Collier focus on sexual harassment, an issue that is pervasive not only in societies but also in political institutions around the world. The authors provide a comparative analysis of the development of sexual harassment legislation in the UK, Canadian, and US legislatures and show how in each of these legislatures sexual harassment has historically not been seen as a serious breach of ethics regulations. More recently, in each legislature new legislation has been ushered in, but whether these new rules will adequately address ingrained cultures of sexism and harassment remains an open question. The failure of legislatures to address these issues, both historically and currently, risks undermining public trust in these institutions, especially at a time when social norms related to sexual harassment are rapidly evolving.

Structural limitations and cultural norms that shape women's political experiences are recurring themes in the first two sections of the volume. Authors show that many formal and informal barriers to women's political power and representation remain. Women candidates, legislators, and party leaders must continuously navigate the gendered distribution of power in politics. This unequal distribution is unlikely to change until more women enter politics, which will hopefully normalize the presence of women and shift the balance of power. In the third part of the volume we therefore turn our attention to policy solutions that may produce such a shift, namely gender quotas.

Setting the stage, Hinojosa, Kittilson, and Williams offer an overview of gender quota implementations across the world. The authors review the impact of electoral systems, thresholds, placement mandates, enforcement mechanisms, and financial incentives, as well as various loopholes that parties have exploited, to explain cross-national variation in the success of gender quotas.

In the following chapter, Tan reviews the implementation of gender quotas across twenty-five Asian countries. In line with Hinojosa et al., Tan finds that gender quotas unequivocally increase the number of women politicians, but that important variation exists in the levels of success obtained. Specifically, Tan highlights the importance of a better understanding of how women candidates are nominated and selected – the "secret garden of politics" – in patriarchal societies and dynastic, weak party systems.

The following two chapters discuss electoral quotas in the Canadian context. Maillé reviews the historic lack of support for gender quotas in Canada, where women's groups have tended to advocate for training programs rather than quotas. Sociopolitical norms surrounding merit and affirmative action have long prevented the implementation of quotas in Canada. Yet, through the example of the informal – and successful – campaign for gender equality in the 2018 Quebec provincial election, Maillé illustrates the space that exists in the Canadian context for the implementation of gender quotas.

This analysis is followed by Franceschet's chapter, which discusses Canadian resistance to quotas on the basis of the particular features of Canada's political system. Using evidence of gender quotas worldwide, Franceschet shows that such quotas can be successfully implemented in countries with single-member district electoral systems; that quotas have been implemented in systems that, like Canada, value autonomy in candidate selection; and that quotas do not reduce the quality of elected officials. This section on gender quotas thus ends with the conclusion that not only have gender quotas been shown to be an effective means to improve women's representation in politics, but there are no compelling reasons why gender quotas would not work in Canada, and in other countries operating in largely majoritarian and/or localized representation frameworks.

The fourth and final part of the volume considers new perspectives on the study of women in politics. This section offers critical reflections on *why, how, and who* to study when we examine women's participation in politics. In the first contribution to this section, Dittmar advises scholars and advocates on how to strategically make the case for women's representation in politics. Specifically, Dittmar argues that women's representation cannot be seen as a monolithic enterprise, either in terms of the actors we study or the impact we think women can and should have on the political process. Finally, Dittmar maintains that we risk imposing a double standard on women and minority politicians by requiring them to justify their disruption of the status quo, rather than asking white men to justify their continued over-representation in politics.

In the next chapter, Och explores the distinction between presence and power and argues that the study of women's representation should be more aware of the role played by critical actors in political decision-making. This implies that women need not just be present in politics, but rather should have access to key positions of power where they can act as gatekeepers, agenda setters, and political insiders. Ignoring these sites of power, and their gendered dynamics, produces a superficial understanding of women's representation in politics.

Liu highlights a different challenge and draws attention to scholarship on stereotyping, arguing that more attention needs to be paid to intersections of multiple identities. Liu highlights particular challenges faced by women with queer or racialized identities, and suggests that future studies need to expand their scope to capture the multilayered identities of women.

Following on this theme, Tremblay challenges existing scholarship by drawing attention to the heterosexual lens that underlies most scholarship on women in politics. As Tremblay points out, most of that work assumes that the women who participate in politics are heterosexual and cisgender. In ignoring these dimensions we risk perpetuating the hegemonic "heterosexual fantasy" present in society, and erroneously adhere to a limited vision on who counts as a woman in our research.

In the final chapter of the volume, Bashevkin returns to the central theme: although important advances have been made in women's access to power and representation in politics, these advancements remain fragile, and challenges persist. Drawing on various examples from Canada, Bashevkin shows that women's increased levels of participation are easily halted or reversed and that women who operate in the male-dominated political arena face an increasingly threatening environment whilst also having to combat resistance from within their own parties.

Together the chapters in this volume provide a comprehensive overview of women's access to power and women's political representation in Canada and beyond. The chapters show that women face many informal and formal barriers not just when they seek to gain access to political power but also once they have gained that power. Although entry of more women into politics is not a silver bullet, it is unlikely that gendered power dynamics will change until more women do so. As the chapters in section 3 suggest, gender quotas may be a clear path towards such increased representation. Yet, as discussed in some of the volume's other interventions, descriptive representation does not necessarily lead to the substantive representation of women's interests. What is more, the current expansion of women's inclusion in politics has mostly involved white, upper-class, heterosexual, and cisgender women. True representation requires diversity. When women in politics are no longer considered a novelty, we may start to observe more substantive shifts in power dynamics and political norms. Until then, women's access to political power and representation remains fragile.

NOTES

1 Data from https://data.worldbank.org/indicator/SG.GEN.PARL.ZS.
2 https://ourworldindata.org/grapher/proportion-of-women-in-ministerial -positions?tab=chart&time=2005..2016.
3 It's worth pointing out that the top three ministerial portfolios held by women worldwide in 2019 involve social affairs; ministeries related to family, children, and the disabled; and the environment. Data from https:// www.unwomen.org/-/media/headquarters/attachments/sections/library /publications/2019/women-in-politics-2019-map-en.pdf?la=en&vs=3303.
4 Data from Inter-Parliamentary Union, January 2020, https://data.ipu.org /women-ranking?month=1&year=2020.

PART ONE

Canadian Perspectives on Women in Politics

1 Women's Representation in Canadian Federal Cabinets, 1980–2019

ROOSMARIJN DE GEUS AND PETER JOHN LOEWEN

On 4 November 2015 newly elected prime minister Justin Trudeau presented his first cabinet to Canadians. The cabinet made international headlines for being one of the most diverse in Canadian history in its ethnic and gender composition. Trudeau stated that he wanted to "present to Canada a cabinet that looks like Canada."[1] An important feature of this cabinet was its gender parity, promised during the campaign, with fifteen male and fifteen female cabinet ministers (excluding the prime minister). When asked why it was important to have an equal split between genders, Trudeau famously replied, "because it's 2015,"[2] vocalising the sentiment that in 2015 gender parity in politics should no longer be considered remarkable. Yet despite the sentiment, and although the Trudeau cabinet was not the first globally to reach gender parity – Chile, France, Spain, Italy, and Sweden, for instance, have all seen gender parity cabinets – gender parity cabinets remain relatively rare (Franceschet, Anneseley, and Beckwith 2017; Annesley, Beckwith, and Franceschet 2019).

In this chapter we explore how the cabinet appointments made by Justin Trudeau compare to cabinet appointments throughout the tenure of seven preceding Canadian prime ministers. Table 1.1 provides an overview of these governing periods.[3] Note that each prime minister usually presides over multiple cabinets, since these may change due to reshuffles, resignations, scandals, or general elections.

We first discuss the existing literature on gender and cabinet appointments and then consider the various types of representation that may be achieved through the appointment of women to cabinet positions. This is followed by an analysis of the gender composition of Canadian federal cabinets in the period 1980–2019. We find that while substantial gains have been made in some forms of representation, women still hold less important cabinet roles than men. Substantive representation, then, lags behind descriptive representation.

Table 1.1. Overview of Canadian Governments, 1980–2019

Date	Ministry	Prime Minister
March 1980–June 1984	22nd	Pierre Elliot Trudeau
June 1984–September 1984	23rd	John Turner
September 1984–June 1993	24th	Brian Mulroney
June 1993–November 1993	25th	Kim Campbell
November 1993–December 2003	26th	Jean Chrétien
December 2003–February 2006	27th	Paul Martin
February 2006–November 2015	28th	Stephen Harper
November 2015–present	29th	Justin Trudeau

Women in Cabinets

The proportion of women in cabinets has increased worldwide, but gender parity cabinets remain rare. There are various reasons for the sustained under-representation of women in cabinets in Canada and elsewhere. Claveria's (2014) distinction between generalist and specialist systems highlights some of the key issues (see also Bauer and Okpotor 2013). Specialist systems tend to have more women in cabinet than do generalist systems. In a specialist system, cabinet ministers are recruited on the basis of subject-specific expertise, and the selection pool of candidates consists of the whole of society. In a generalist system, on the other hand, cabinet members are drawn from a pool of political insiders, most often members of Parliament. In such a system, cabinet posts may be offered for a variety of functional reasons, whether policy experience, political seniority, or political loyalty. Since women tend to be under-represented both in Parliament and in the higher echelons of parties, this imbalance is easily replicated when selecting on the basis of these criteria (Annesley and Gains 2010). In both generalist and specialist systems women face gendered assumptions about who qualifies as a suitable candidate to become a cabinet minister, and in both systems prime ministers tend to be male, increasing the risk of selection from a male-dominated network. Moreover, in both generalist and specialist systems, various degrees of balance across several descriptive characteristics (region or religious confession, for example) may be prioritized, limiting the ability to balance on gender.

Despite these limitations, the number of women in cabinets has increased worldwide in recent decades (Stockemer and Sundström 2018). Yet even where important advancements have been made, women remain under-represented in some of the most powerful and high-profile posts, such as those of Foreign Affairs, Finance, and Defence (Barnes and Taylor-Robinson 2018).[4]

The Importance of Women in Politics:
Types of Representation

The desire to increase the number of women in cabinets is at least partially rooted in the idea that politicians will pursue politics and policy in the interests of those who are like them. In academic parlance, this is the link between descriptive and substantive representation, first identified by Pitkin (1967). Here, "descriptive representation" refers simply to women's numeric representation or presence within political institutions. "Substantive representation," on the other hand, refers to the representation of policy views, interests, and preferences of women. Women's descriptive representation is often thought to result in women's substantive representation because women politicians are thought to be more likely to act in line with women's interests and promote legislation focused on equality (Swers 2002; Lowande, Ritchie and Lauterbach 2019). Despite the implied link between descriptive and substantive representation, it is important to point out that women do not necessarily represent women's interests. Moreover, it is often difficult in practice to ascertain what are "women's issues" or interests, since women as a group are heterogeneous and hold a variety of different – and potentially conflicting – opinions on policy matters (Celis et al. 2008; McAndrews et al. 2020).

A third type of representation, symbolic representation, is often added to further capture the potential benefits of women's participation in legislative politics. Symbolic representation can be defined as the "power to evoke feelings or attitudes" (Pitkin 1967, 97). Symbolic representation, which can exist without substantive representation, refers to the idea that the incorporation of women in the political process provides a signal of inclusion. Since women worldwide report lower levels of interest in, knowledge about, and engagement in politics, symbolic representation is thought to have important trickle-down effects that may reduce these gender gaps.

The evidence of such symbolic representation is mixed. Various studies have found that when the share of women in legislatures increases, women's political activity, knowledge, and sense of efficacy rise and beliefs about women's ability to govern improve (Atkeson 2003; Atkeson and Carrillo 2007; Alexander 2012; Barnes and Burchard 2012). Other studies have found no clear link between women's increased representation and women's political engagement. Rather, these studies find that higher numbers of women in legislatures increase trust in and satisfaction with democracy amongst *both* men and women (Lawless 2004; Karp and Banducci 2008). Liu (2018) even finds that the presence of female legislators has a negative effect on women's participation in politics in East and South East Asia.

Some have argued this mixed evidence is due to the focus on women legislators rather than executives. The potential symbolic representational effects are thought to be greater for women in positions of executive power, emphasizing the importance of the inclusion of women in cabinets. Political executives are more powerful and visible than legislators and are more instrumental in initiating new policies (Schwindt-Bayer 2017; Alexander and Jalalzai 2020; Barnes and Taylor-Robinson 2018). Various studies have found that the presence of women in executive office (heads of government or members of cabinet) indeed has a positive effect on women's political participation. For example, using a survey experiment in Brazil, Schwindt-Bayer and Reyes-Household (2017) show that the presence of a female governor increases women's interest in politics. Liu and Banaszak (2016), using a cross-national analysis, find that an increase in the proportion of women in cabinet leads to higher levels of voting and party membership amongst women. Similarly, Alexander and Jalalzai (2020) find in another cross-national study that the presence of a female head of state increases women's likelihood of voting in elections. However, the authors also find that the presence of female heads of state increases levels of political interest and shifts gender-role perceptions for *both* men and women. In line with this finding, Barnes and Taylor-Robinson (2018) show that the presence of women in high-profile cabinet positions (Foreign Affairs, Defence, and Finance) increases government satisfaction amongst both genders (also see Atkeson and Carrillo 2007). Although this finding undermines the idea that female role models exclusively affect women's attitudes, it suggests that the increased representation of women in politics may have the additional benefit of increasing support for democratic governance amongst the entire population.

Women in Canadian Federal Cabinets

While we have growing cross-national evidence on how the presence of women in cabinet positions affects citizens' views and participation, we lack more basic detailed knowledge about why and when women's representation in cabinets has increased and decreased. In this section we provide an overview of women in federal cabinet positions in Canada in the period 1980–2019. We start with the government of Pierre Elliot Trudeau in 1980 and end with the governing period of Justin Trudeau in 2019 (see also Table 1.1). We assess the development of women's descriptive, substantive, and symbolic representation over this period.[5] For these analyses, we collected data on all Canadian cabinet ministers from 1980 to 2019. Data were collected from the "Guide to Canadian Ministries," a resource provided by the Canadian government.[6] The guide provides the names of all cabinet ministers and the day they were appointed. We manually coded the gender of each cabinet minister throughout this period.

Descriptive Representation

Figure 1.1 shows the proportion of women in each Canadian cabinet at the *start* of each ministry (i.e., the start of the governing period of a particular prime minister) over the period 1980–2015. Note that for comparison purposes Figure 1.1 shows the proportion of women that were in cabinet on the *first day* that the respective prime minister was sworn in and therefore excludes the various cabinet shuffles or newly elected cabinets that occurred during a prime minister's tenure.[7] We expect to see a maximum level of balance, in terms of both gender and ethnicity or regional balance, at the start of each ministry since many – unforeseen – events may occur throughout a governing period. Certain cabinet ministers may under- or over-perform or a particular political crisis may erupt, resulting in multiple shuffles that will complicate the attempt to achieve a desired balance or parity throughout a governing period.

Note that in Figure 1.1 prime ministers are included in the count of the cabinet ministers. Cabinet positions have changed over the course of the three decades under study, but cabinet ministers were included if they were considered part of the cabinet at the time they held office.[8] Although several individuals held dual or even multiple cabinet positions, each individual was only counted once per cabinet.

Figure 1.1 shows that there has been a clear increase in the percentage of women in the first cabinets of each prime minister's tenure since 1980. Moreover, the increase of women in cabinet positions has surpassed the percentage of women elected to parliament (grey dotted line).[9] As such, descriptive representation in Canada is currently achieved more through appointed (cabinet positions) than elected office (parliamentary election). Figure 1.1 also clearly shows the impact of Justin Trudeau's commitment to gender parity in his first cabinet appointed in November 2015. Trudeau effectively doubled the conventional proportion of women in Canadian cabinets, which was approximately 25 per cent under the preceding prime ministers, Harper and Martin.

Substantive Representation

As discussed above, substantive representation is difficult to measure due to the question of what counts as "women's views or interests," as well as questions as to how to measure representation (i.e., through

Figure 1.1. Percentage of Women in Canadian Cabinets and Parliament at the Start of Each Ministry, 1980–2015

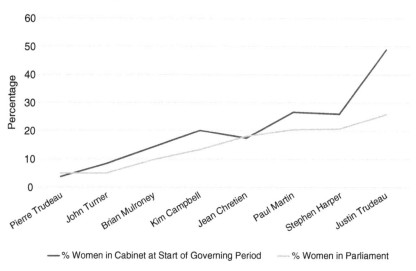

bills, laws, votes, or speeches). We argue that one way in which a government may pursue substantive representation of women is through the appointment of women to a varied set of cabinet positions. In doing so, governments ensure that women's influence (through policymaking and agenda setting) is not limited to a certain topic (i.e., childcare or gender equality), but rather is present across a range of topics. To get a sense of women's appointments to cabinet positions in Canada we provide an overview of the number of men and women appointed to a selected set of cabinet positions over the entire period 1980–2019.

Figure 1.2 shows a simple count of the number of men and women that were appointed to various cabinet portfolios at any point throughout the tenure of Pierre Trudeau (1980–84), John Turner (1984), Brian Mulroney (1984–93), Kim Campbell (1993), Jean Chrétien (1993–2003), Paul Martin (2003–06), Stephen Harper (2006–15), and Justin Trudeau (2015–19).[10] Cabinet portfolios have changed over the course of these three decades, and thus we focus on a selected set of positions that have remained stable over the years. This results in a set of sixteen cabinet portfolios (including the prime minister) that were present in each of these governing periods. Note that an individual may be counted more than once – this occurs when they were reshuffled during the period of government of a prime minister, or if they held two separate cabinet positions simultaneously. Figure 1.2 thus shows the number of men and women that were appointed to a particular portfolio at any point throughout the period 1980–2019. The figure does not account for the fact that some portfolios – as well as some ministers – see more turnover than others.[11] The figure further excludes associate ministers (such as associate minister of defence or finance).

Because the figure shows counts (the raw number of men and women holding each position), women are under-represented in each category, with the exception of the Department of Health. Several trends are notable. Over the period under study the only cabinet position that has seen more women than men appointed is the Department of Health. Women are relatively well represented in the departments of Labour, the Environment, and National Revenue. They are poorly represented in Finance, Defence, Foreign Affairs, the Prime Minister's Office (PMO), Transport, and Agriculture.

Using the typology created by Krook and O'Brien (2012) to classify ministries as either "masculine," "feminine," or "neutral," we clearly observe an under-representation of women in ministries that are considered to be masculine in nature – Finance, Foreign Affairs, Defence, Transport, and Agriculture – whereas women are, as noted above, over-represented in Health, which Krook and O'Brien (2012) classify as "feminine." Women ministers in Canada are further well represented in the Ministry of the Environment, which Krook and O'Brien (2012) classify as "neutral." The only masculine cabinet position in which women are well represented over time is the Department of Labour. Yet it must be noted that in the Canadian context the Labour department is responsible for several policy areas that may be considered more "feminine," such as employment equity, workplace standards, and employment insurance – which includes maternity policy. The portfolio has much less to do with the rough and tumble of union politics, given the low rate of unionization in Canada and the liberal democratic nature of the capitalist state (Esping-Anderson 1990).

How does Justin Trudeau's period in government compare to those of previous decades? Despite significantly improving descriptive representation, the cabinet appointments made by Trudeau in the period 2015–19 replicate many of the same, gendered, patterns of substantive representation present in the previous period. Figure 1.3 shows the number of men and women appointed to the selected cabinet positions throughout 2015–19. The top two cabinet positions for women were Health and Labour, and more women than men were appointed to International Trade. An equal number of men and women were appointed president of the Treasury. However, no women were appointed to key ministries such as Finance or Defence

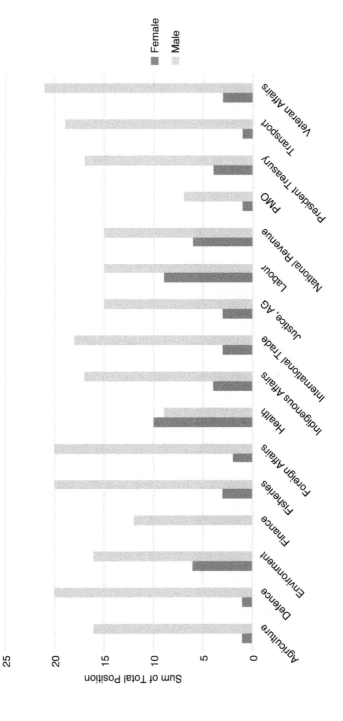

Figure 1.2. Number of Men and Women Appointed to Various Cabinet Portfolios, 1980–2019

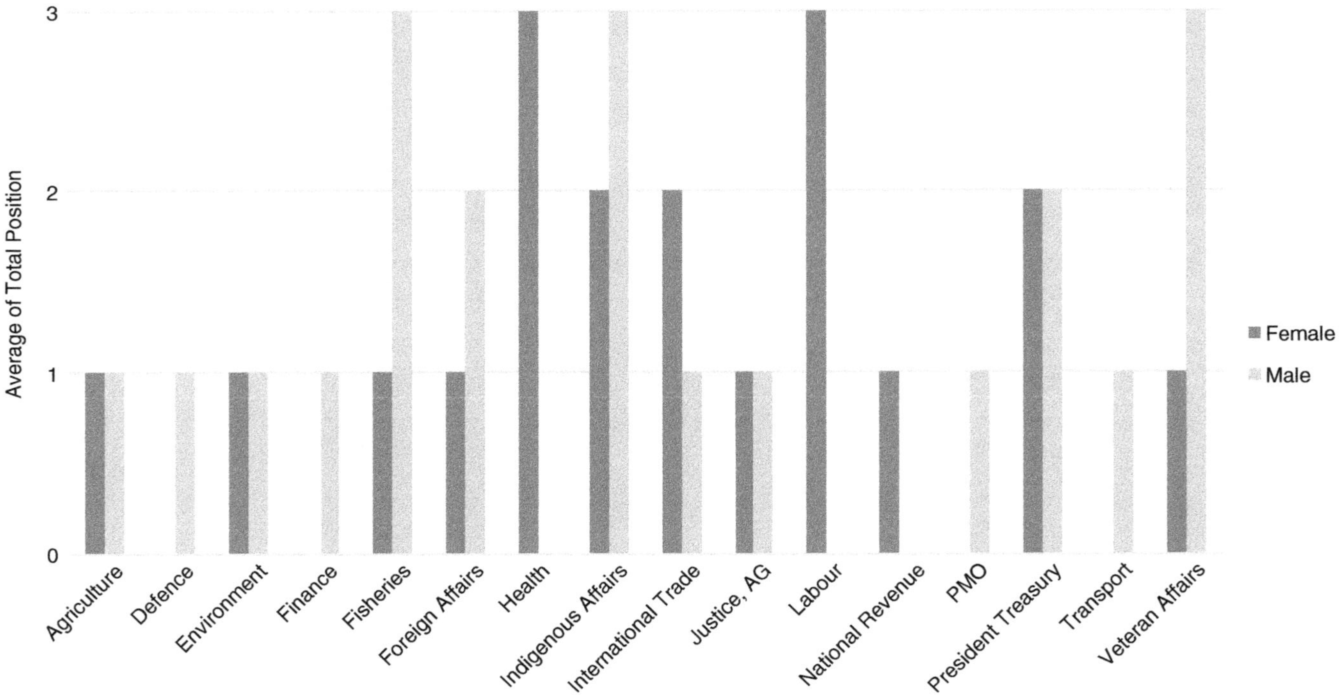

Figure 1.3. Appointments to Cabinet during Justin Trudeau's Government (2015–19), by Gender

in the 2015–19 period. Trudeau made two remarkable appointments in his first period in government. In 2015, he appointed Jody Wilson-Raybould as minister of justice and attorney general of Canada. This made her only the third woman to hold the post, and the first Indigenous person to do so. What is more, in 2017 Chrystia Freeland was moved from International Trade to Foreign Affairs, making her only the third woman in Canadian history to hold this position. Yet neither of these appointments were carried through to 2019. As also discussed in the chapter by Bourgeois in this volume, Wilson-Raybould was demoted in January 2019 to the Department of Veteran Affairs after a public disagreement with the prime minister over the SNC-Lavalin Affair. She soon left that post. The prime minister later removed her from caucus. Wilson-Raybould was replaced in the Justice portfolio by David Lametti, who continued in the post after the 2019 elections. Chrystia Freeland also did not return to Foreign Affairs after the 2019 elections. She was instead appointed minister of Intergovernmental Affairs and deputy prime minister; it is unclear whether this should be interpreted as a promotion.

It is worth noting that throughout Justin Trudeau's tenure he has appointed two men to lead the Department of Families, Children and Social Development, going against a general trend in which women tend to be appointed to this position. After the 2019 general elections, Trudeau initially did not appoint a woman to any of the key departments of Finance, Foreign Affairs, Justice, or Defence – replicating the gendered pattern of cabinet appointments that exists worldwide. Women instead were appointed to lower-status departments such as International Trade and International Development and as associate minister of finance. What is more, women were appointed to newly created (and hence less established) cabinet positions with responsibilities for diversity, inclusion and youth; digital government; seniors; and middle-class prosperity. Importantly, none of these positions are as heads of stand-alone departments. Instead, the women appointed to these newly created positions are effectively junior ministers within another minister's department.

Symbolic Representation

"Symbolic representation" refers to the potential for women's participation in politics to signal inclusion, which may have important trickle-down effects on women's further participation in politics, knowledge of political affairs, and levels of political ambition (Atkeson 2003; Atkeson and Carrillo 2007; Alexander 2012; Barnes and Burchard 2012). Many of these trickle-down effects can only be assessed in several years' time. Specifically, research suggests that higher levels of women's representation have a particularly strong effect on adolescents' attitudes (Wolbrecht and Campbell 2007; Dassonneville and McAllister 2018). As such, young women who grew up during Justin Trudeau's government might show higher levels of engagement and participation in years to come, as Justin Trudeau maintained gender parity in his cabinet throughout his first period as prime minister. His continued commitment to gender parity has been interpreted as demonstrating a deeply held belief in the importance of women's representation that goes beyond simply fulfilling an election promise. At the same time, the 2019 resignation from cabinet (and subsequent expulsion from the Liberal Party) of two of Trudeau's most prominent female ministers, Jody Wilson-Raybould and Jane Philpott, has led some to question his image as a champion of women. Furthermore, the changes in some key cabinet positions in Trudeau's newly appointed cabinet in November 2019, in which women were largely overlooked for high-profile positions, highlight the importance of distinguishing between numeric and substantive representation, the latter of which requires a more deeply held belief in women's added value in politics.

Another way in which gender parity in cabinet may manifest symbolic representation is through the creation of a cultural norm if it provides a new benchmark for women's inclusion in government. Although it seems unlikely that all future governments will meet the parity threshold, future prime ministers might at least be asked to justify any divergence from this standard. For example, then-Conservative party leader Andrew Scheer was asked in the 2019 election campaign whether a Conservative cabinet would include an equal number of men and women. Scheer replied that the best candidates would be chosen, and that this might well result in even more women in cabinet than under Trudeau ("Federal Election" 2019). However, in Alberta, Premier Rachel Notley appointed a gender parity cabinet in 2015, but her successor in 2019 failed to follow suit, highlighting the fragile and non-linear nature of any progress towards gender parity.

Concluding Remarks

This chapter has explored the representation of women in Canadian cabinets in the period 1980–2019. We examined the development of women's representation in cabinets in Canada and assessed the importance of the gender parity cabinets that were appointed by Justin Trudeau. While Trudeau's first cabinet in 2015 significantly increased the descriptive representation of women in cabinet, it also failed to upend the pre-existing and clear patterns in the division of cabinet portfolios in Canada over time. Although the Trudeau government initially broke through some of these (e.g., Foreign Affairs and Attorney General), others were kept in place in 2015 (Defence and Finance). Furthermore, several gains in substantive representation of women made in Trudeau's first period in office in terms of were reversed in his second period. This suggests that although descriptive representation is an essential first step, substantive representation does not necessarily follow. What is more, progress towards gender equality is both fragile and non-linear. Whether women's descriptive and substantive representation in Canadian cabinets persists will strongly depend on the choices of future prime ministers and their commitment to the equal representation of women in Canadian politics.

NOTES

1 https://www.theatlantic.com/international/archive/2015/11/canada -cabinet-trudeau/414280/.
2 https://www.theguardian.com/world/2015/nov/04/canada-cabinet -gender-diversity-justin-trudeau.
3 In Canada the period of government of a prime minister is referred to as "the ministry," which may span multiple elections. As such, Justin Trudeau's tenure as prime minister is referred to as the "Trudeau ministry," which is the twenty-ninth ministry of Canada. This means that the Trudeau ministry encompasses various cabinets.
4 Canada, for example, has only three times had a female minister of external affairs or foreign affairs (Flora MacDonald, Barbara McDougall, and Chrystia Freeland) and once a female minister of defence (Kim Campbell).
5 See also Bauer and Okpotor 2013, who apply this approach to cabinets across sub-Saharan Africa.
6 https://guide-ministries.canada.ca/dtail.asp?lang=eng&mstyid =23&mbtpid=1, accessed 16 October 2019. The data for Trudeau's cabinet are taken from https://www.ourcommons.ca/Members/en /ministries?ministry=29&precedenceReview=91&province=all&gender =all&lastName=all, accessed 16 December 2019.
7 The only exception is the government of Kim Campbell, whose cabinet included several ministers who were appointed under Mulroney but kept their positions under Campbell.

8 This means that the count of cabinet members includes the secretary of state of Canada, the secretary of state for external affairs (now minister of foreign affairs), the solicitor general, ministers of state, the deputy prime minister, the postmaster general, and the associate minister of defence. Not included is the deputy leader of the government in the House of Commons, a position that existed under the government of Paul Martin but was not part of the cabinet. Also not included are additional secretaries of state that existed under Chrétien.

9 Data for parliaments from https://www.cbc.ca/news2/interactives/women -politics/, accessed 17/10/2019.

10 Acting ministers are excluded from the counts.

11 Note that during Justin Trudeau's tenure there were two departments responsible for Indigenous affairs: the Ministry of Crown-Indigenous Relations and the Ministry of Indigenous Services. For the counts of the number of men and women in the portfolio of Indigenous affairs in Figures 1.2 and 1.3, these two ministries are counted together.

2 Do Women Get Fewer Votes in Ontario Provincial Elections?

SEMRA SEVI, ANDRÉ BLAIS, AND VINCENT AREL-BUNDOCK

Despite making up more than half of the population, women rarely make up more than 30 per cent of legislatures around the world. Indeed, they remain a significant unrepresented group in elected assemblies (Putnam 1976). While the percentage of women legislators has increased worldwide, the mean is still 24 per cent as of 2019 across 193 member countries of the Inter-Parliamentary Union (2019). There is of course substantial variation across and within countries at different levels of government. In 1902, ahead of her time, Margaret Haile was the first Canadian woman candidate to stand in a provincial election in Ontario. Yet women in Ontario were not given the right to vote until 1917.

The study of women in politics is extensive and covers the political participation of women (Campbell and Wolbrecht 2006; Dolan 1998; Herrnson et al. 2003; Plutzer and Zipp 1996), the gender gap (Dassonneville and McAllister 2018; Karp and Banducci 2008), descriptive and substantive representation (Chattopadhyay and Duflo 2004; Lott and Kenny 1999), quotas (Matland 2002), and the impact of different electoral systems on the presence of women in politics (Norris 1985). These studies are rich and extensive. Yet they usually study elections at a given point in time, providing a snapshot context of women's participation in politics but not the full picture.

Using a unique dataset from 1902–2014 (Sevi 2021), this chapter examines women's electoral presence in the Canadian province of Ontario over a long period of time. Existing research suggests that women are roughly equally represented at the federal and provincial levels in Canada. In a recent publication, Sevi et al. (2019) show, in a study spanning from 1921–2015, that women's representation at the federal level in Canada had increased to 25 per cent by 2015 and that female politicians are not disadvantaged at the polls compared to male candidates. Building on this research, we provide a new and comprehensive examination of the representation of women in Ontario over a similar time frame. We probe one simple question: do women get fewer votes than men at the provincial level over time? The answer to this question has important implications for the policies that could or should be adopted to increase the representation of women in politics.

Women in Ontario Elections

We collected historical data for all 7,596 unique candidates who ran for provincial elections in Ontario from 1902–2014.[1] We make use of the R package genderizerR, which infers the gender of candidates based on their first names. GenderizerR is based on the genderize.io API, which is a web scraping tool (http://genderize.io), and provides a likely gender and probability score for each candidate. We kept all the probabilities. We then verified each entry manually on two different occasions. This large dataset allows us to compute precise estimates of the difference in the electoral fortunes of men and women candidates over time and is the most comprehensive examination of women's representation in Ontario. We also account for party effects and time trends.

Figure 2.1 shows the percentage of female candidates in Ontario over time. While the proportion of female candidates has increased over time, under-representation of women persists. The percentage of women candidates has increased from just over zero in 1902 to just over 25 per cent in 2014. During the same period, the percentage of women legislators increased at Queens Park from just over zero in 1902 to about 35 per cent in 2014. At the federal level, the percentage of women candidates has increased from just over zero in 1921 to about 28 per cent in 2015, while the percentage of women legislators increased from just over zero in 1921 to about 25 per cent in 2015 (Sevi et al. 2019). In other words, there seem to be more female legislators at the provincial level than at the federal level.

One reason for this could be that women are more easily elected at lower levels of government. This finding can be compared to previous research, which has produced mixed results on whether lower levels of government attract more women and whether women do better in elections at lower levels of government (Blais and Gidengil 1991; Tolley 2011). Whereas Blais and Gidengil (1991) find that women get a municipal advantage, Tolley's (2011) findings suggest that regardless of the level of government, the proportion of women legislators is about the same. One potential reason for conflicting findings is data limitations; previous studies do not have longitudinal data over an extended period of time. The research presented here is based on a longer duration and is thus able to shed new light on the electoral presence of women.

Figure 2.1. Representation of Women in Ontario Provincial Elections

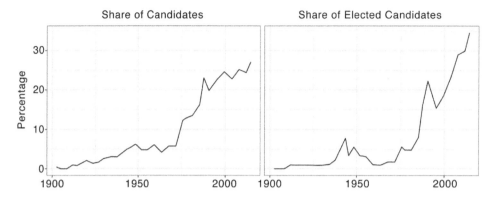

As Figure 2.1 shows, both the number of women candidates and the number of women elected to office have increased over time in Ontario. However, we are interested in seeing if female candidates are more or less successful at obtaining a seat in the Ontario legislature than their male counterparts. To explore this question, we conducted regression analysis. Since we are interested in women's electoral performance, the dependent variable is the candidates' vote percentage. We ran a series of ordinary least squares (OLS) regression models, first focusing on the bivariate association between a candidate's vote share and her gender. The first column in Table 2.1 shows that, on average, the vote share of female candidates is approximately 8.6 percentage points lower than the vote share of male candidates, suggesting that on average women fared worse than men in Ontario provincial elections. However, a variety of factors may explain this gender gap. In model 2 we include election fixed effects. This allows us to take into account that the proportion of women candidates has increased substantially over time, as has the number of candidates running in each constituency. This means that the mean percentage of votes obtained by each candidate has been declining, which reduces the size of the estimated gender gap from 8.6 percentage points to 1.8 percentage points. However, there might be other confounding variables. For example, one might expect that women run for minor parties more often than men; the gap in vote share may simply reflect that fact. Another explanation could be that parties nominate women to ridings where their chances of winning are low (Thomas and Bodet, 2013). Model 3 adds party-riding fixed effects, which allows us to take into account the differential popularity of the parties in the various ridings, and thus to

Table 2.1. The Gender Gap in Ontario

	(1)	(2)	(3)	(4)	(5)
Woman	−8.6	−1.8	−1.3	−1.3	−1.3
	(0.5)	(0.5)	(0.4)	(0.3)	(0.3)
Vote share lag	–	–	–	0.6	0.5
	–	–	–	(0.0)	(0.0)
Incumbent	–	–	–	–	3.0
	–	–	–	–	(0.3)
Distance from contention	–	–	–	–	0.0
	–	–	–	–	(0.0)
Constant	29.6				
	(0.2)				
R^2	0.02	0.21	0.81	0.80	0.80
Adj. R^2	0.02	0.20	0.73	0.79	0.79
Election fixed effect	No	Yes	Yes	No	No
Party-election fixed effect	No	No	No	Yes	Yes
Party-riding fixed effect	No	No	Yes	No	No
N	11,918	11,918	11,918	8,478	8,478

Notes: Robust standard errors appear in parentheses. All models are OLS regression models with candidate vote percentage as the dependent variable. All coefficients are significant at the .001 level.

implicitly compare the vote shares of men and women candidates running for the same party in the same riding. This further reduces the vote gap to 1.3 points. Finally, in models 4 and 5, we add party-election fixed effects and vote share in the previous election, whether a party is the district-level incumbent, and their distance from contention.[2] The vote gap is estimated to be 1 percentage point, exactly as in model 3. These data thus suggest that there may be a very small gender gap in Ontario provincial elections. Indeed, the results in Table 2.1 suggest that the gender gap in representation may mostly come from candidate selection and party attitudes towards male and female candidates.

The next question is whether that gap has decreased over time. We therefore tested a new model that replicates model 4 (but only includes party fixed effects), adding an interaction between gender and a continuous year variable. If the gap is decreasing the interaction term should be positive, meaning that the negative association between "women" and "votes" decreases over time. This is precisely what we find. Figure 2.2 shows the estimated marginal effect of gender over time. We can see that in 1902 the gender gap in vote share was just over 5 percentage points but by 2014 it is statistically indistinguishable from zero.

Figure 2.2. Marginal Effect of Gender on Vote Share

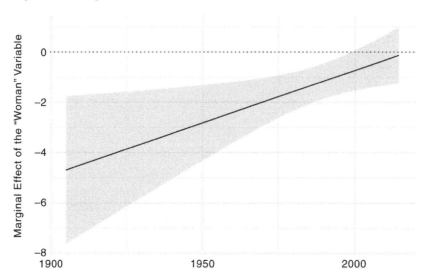

Discussion

The findings discussed above regarding the electoral performance of women candidates in Ontario provincial elections are strikingly similar to the results of our previous research on the gender gap in Canadian federal elections. At first glance, there is a huge gap, 8.6 points in the former case and 8.4 points in the latter. But as soon as we include election and party-riding fixed effects or we control for previous party performance in the riding and incumbency, the gap shrinks and becomes very small. Furthermore, the data indicate that the gap may well have existed in the past but has now disappeared.

We should stress that our data allow us to estimate the overall net association between gender and votes. It is possible, for instance, that women candidates get fewer votes among some groups (let us say old men) and more votes among others (let us say young women) and these two factors cancel each other out. Such possibilities can and should be explored with the appropriate survey data, that is, the Canadian Election Study.

Finally, we need to reiterate that our design is observational and as such may suffer from an omitted variable bias. This would be the case if some unmeasured candidate characteristic is correlated with both gender and electoral performance. For instance, if women are higher quality candidates than men and if higher quality is associated with more votes, then our estimate of the gender gap would be biased towards zero. This is precisely what is reported by Fulton (2012, 2014) in the American case. But the only study that has examined that possibility in the Canadian case, that of Black and Erickson (2003), finds that controlling for candidate quality does not affect the overall results. Clearly more work needs to be done to test the robustness of our findings.

NOTES

1 The first woman to run for a seat at the Ontario legislature did so in 1902.
2 This variable indicates the difference between a given party's vote share and the winner's vote share in the previous election.

3 News and Political Legitimacy: Gendered Mediation of Canadian Political Leaders

LINDA TRIMBLE

News organizations play a crucial role in introducing, describing, and evaluating political leaders. Because much of what citizens know about leaders is produced by mainstream media outlets, it is essential to investigate the ways in which news representations of politics and politicians are shaped by understandings about gender. In this chapter I explore whether media coverage questions women's political legitimacy on the basis of their gendered identities. To do so, I draw insights from my book about female prime ministers, my collaborative research on gendered mediation of Canadian national political party leadership candidates, and a new project examining media representations of Canadian and Australian premiers.

Women's political legitimacy is influenced by the news value of unexpectedness, which directs attention to the out-of-the-ordinary (Wagner et al. 2017, 477). The presence of women in party or government leadership roles remains highly unusual in Canada, especially at the national level. Kim Campbell, the first and only woman to have served as the country's prime minister, is one of just four women to have led a federal political party. Since Campbell's resignation in 1993, no woman has won the leadership of either of the two parties that have formed government at the federal level. Canada's ten provinces and three territories offer greater opportunities, as evidenced by larger numbers of female party leaders (thirty-one to date)[1] and provincial and territorial premiers (a total of twelve). Still, women leaders are rare at any level of government. While over three hundred people have served as first minister at the federal or subnational level, only thirteen of them have been women.[2] By emphasizing gender novelty, media coverage of Canadian federal party leadership candidates, prime ministers, and premiers highlights the unusualness of women seeking power and foregrounds the ways in which their personas, personal lives, and performances are different from those of the men who typically ascend to the top jobs. In this fashion, journalists and news commentators raise doubts about women's suitability for and capacity to succeed in political leadership roles. Yet as emerging research on Canadian and Australian premiers indicates (Trimble et al., 2019), increased representation of women in leadership roles has the potential to challenge the cultural association of men and masculinity with the enactment of party and government leadership.

National Party Leadership Candidates

Since attaining the leadership of a political party is the sole pathway to government leadership in parliamentary systems (O'Brien 2015), research on newspaper coverage of party leadership candidates offers valuable insights into the gendering of women's political aspirations and performances by the press. News is gendered when it views actors and events through the lens of gender-based identities, skills, roles, and assumptions, for instance by assuming women are less competitive or capable than men, or indicating that men who express emotion are weak. I lead a team engaged in a large-scale project examining a census of news stories about national party leadership competitions published by Canada's opinion-leading, highest-circulation national newspaper, *The Globe and Mail*. Analysing reporting about thirteen leadership competitions held over a thirty-seven-year period (1975–2012) allows us to compare coverage of eleven competitive women and nineteen men, for a total of thirty leadership contenders. Four of these women were successful in their bids: former New Democratic Party (NDP) leaders Audrey McLaughlin and Alexa McDonough; former Progressive Conservative (PC) Party leader Kim Campbell; and former Green Party leader Elizabeth May. This study affords rigorous gender-based comparisons of leadership candidates' levels of news visibility, as well as evaluations of women's suitability for and capability in the role of party and government leader.

Visibility

The *Globe and Mail* devotes considerable attention to the individuals seeking party leadership roles (Sampert et al. 2014, 288). Candidates are front and centre of the media gaze, especially those who are pegged as likely victors. News coverage is vital to a successful campaign because reporting about the competition identifies which challengers should be taken seriously (Goodyear-Grant 2013, 24–5). Insufficient attention from news outlets can undermine efforts to raise money, attract volunteers, and disseminate information to party members. As such, it is important to determine whether or not women aspiring to elite political leadership positions have a news visibility problem.

To comprehensively gauge the level of attention given each candidate in the *Globe's* reporting, our team determined whether they were mentioned in the news story and made more prominent by being foregrounded in the headline, named first in the body of the story, mentioned several times, and directly quoted (Wagner et al. 2017). Enhanced prominence signals a candidate's perceived importance in the race. Overall, men candidates are more visible in the *Globe's* reporting than women (Wagner et al. 2017, 482). However, this advantage disappears when competitiveness is taken into account. The greater the perceived likelihood of the candidate winning the race, the more the candidate became the focus of news coverage, regardless of gender identity. Novelty is also a factor, as individuals viewed as groundbreaking because they were the first of their social group to seek or win the party leadership – and, in the case of Campbell, the prime minister's role – enjoyed higher levels of visibility than non-novel competitors (Wagner et al. 2017, 477). While significant, novelty has considerably less impact than competitiveness in prompting media attention to leadership contenders.

What does this mean for media evaluations of women's political *viability* – their anticipated likelihood of gaining power? First, only those seen as capable of winning the race are heavily profiled in the news, and a variety of gendered factors shape the capacity of a candidate to raise sufficient funds to be noticed by press and party alike. Second, while women's news visibility improves as their competitiveness increases, gender undoubtedly influences perceptions of viability *before* they enter the competition, when attention from the media is essential to generating momentum, raising funds, and earning endorsements. Third, visibility does not in and of itself confer legitimacy. A political actor may be in the media spotlight yet be evaluated as lacking the "right stuff" for leadership. Gender differences in personalizing tropes and assessments of leadership skills and attributes are revealed by examining the meanings constructed by news about the suitability and capability of leadership candidates.

Suitability

The phenomenon of news personalization weaves attention to personal attributes and "private" lives into stories about political ambitions and performances (Hirdman et al. 2005; Langer 2010). By politicizing bodies and families, personalization questions women's suitability for the job of party leader (Trimble et al. 2013). Attention to their gender identities casts women as outsiders to politics, and peering into their family lives reinforces gender stereotypes, underscoring the presumption that women should take care of the family and domestic routines while men take charge of politics. To assess the degree to which various personalizing themes are employed in depictions of Canadian national leadership candidates, we looked for explicit references to gender identity, age, physical appearance, sexual identity or sexualization, upbringing, marital situation, and children (or mentions of childlessness). The *Globe's* reporting focused more attention on these personal dimensions for women than for men. Notably, women who were highly visible because of their celebrity status or likelihood of winning the race had their personas and personal lives profiled (Trimble et al. 2013, 473).

As qualitative analysis of the leadership campaign coverage revealed, only certain types of bodies are seen to personify political leadership (Trimble et al. 2015). Men who met expectations of the ideal political physique were characterized as authentic sites of political leadership because of their size, dynamic comportment, and physical gravitas. In contrast, the bodies of women, especially those seen as extraordinary because of their proximity to power, were depicted as incompatible with the performance of leadership. Kim Campbell, high-profile celebrity candidate Belinda Stronach, and the NDP's first woman leader Audrey McLaughlin were presented as politically restrained and diminished by the size, demeanour, and adornment of their bodies (Trimble et al. 2015, 322). While several men competitors were described as "big," "tall," and "burly," situating their bodies as sites of power, Campbell's petite stature was emphasized with lexical choices such as "small" and "diminutive" (321). By sexualizing these women – Campbell was deemed the "pin-up prime minister" and Stronach a "blonde bombshell " – the reporting undermined their legitimacy (322) The *Globe's* coverage of Rosemary Brown racialized her 1975 campaign for the NDP leadership by labelling her "a black woman" and "black female" (323). As these examples illustrate, the gendered and racialized features of women's bodies are foregrounded for their unusualness, marking them as "aberrant and inauthentic" in their quest for political power (322; also see Tolley 2016). By directing attention to women's embodied identities, physiques, sexual attractiveness, and intimate relationships, news coverage infers they do not belong in political leadership roles.

Capability

Are women presented as capable political leaders? Analysis of the *Globe's* reporting offers answers to questions about how female party candidates' leadership skills are described and interpreted (Wagner, Trimble, and Sampert 2018). We found that the women who were front and centre of the *Globe's* interrogation of leadership qualities were more frequently appraised than equivalent men candidates, and these evaluations were markedly more negative in their tone and emphasis.

Analysis of the words and phrases used to describe leadership attributes pinpointed four dominant themes: language skills (proficiency in both of Canada's official languages); communication skills (the ability to speak and debate clearly and in ways that resonated with audiences); intellectual substance (the intelligence and knowledge necessary to offer substantive policy ideas); and political experience. We found no gender differences in evaluations of bilingualism. However, heightened attention coupled with more negative assessments appeared in depictions of three high-profile women: Campbell, McLaughlin, and Stronach. Their speeches were deemed uninspiring, stilted, and inauthentic, and their intelligence, expertise, knowledge, and experience were either downplayed or belittled. In contrast, men received complimentary coverage of their leadership strengths and limited attention to their weaknesses (Wagner, Trimble, and Sampert 2018, 15).

Most of the comments about intellectual substance were directed at Campbell, who was described as smart but arrogant, and hence insufficiently humble for her intelligence to be regarded as a virtue. Campbell's coverage also reflected the *Globe's* tendency to characterize women as political neophytes even when their experience was similar to or greater than that of their male competitors. Despite having served in the high-profile cabinet posts of Defence and Justice, Campbell was judged insufficiently experienced and thus "unsuitable" for the top job. Yet her primary competitor in the leadership race, Jean Charest, who had held only junior cabinet portfolios, was said to have "the makings of a prime minister" (Wagner, Trimble, and Sampert 2018, 13). And even though she was poised to assume the exalted role of prime minister, Campbell was represented as passive, inactive, or ineffective in her exercise of power (Gerrits et al., 2017). When journalists foreground the incongruity between women's gender identities and the performance of political leadership in this fashion, they cast doubt on women's credibility and capacity to succeed.

Women Government Leaders

What happens when a woman rises to the top? Does the power and gravitas of the first minister's role confer a legitimacy advantage to any woman who achieves the position, or does her gender-based unusualness work to challenge perceptions that she is suitable for the job? Research on government leaders helps answer these questions, with findings underscoring the importance of gender novelty for the mediated legitimacy of female government leaders (Falk 2010, 35–6; Meeks 2012, 184; Tolley 2016, 41).

My study of women prime ministers included analysis of national and regional newspaper stories about Campbell during three key career phases: after she was sworn in as Canada's prime minister, a month-long governance phase; the 1993 election campaign; and her resignation from the leader's role after her party's electoral defeat (Trimble 2017). Because she became prime minister at a time when elite women politicians were rare, Campbell's ascent was remarkable. She was a "famous first," and her gender novelty ensured a visibility advantage. Campbell was profiled in significantly more news stories than her electoral competitor, Liberal leader Jean Chrétien, for instance (Trimble 2017, 28). Yet news reports raised doubts about Campbell's suitability for and capability in the role of prime minister.

Throughout her four months in office, Campbell's unusualness was foregrounded with the "first woman" label (Trimble 2017, 75, 78). The practice of gendering political nouns – that is, specifying the gender of the political actor with phrases such as "the *female* prime minister" – positioned Campbell's performance as aberrant. In contrast, Chrétien was articulated as an ordinary guy, a man of experience and action who was said to be "looking very prime ministerial." Campbell was never represented as looking like a government leader; instead, she was evaluated as too small, weak, and overtly feminine to be convincing in the role (132–4). Most damaging was news coverage that questioned her ability to effectively challenge the ideas of her electoral opponents or, for that matter, to speak authoritatively and convincingly to Canadians (156–8, 198). When she was campaigning in the general election, Campbell was described as shrill, strident, whiny, impulsive, and unable to restrain herself from lobbing self-destructive "verbal bombshells" that exploded her party's chances at the polls (198). Overt condemnation of Campbell's speech acts revealed considerable unease with a woman in power.

Canadians have seen only one woman serve, and very briefly, in the prime minister's role, and that was almost thirty years ago. By contrast, women are considerably more prominent and electorally successful at the subnational level. To date, twelve women have led provincial or territorial governments, with nine rising to power since 2010. And for over a year Canada's four most populous provinces were led by women.[3] Women leaders are more successful, too. In contrast to Campbell, who was selected to lead a party destined for electoral defeat, six of the eight women premiers brought their parties to victory in general election campaigns, and former BC premier Christy Clark made history by governing for six years and winning two elections.[4] Tangible evidence that women can win, coupled with their high-profile governance of powerful provinces, may have disrupted the "unspoken cultural association that politicians ... must be men" (Falk 2010, 93).

New research with international collaborators (Trimble et al. 2019) explores this possibility by analysing reporting by leading national and regional newspapers about twenty Canadian and Australian premiers: five women in each country and their immediate male predecessors.[5] The sample is unique in featuring four jurisdictions, including two Canadian provinces, in which a second woman has attained the premiership, allowing us to gauge differences in media representations based on gender incongruity. Comparing novel and non-novel women leaders reveals that news coverage changes when more than one woman has broken the metaphorical glass ceiling.

The research team examined newspaper stories published during the first week after each premier's election to the role. In introducing new leaders to the public, journalists foster powerful first impressions of their political identities and capabilities (Trimble et al. 2019). By measuring the frequency and intensity of eight indicators of media personalization, we determined that female premiers experienced higher levels of attention to their gender identities, bodies, and personal lives than was the case for the men who preceded them. Importantly, this difference disappeared when gender novelty identity was controlled for. While the first women to become premier in their jurisdiction experienced higher levels of personalization than do men premiers, subsequent women are no more likely than their male predecessors to be described in ways that highlight their personas or personal lives. As these findings suggest, the symbolic impact of women's presence in high-prestige positions shapes news representations of government leaders by normalizing the sight of women in high political office. When a woman leader is no longer regarded as incongruous because of her gender, news writers rely less heavily on gendered norms and stereotypes to tell the story of her rise to power.

Does News Coverage Present a Barrier to Women's Leadership?

Analysis of reporting about Canada's lone woman prime minister and eleven female candidates for the leadership of national political parties shows that women who are set to break barriers or who have other qualities that make them intensely newsworthy do not experience a visibility disadvantage. Indeed, they are prominent in news coverage. Unfortunately, this type of scrutiny featured delegitimizing characterizations of their bodies, racial identities, and personal lives, as well as criticism of their political experience and acumen. Gender incongruity is heightened in news reports of these women's political aspirations, prompting questions about their suitability for high political office. News representations of Campbell, in particular, presented her as unable to exercise power in an authentic and agentic manner.

A major limitation of this research is the absence of a recent case in which a woman was selected to lead a governing party or a party in contention to form the government at the national level. It is not possible, therefore, to determine whether a highly competitive woman candidate for a major federal party would encounter similar treatment today. Researchers should turn to the subnational level for a larger sample of success stories. Six of Canada's eight women provincial premiers secured the role by mounting successful leadership campaigns while their party was in government. Analysis of their campaigns would help determine whether, over time, journalists and commentators focus more on competitiveness and viability than on gender novelty and stereotypes.

New research on reporting about Australian and Canadian premiers shows that while "firsts" will continue to be singled out for the personal and identity characteristics distinguishing them from the white heterosexual men who typically win party and government leadership roles, news coverage does not invariably present obstacles to women's leadership. When the sight of a woman as leader is no longer unusual, reporting is considerably less gendered in its emphasis on personalizing themes. In exploring the effects of gender novelty on news characterizations of premiers' gender identities, family lives, and leadership skills, this research takes important steps towards understanding the impact of symbolic representation – the increased presence and concentration of women in powerful leadership roles – on gendered mediation of political leadership.

NOTES

1 This total does not include women who served as interim leaders or whose parties did not have legislative representation while they held the leadership position.
2 See https://nosecondchances.ca/ and www.pathway2premier.com.
3 From Kathleen Wynne's rise to the premiership of Ontario in February 2013 to Quebec premier Pauline Marois's defeat in a general election in April 2014, four women served as premier: BC's Christy Clark and Alberta's Alison Redford held power at the same time.
4 That said, Clark's second term as premier was short lived, as her minority government lost a confidence motion just three months after the election.
5 See www.pathway2premier.com.

4 Adversarial Politics: Understanding the Colonial Context of Indigenous Women's Political Participation in Canada

ROBYN BOURGEOIS

Under Prime Minister Justin Trudeau's Liberal government, Indigenous women received unprecedented access to the federal seat of political power in Canada, epitomized by the 2015 appointment of Kwakwaka'wakw lawyer Jody Wilson-Raybould – or Puglaas ("a woman born to noble people"), as she is known in the Musgamagw Tsawateineuk/Laich-Kwil-Tach society she comes from – as the attorney general (AG) and minister of justice for Canada. Wilson-Raybould's tenure as AG was seemingly unperturbed until her sudden redeployment to the Ministry of Veterans Affairs on 14 January 2019. Within a month, Wilson-Raybould resigned from Trudeau's cabinet amid allegations that the Prime Minister's Office had attempted to influence her decision to pursue criminal prosecution of Montreal-based engineering company SNC-Lavalin, on charges of corruption and fraud relating to their business dealings in Libya. In the aftermath of this resignation, the prime minister and his government have maintained their innocence while simultaneously engaging in "character assassination" by portraying Wilson-Raybould as "difficult," "incompetent," and "not a team player" (Green et al. 2019). Coming quickly to her defense have been Indigenous peoples including, most prominently, her father Bill Wilson, a Musgamagw hereditary chief, who described the prime minister's treatment of his daughter to *Maclean's* magazine as a "kick in the teeth" (Edwards, 2019).

To help Canadians understand the politics at play when Indigenous women like Jody Wilson-Raybould opt to participate in Canadian state politics, this chapter offers a brief but necessary political history lesson grounded in Canada's existence as a colonial nation state. While most people have the privilege of participating in Canadian state politics as citizens, Canada's historical and ongoing domination of Indigenous peoples, their sovereign nations, and their lands ensures that Indigenous women's political participation is inherently adversarial: the colonized engaging their colonizer. Through a succinct overview of Canadian history, this chapter establishes Canada's historical and ongoing existence as a colonial nation state fundamentally invested in domination and violence directed at Indigenous peoples. This is followed by an unpacking of the political terrain that this historical and ongoing Canadian state investment in colonialism creates for Indigenous women who opt to participate in Canadian nation state politics through consideration of Wilson-Raybould's specific experience.

While I write this chapter in solidarity with Indigenous peoples and sincerely hope that they benefit from this analysis, I want to acknowledge the primary audience for this chapter: non-Indigenous people in Canada. As someone with mixed racial ancestry – Nehiyaw (Cree) and white settler – I walk in two worlds and one of my gifts, as my Cayuga father-in-law and other Elders like to remind me, is facilitating discussion and knowledge transference between these worlds. True reconciliation – decolonization and the regeneration of Indigenous sovereignty and self-determination – requires the support of white settlers willing to learn and participate in the dismantling of Canadian colonialism, and I write with the hope that this chapter might contribute to this process.

Because of the complexities of language and differences in understanding, I must offer a brief explanation of language usage pertaining to Indigenous peoples in this chapter. The term "Indigenous" refers to First Nations, Métis, and Inuit peoples, those commonly referred to as "Aboriginal" in Canadian society. I have refrained from using "Aboriginal" out of respect for Indigenous leaders who deem this term state-produced and colonial; and while "Indian" is equally problematic, I use it here strategically to draw attention to the operations of the Indian Act. Finally, I privilege using Indigenous names for specific nations/communities.

Your Home on Native Land: Canada and Colonialism

The distinct conditions under which Indigenous women engage in Canadian state politics are the direct consequence of Canada's historical and ongoing existence as a colonial nation state. Colonialism, in simplest terms, involves the theft and occupation of Indigenous lands through domination and elimination of Indigenous peoples by white settler societies. The right of white people to do this is founded on racist ideas about the perceived inferiority of Indigenous peoples, reinforced through violence directed at Indigenous peoples (Razack 2002). This racism works in interlocking ways with heteropatriarchy, meaning that

Indigenous peoples experience colonialism in explicitly gendered ways that not only privilege masculinity over femininity but also eliminate Indigenous queer normativity – recognition of multiple gender roles and gender fluidity and acceptance of 2SLGBTQQIA (two-spirit, lesbian, gay, bisexual, trans, queer, questioning, intersex, and asexual) people from our nations (Simpson 2017). This domination is embedded, and thus continually reproduced, within the institutions of white settler societies – including using the law to make the foundational and ongoing theft and occupation of Indigenous lands and domination of Indigenous peoples legitimate and legal (Culhane 1998; Razack 2002). It is manifested through white settler social, political, and economic control over previously sovereign Indigenous nations and by bringing all facets of Indigenous life under the jurisdiction of the Canadian nation state (Culhane 1998). It is also manifested through violence directed at Indigenous peoples, who represent the ultimate threat to the colonial order of things, as their very existence as the original peoples of the lands stolen and occupied by Canada inherently undermines the legitimacy of the colonial nation state. Indigenous peoples thus are perpetually targeted for elimination, whether legally through assimilation or physically through genocidal violence (Razack 2002).

While it would require a large library of books, multiple post-secondary courses, and numerous learning sessions with Indigenous Elders, knowledge carriers, and community members to cover Canada's colonial history adequately, I offer this brief overview to demonstrate the veracity of the claims made above:

Prior to the arrival of white settlers, many sovereign Indigenous nations lived on Turtle Island, the term many Indigenous peoples use to refer to the lands that now constitute North America, including (specifically in the Canadian region) the Algonquin, Anishinaabeg (Ojibwa/Ojibway), Beothuk, Blackfoot, Coast Salish, Dakota, Dene, Haida, Nehiyaw (Cree), Haudenosaunee (Iroquois), Inuit, Mi'kmaq, Secwepemc, Syilx, and Tlingit. While portrayed as inherently "primitive," "backwards," and "uncivilized" by white settler society as a means of justifying colonial domination (Culhane 1998, 47–8), our land-based civilizations had complex cosmologies and belief systems (Invert Media 2015), language and knowledge systems (Friesen 1999), and social, political, and economic systems that had ensured our collective survival on these lands from time immemorial. In fact, the Haudenosaunee Confederacy – a consensus-based system of governance created and used by the six Haudenosaunee nations (Cayuga, Mohawk, Oneida, Onondoga, Seneca, Tuscarora) united under the Great Law of Peace – served as model for the creation of the United States government (Haudenosaunee

Confederacy 2019), and the freedom and power enjoyed by Haude-nosaunee women in their nations inspired the first feminists in North America (Roesche Wagner 2001). Our generosity and intimate knowl-edge of the land helped untold numbers of early settlers survive under conditions that they considered "harsh" and "dangerous"(Razack 2002, 3). Many of our nations were willing to share this land with white set-tlers but under very specific terms – returning to the Haudenosaunee, for example, in response to increasing numbers of Dutch settlers enter-ing their territory, around 1613 the Haudenosaunee sought the creation of a treaty known as the Two-Row Wampum. (Wampum belts operate as a record and mnemonic device designed to help viewers recall knowl-edge that was traditionally shared orally.) Community knowledge keeper Rick Hill (2013) writes that in the Mohawk language this treaty was referred to as *Teioháte* (two paths/roads) *Kaswenta* (wampum belt) and it consisted of five alternating rows of purple and white beads, with the rows of white beads appearing as two paths down a purple road/ river. Haudenosaunee interpretation of this agreement states that while both Indigenous and non-Indigenous people are welcome to share this land under peace and friendship, neither shall interfere in the lives of the other group (Parmenter 2013, 83–4). In other words, no one would own the land as private property, and while we would show consid-eration of how our actions impacted others, Haudenosaunee national sovereignty was recognized and affirmed.

Colonial white settler society, however, is driven by greed and the desperate need to secure unfettered access to a land base for its exis-tence, and the Canadian nation state was and continues to be established and secured through domination and violence directed at Indigenous peoples. While Canadian colonialism operates through the ideology that *all* Indigenous peoples are inferior to white people and that this perceived inhumanity justifies domination and violence (Razack 2002, 1–2), these beliefs are also distinctly gendered: Indigenous men are por-trayed by white settler society as physically dangerous and a threat to white people, especially white women, so as to justify white male con-trol of these women under the guise of providing protection (Innes and Anderson 2015, 10–11). By comparison, Indigenous women find them-selves trapped in their own racialized "madonna-whore" dichotomy: portrayed as the good and noble "Indian princess" for their willing-ness to assist colonialism, or as the bad "squaw" – inherently sexually available (promiscuous) and thus inherently sexually violable (rapable) (Bourgeois 2017, 260–1) and disposable (Razack 2016). In the historical accounting that follows, I pay attention to how these gendered white settler ideologies play(ed) out in the material world.

The Canadian nation state was established through colonial domination and violence directed at Indigenous peoples. During the years prior to the formal creation of Canada in 1867, this included enslavement (Neeganagwedgin 2012), germ warfare through the purposeful exposure of Indigenous peoples to diseases brought here by white settlers (Finzsch 2008), the introduction of alcohol to Indigenous peoples (Thatcher 2004, 15–16), the destabilization of Indigenous political alliances and increased intertribal conflict through the introduction of colonial mercantilism (Lawrence 2002, 26–8), and treaty negotiations involving coercion and force (Truth and Reconciliation Commission 2015, 1). The legal right of white settlers to occupy Indigenous lands came courtesy of an illegal application of British law: anthropologist Dara Culhane (1998) demonstrates how the existing legal provisions governing the claiming of land for the British Empire when an existing population was present were cast aside in favour of an alternative legal provision invoking the right to claim land deemed empty of people (*terra nullius* – or empty land), on the basis of the perceived racial inferiority of Indigenous peoples. In addition to this legalization of the theft of Indigenous lands, many of the colonial institutions that became pillars of the Canadian nation state began prior to its formal creation in 1867, including residential schools, the confinement of Indigenous peoples to reserve land, legislation controlling Indigenous identity and access to treaty rights, and economic marginalization.

Settler colonial domination is written into the very fibre of the Canadian nation state: the British North America Act that created Canada in 1867 clearly states that the federal government of Canada holds "responsibility" over "Indian peoples and Indian land." This fraudulent right to control Indigenous peoples was actualized in 1876 with the introduction of the Indian Act, legislation that remains – albeit in a heavily amended form – to this day. This racist legislation secures the right of the federal government to (a) determine Indigenous identity ("Indians") and community membership; (b) confine Indians to reservations and control what they can do on this land; (c) impose Western models of governance through elected band councils that, historically (1876–1951) entirely excluded women; (d) attack traditional matriarchal lineage systems in many nations by imposing patriarchal lineage as the priority for establishing who is an officially recognized "Indian"; and (e) unfairly eliminate women as Indians (i.e., those who are officially recognized as Indians under the Indian Act) through sex-discriminatory exclusions related to marrying a non-Indian – exclusions that are not applied to male Indians. It also at one time forced enfranchisement – legal termination of Indian status and imposition of Canadian citizenship – on Indians who sought an education, joined the religious clergy, or enlisted in the military.

The Canadian nation state has attempted to control and destroy Indigenous nations in myriad ways beyond the Indian Act. Deploying racist discourses that deemed all Indigenous women and men to be dysfunctional parents, Canada has illegally and genocidally removed Indigenous children from their families and communities, first through Indian residential schools and then through its child welfare systems. As the final report of Canada's Truth and Reconciliation Commission (TRC) makes clear, the Canadian government pursued these genocidal strategies in order to "divest itself of its legal and financial obligations to Aboriginal people and gain control over their land and resources" (2015, 3). Through the destruction of Indigenous families, these systems attempted to eliminate transmission of Indigenous ways of knowing and doing and promote social assimilation into colonial Canada (2–3), and exposed the majority of Indigenous children to multiple forms of violence, including physical and sexual abuse (105–9).

These patterns of violence are replicated in destructive ways through a process termed "intergenerational effects" (Bombay, Matheson, and Anisman 2014), and this is exploited by the Canadian nation state to justify the ongoing removal of Indigenous children through provincial/territorial child welfare systems (Barker, Alfred, and Kerr 2014). As a replacement for the residential school system, state child welfare agencies have accelerated the destruction of Indigenous peoples through their children, as estimates suggest that there are currently three times the number of Indigenous children in the custody of the state as at the height of the residential system (Baker, Alfred, and Kerr 2014, E534). Youth exposed to the Canadian child welfare system, argue Barker, Alfred, and Kerr, "are among society's most vulnerable citizens" and face detrimental consequences, including increased risks for experiencing homelessness, mental health issues, addictions, and incarceration (2014, E434). We also know from the final report of the National Inquiry into Missing and Murdered Indigenous Women, Girls, and 2SLGBTQQIA people (2019) that involvement with these child welfare systems is a significant contributing factor to physical and emotional violence.

Finally, while Indigenous peoples are dominantly understood in contemporary Canadian society as being an economic burden on the state – welfare dependent and financially draining Canada through treaty monies and land claims – this ideology elides two core truths: (1) the economic marginalization of Indigenous peoples is the direct consequence of colonial domination and the actions of the Canadian nation state; and (2) the paltry amount of funding spent on meeting existing treaty obligations is dwarfed by what the Canadian nation state has earned through the illegal theft and occupation of Indigenous lands, exploitation of these lands and their resources; exploitation of Indigenous bodies; and taxation of Indigenous peoples. Colonialism disrupted existing Indigenous patterns of subsistence by forcibly removing Indigenous peoples from their traditional lands (Bourgeois 2015); confining them to reserves that rarely aligned with traditional land use patterns and consisted of the least arable lands, those unwanted by white settler society (TRC 2015, 1); and introducing colonial mercantilism and capitalism (Lawrence 2002, 26–8). Through the Indian Act, the Government of Canada attacked Indigenous patterns of wealth redistribution by outlawing of ceremonies like the Potlatch and secured the right to control what Indians can do on and with reserve land.

With limited access to economic capital, Indigenous peoples have had few opportunities to own the means of capitalist production and profit; consequently, most Indigenous peoples end up serving as part of the exploitable labour force, where they face limited opportunities thanks to well-documented long-term racial discrimination in the Canadian labour market (Fernandez and Silver 2017). Given Indigenous peoples' marginal and precarious standing within Canada's national economy and thus high rates of abject poverty, welfare dependence has long been an important mode of survival for Indigenous peoples in Canada. However, historian Hugh Shewell (2004) has documented that increasing welfare dependence among Indigenous peoples was a fundamental governmental strategy for extending Canadian colonial control: the more Indigenous peoples were dependent on the state for money, the more Canada could exert control over Indigenous nations. This history of purposeful colonial economic devastation and exclusion is elided in Canadian society: the violence is erased by racist discourses portraying Indigenous people as lazy and a financial burden to Canada, discourses that incite hatred and discrimination towards Indigenous people.

Adversarial Politics: Indigenous Women and Canadian Political Participation

Given this history of settler colonial domination, Indigenous women like Jody Wilson-Raybould who opt to participate in Canadian nation state politics face an inherently adversarial political terrain defined by the relationship of conquest: the dominated engaging those who dominate them, or, in the language of the anti-violence sector, the abused confronting their abuser. Choosing to be active in Canadian political systems, as such, carries distinct perils for Indigenous women, for everything they do to politically strengthen the Canadian nation state risks further colonizing and destroying Indigenous peoples. While this risk leads many Indigenous women to turn their back on Canadian political participation, others see their participation as essential for decolonization and social change: Jody Wilson-Raybould, for example, saw her role as minister of justice "as ensuring our country's laws and policies actually do change based on the recognition of [Indigenous] rights" (2019, 51).

The adversarial colonial nature of Canadian politics was exposed in the post-resignation treatment of Jody Wilson-Raybould, which replicated historical patterns of Canadian colonialism operating around notions of "good" and "bad" Indigenous women. Wilson-Raybould began as the good "Indian princess": by appointing a strong Indigenous woman with powerful leadership ties to her Indigenous community to one of the highest political positions in Canada, Prime Minister Justin Trudeau and his Liberal government established significant "street cred" in their commitment to "reconciliation" and improving Canada's relationship with Indigenous peoples, and likely secured greater Indigenous and non-Indigenous support. As long as Wilson-Raybould worked productively with the Government of Canada, she was hailed as a valuable member of caucus. However, when she refused to offer legal lenience to SNC-Lavalin under pressure from the prime minister and his government, she became the bad Indian and was cast out: she was portrayed as "difficult" and "not a team player," demoted from her political power position, and forced to resign from cabinet in order to preserve her political integrity.

Ironically, this colonial defamation and expulsion of Wilson-Raybould seems to have backfired for Trudeau: the SNC-Lavalin affair brought into question the integrity of his government, and while he easily won a majority government in the 2015 election, he was reduced to a minority government in 2019. At the same time, Wilson-Raybould was re-elected in her riding of Vancouver Granville and sits in the House of Commons as an independent member of Parliament.

Conclusion

This chapter's attention to Canada's historical and ongoing existence as a colonial state rooted in domination and violence directed at Indigenous peoples in order to secure and retain unfettered access to stolen Indigenous lands is meant to expose for Indigenous and, especially, non-Indigenous readers the potentially genocidal perils of Canadian political participation faced by Indigenous women (and, indeed, all

Indigenous peoples) and, thus, properly contextualize Prime Minister Justin Trudeau and his government's treatment of Jody Wilson-Raybould as a colonial response. The Canadian political terrain is in no way equitable or a "level playing field" when it comes to Indigenous women; instead it is overdetermined by colonialism and historical and ongoing power dynamics that drastically favour colonial Canada at the direct expense of Indigenous peoples. Instead of an act of democratic citizenship, Indigenous women's political participation is innately adversarial: the colonized versus the colonizer. And as the treatment of Jody Wilson-Raybould makes clear, the Canadian colonial state is happy to accord political power to Indigenous women when it fits their agenda but will just as happily take it away if those Indigenous women stand in their way … and will defame them in the process.

This vicious colonial Canadian state political attack against an Indigenous woman leader attempting to do her job with integrity will likely have a chilling effect on Indigenous women's involvement in Canadian state politics. It is a reminder that the political terrain is inherently adversarial and the colonial state won't hesitate to eliminate a "bad Indian" to advance its own interests, which include ongoing colonial domination over Indigenous peoples and unfettered access to our lands. Why would any Indigenous woman want to participate in Canada state politics?

PART TWO

Comparative Perspectives on
Women in Politics

5 Missing the Wave? Women Congressional Candidates Who Lost in the 2018 Election

JULIE DOLAN, PARU SHAH, AND SEMILLA STRIPP

"More women running that ever before" was a common headline for the 2018 US congressional elections, which led to much speculation about a potential "pink wave." Noting the historic influx of female candidates, we attempt to uncover what changed the calculus for so many women between 2016 and 2018: with a newly elected president who had zero political experience, were they less apprehensive about their own qualifications? More heavily recruited by the parties and other political players? All of a sudden less encumbered by family responsibilities? Or just plain fed up with the status quo?

Using a unique dataset of in-depth qualitative interviews of women who ran in a 2018 congressional election across the United States, in this chapter we examine these women's motivations for running, the support they received and challenges they faced, and their plans for the future. We focus on the women who wanted to be part of that wave, but who lost in either the primary or general election.

We do so for a couple of reasons. First, just about everything we know about female candidates comes from analysing those who won or through making inferences about the qualities of those who emerged victorious (Carroll and Sanbonmatsu 2013; Palmer and Simon 2012; Pearson and McGhee 2013). But given that approximately three times more women lost than won their congressional bids in 2018, focusing solely on the winners likely paints a skewed portrait of women's experiences on the campaign trail. Second, focusing on the losers is instructive for predicting what comes next. Anecdotal and quantitative data show that women are less likely than men to run again after suffering a congressional loss (Wasserman 2018; Witt, Paget, and Matthews 1994). Yet previous studies of electoral loss have largely ignored women and have not specifically asked women about their experiences or future plans after loss (Kim 1970). With nearly one hundred women deciding to run again for Congress in 2020 after losing their 2018 bids (Center for American Women and Politics 2018), the time is ripe for such analysis.

Overall, our results point to the persistence of structural challenges in shaping women's candidacies, especially family responsibilities and lack of party support. But our interviews also call into question the conventional wisdom about women's self-doubt dampening political ambitions. We conclude with implications of this research for the broader scholarship on candidate emergence and women's leadership.

Telling Their Story

To better understand the experiences and motivations of the women who ran and lost in the 2018 election, we spoke with them directly. Between August 2018 and January 2019, we emailed all female primary and general election losers for whom we could find email addresses, inviting them to share their story with us. In all, we interviewed fifty-five women (fifty-two House and three Senate candidates) who lost in either the primary or general.[1]

We asked each woman approximately ten questions about her experiences running in 2018, including open-ended questions about motivations to run, apprehensions and challenges, support and recruitment, lessons learned, and next steps. We relied on qualitative interviews to ensure that we were not limiting the range of response possibilities, inviting each woman to identify and share, in her own words, the most important pieces of her own story. Our interviews averaged 41 minutes in length, ranging from 15 to 111 minutes.[2]

Why Did You Run? What Motivated You?

What motivated these women? The majority identified more than one factor, but the most common impetus was the desire to make Congress more representative of the people (60 per cent), emphasizing the value of electing not only more women and people of colour but people from different occupational backgrounds and walks of life. As one woman captured the sentiment:

> I think a diversity of voices ... should be there because I think democracy best works when its representatives reflect their community.

The second most commonly cited reason for running was frustration and anger with the status quo (46 per cent), combined with a sense of urgency about making change. As one woman said:

I was afraid for our country … [the Trump administration] is an authoritarian regime which does not respect the rule of law and which will slowly tear down, not just the legislative accomplishments of the Obama administration, but the civil rights that many of us consider most basic and perhaps even human rights.

The third most common factor shaping women's decisions to run in 2018 was that the timing was right (38 per cent): the incumbent had just stepped down or the timing was particularly good for career or family reasons. Yet even so, very few of these women characterized their decisions to run as motivated by ambitions for higher office or to gain power, reasons more typically offered by men than women (Costantini 1990). Instead, they usually spoke about how they brought the right skill set, connections to their community, and history of public service to take advantage of the opportunity.

Apprehensions and Challenges

QUALIFICATIONS
One of the primary explanations for women's reluctance to run is that they often doubt their own qualifications or spend far more time amassing experience in lower-level offices before making a bid for an office like Congress (Bledsoe and Herring 1990; Fox and Lawless 2004). And while some of our interviewees expressed such reservations, many considered that the stakes were too high to remain on the sidelines. For example, after deciding against pursuing a seat on her city council in 2016, one candidate revealed how the 2016 election prompted her to re-evaluate:

[In 2016], I decided not to run because I wasn't sure. I wanted to take more time to research it, I wanted to take more time to be totally positive in my decision. And I had a lot of self-doubt, but it kind of all evaporated because I realized all my self-doubt means nothing and it's just a barrier that's holding me back from doing something that could benefit other people and make other people's lives better … That's kind of what pushed me over the edge to run in 2017 were my fears in 2016.

Importantly, many interviewees revealed that a far more frequent worry than self-doubt was the concern that others would not take them seriously as candidates. Many tell stories of being entirely underestimated by members of their communities as well as local party members. Even women who had already won elective office were subjected to such voter misgivings, such as one locally elected woman, who heard things like "You're not ready. You're too young. Why do you think you can run? What makes you think that you're congressional?"

These women's stories revealed new insights about how perceived qualifications shape their decisions to run. Rather than doubt their own capacities, more often these candidates spoke to the ways in which others undervalued or discredited their qualifications. Of course, all of these women ultimately decided to run – whether such apprehensions hold back other women is worth pursuing in more depth.

FAMILY RESPONSIBILITIES

Previous research points to women's many hats as another reason women may not enter the electoral field – concerns about work-life balance and fulfilling all expectations are often cited as deterrents (Mandel 1981; Silbermann 2014). Based on our interviews, we conclude that women's family responsibilities still weigh heavily on women's decisions to run, with many waiting until their children were grown before launching candidacies. The average age of our interviewees was fifty-one, and the majority of these women (68 per cent) have children. However, only 20 per cent had school-aged children living at home when they ran. Many shared their apprehensions about how their candidacies would affect their kids and family, not only in terms of loss of privacy but also whether there were enough hours in the day to mount a campaign. As one woman stated:

> I was a little bit apprehensive about what it would mean for my family, the scrutiny. I wondered what the time commitment would do. I have kids. I've got four kids and so I didn't know what my day-to-day life would really look like. Like how many hours of the day this would take for me and for my family.

THE ROLE OF MONEY

The most common reservation mentioned by interviewees centred on the role of money in elections and their ability to raise sufficient funds to compete (24 per cent). As we discuss later, very few received any support or backing from their party or organizations such as EMILY's List, the most influential political action committee (PAC) devoted to supporting women's candidacies, so such a finding is understandable. Not only did these women worry about the challenge of raising money, but many shared stories of losing their primary to men who were less experienced but wealthy and willing to spend whatever it took to secure the nomination. As one woman in a crowded primary offered, one of her primary opponents had "zero legislative experience. He just woke up one day and said, 'Hey, you know, I'm a millionaire. I deserve to buy the seat.'"

Others reported very similar experiences:

> What I've learned from watching not only my race but other races is it's not necessarily the most qualified candidate or the best candidate for the job who comes out ahead. Unfortunately, I think the most important lesson is if you don't have lots of money up front ... it doesn't matter how good you are. And I was beaten by a man in his early forties who put over two million of his own money into the race. And [a supporter of his] spends another million. And that's for a primary.

Another theme echoes previous research: women simply must work harder than men to raise campaign funds (Carroll and Sanbonmatsu 2013).

> You know, nobody wants to give you money. It doesn't matter if they're your best friend or someone you've never met before, like nobody wants to give you money and no one wants to give you as much as you want them to give you.

Party Support and Encouragement

How often were women encouraged to run? Might the historic numbers of female candidates be attributed, in part, to increased party efforts to support female candidates in 2018? To gauge party support, we asked women if anyone had recruited or encouraged them to run, and we followed up with a question specifically inquiring about party support if they had not credited the party in their response.

The most common response from our interviewees was that they were essentially ignored or left to their own devices, receiving either token or no support from their political party (38 per cent). And despite the parties' usual claims to remain neutral in the primary, a sizeable number of women (30 per cent) learned that the party had someone else in mind for the position. Some women did report receiving slightly more support, about equal to the numbers who reported that they were either discouraged or sabotaged by fellow partisans or the party apparatus (approximately 20 per cent for each).

If we recall that most of our interviewees were engaged in primary races, the fact that they received so little support from their party is not particularly surprising, as the party often remains neutral during primaries. As mentioned above, however, many learned that the party, despite its claims of neutrality, was working behind the scenes to support someone else.

> I met with the party leader ... and she was warm and encouraging on a personal level, but neutral, and she said she was going to be neutral with all the candidates since it was a primary. But the Democratic Party in general, the establishment was definitely upset with me running. They had another candidate kind of picked out for the seat.

Even after advancing to the general election, women did not necessarily receive additional support. As one woman, a primary winner, reported:

> I never spoke to a single person from the DCCC [Democratic Congressional Campaign Committee]. I reached out, never got any response. The state party, the first conversation I had with them after the primary was cordial. It was, "Good for you. That was an exciting win. Basically the good news is we're not going to tell you what to do with your campaign. The bad news is we have nothing for you."

Such explanations make sense, especially in districts heavily tilted towards the opposing party. And a number of women running in difficult districts report that members of the party essentially discouraged them from running, suggesting that the party had for all practical purposes given up on the congressional district and did not have the capacity to get behind their campaigns. Yet for a handful of women, the party provided more than token support, such as small donations, assistance with phone banking, being included on coordinated campaign mailers, and campaign assistance from elected members of the party. To be clear, none of these women credited the party with much support; they simply acknowledged that they had received *some* assistance along the way.

Although the parties were not particularly involved in encouraging or recruiting these women to run, the majority of our candidates received encouragement from elsewhere and often credited such votes of confidence as key to their decision to run. Elected officials, progressive individuals and groups, and friends and family were the most likely sources of encouragement, but colleagues, fellow church members, and neighbours similarly offered their support at key moments when our candidates were pondering a run. This finding reflects the value of such practices for female candidates, who are more inclined than male candidates to require prodding and support (Carroll and Sanbonmatsu 2013; Crowder-Meyer 2013; Lawless and Fox 2012).

Lessons Learned

We asked all of our interviewees to reflect upon the lessons they learned on the campaign trail. And like their motivations for running, most of the women listed more than one lesson learned. In general, their responses fell into three categories: lessons related to the actual process of campaigning, insights about voters and their larger communities, and personal lessons.

The two most commonly mentioned campaign lessons were the value of money and the importance of a strong campaign team, offered by nearly 25 per cent of the women. While many indicated they realized fundraising would be important going into the race, they did not fully appreciate just how much time they would need to spend dialing for dollars, or just how expensive communicating their message across the district would prove. Quite a few candidates had also pledged not to accept PAC money and none were able to self-fund their campaigns.

Perhaps relatedly, many interviewees emphasized the importance of a strong campaign team, either as hired hands or volunteers. The comments of those who relied more heavily on volunteers than paid staff were almost entirely positive; using volunteers was viewed as an indicator of the candidate's ability to inspire and motivate the grassroots. As one said:

> I also learned that the greatest way that I believe can really get a campaign going, is do it organically. Organically in the sense that I didn't have paid people knocking on doors. I had volunteers. Volunteers who believed in our cause, who believed in our message, and that is absolutely priceless.

Another common sentiment voiced by our interviewees was the value of directly engaging voters. Whether articulated as a positive force for getting to know one's community or as an activity they wished they could have engaged in more frequently, many women highlighted the importance of going directly to the people and hearing them out. They learned to engage voters across a multitude of issues and perspectives, felt deeply appreciated for taking the time to listen, and often characterized their interactions with voters as the lifeblood of democracy.

A number of women also emphasized how their campaigns taught them much about themselves and provided excellent opportunities for personal growth. They spoke about developing many skills as the campaign wore on – public speaking, asking for money, trusting their own instincts, and developing a thicker skin. And with such learning experiences, their self-confidence often grew. As one woman explained, she initially worried about her personal appearance and how photos might portray her as an "ugly woman." She admitted having a "deep, deep concern … that I would appear to be this angry, ugly, wrinkled, down at the mouth, serious, angry woman." Yet, much to her delight, the campaign dispelled such worries and led to increased self-confidence:

> I'm incredibly comfortable in my own skin now … I am photogenic. I take beautiful photos, even when I'm angry, when I'm pointing my finger, or I'm sneering … I am a very talented and very intelligent person. I had deep understanding of the issues that were involved … [and people] respected my knowledge.

Next Steps

What comes next for these women? Despite the very difficult roads many of the women faced, the often physically and mentally demanding campaign cycle, and the ultimate loss, only five women said they would not run again. Thirty-one were very positive about their future prospects, excited about the lessons learned, and ready to apply them the next go-around, and another eighteen responded "maybe." A common refrain was, "I'll be ready next time." And for the women unsure of their future plans, many were determined to help other candidates by building upon the lessons they learned.

Conclusion

This project began with a simple question about the women who decided to run in 2018, and then lost: what motivated them and what challenges did they face? Do the traditional theories about why women run fit the facts today, or have those facts shifted? As we described above, many of the traditional reasons for female under-representation in political candidacies still hold true: female candidates are often discouraged from running, even by their party; they struggle with fundraising; and family responsibilities and concerns continue to weigh heavily on their decisions.

Yet one unexpected finding from these interviews is the nuanced role of self-confidence in shaping women's decisions to run. Two-thirds of these women were first-time candidates, with the vast majority telling us that they had never considered running before. And to be sure, a very small number explicitly shared reservations about their capacity to perform. But far more common was the experience of being underestimated on the campaign trail, answering to and dealing with *others* who called into question their qualifications. And while our interviewees ultimately decided to throw their hat into the ring rather than remain on the sidelines, we argue that their experience on the campaign trail nonetheless sheds light on other women's reluctance to run for office. Even after amassing impressive credentials, women are accustomed to having others downplay their accomplishments or question their capacities, especially when attempting to enter masculine fields. That is, women's calculus about their own qualifications in contesting elected office is likely a mix of their own self-doubts and a healthy appreciation of the ways in which others will routinely dismiss their abilities. We argue that developing a better understanding of which weighs more heavily on women's decisions to run (or not run) is important for addressing the gender gap in political candidacies.

In addition, we argue for building a more comprehensive understanding of the factors that shape women's decisions to run after suffering a loss. Noting that more than half of our interviewees told us they were planning to run again at some point in the future, we are especially interested in determining what separates these women from those who expressed greater reluctance following their 2018 loss. While we know a fair bit about gender and the decision to run for office, none of this scholarship systematically examines the role of loss in shaping future political ambitions. Is the decision to run again a function of the competitiveness of their previous election? A commitment to continue fighting for the things that inspired the first run? Alternatively, might women decide against running after experiences of being ignored by their party and dismissed by voters? By investigating these questions with women who have already ran and lost one election, we hope to shed light on this important, yet overlooked, component of political ambition.

NOTES

1 Although not a randomly selected sample, the women we spoke with were similar to the population of women who ran for a House seat in 2018 and lost. Specifically, the vast majority were Democrats (84 per cent), and over half ran as challengers (54 per cent). In 2018, 75 per cent of all female congressional candidates were Democrats and 55 per cent ran as challengers (data from the Center for American Women and Politics).

2 We promised all of the women confidentiality and replaced their names with codes. Interviews were recorded and then transcribed by temi.com. We cleaned the coded transcripts and used NVivo to analyse the results.

6 Black Women's Hair Matters: The Uneasy Marriage of Electoral Politics and (Dis)Respectability Politics

NADIA E. BROWN

I know that I looked respectable.

– Delegate Aisha Braveboy (D-MD)

The act of balancing racialized/gendered stereotypes and one's self-presentation is often a difficult negotiation for Black women candidates and elected officials. Yet this issue is often seen as frivolous or trivial in mainstream discussions of candidates and is not discussed in political science literature. In this chapter, I examine the importance of and challenges surrounding Black women's personal appearances on the campaign trail or within legislative bodies to conclude that respectability politics influences the self-presentation of Black women political elites.

Black women crafted "respectable" norms for themselves and their communities as a method of combatting race/gender-based aggression and discrimination against them. During the Reconstruction Era and early Jim Crow, Black clubwomen endorsed white Victorian norms in attempts to uplift the Black race (Higginbotham 1993). They attempted to outperform white upper-middle-class culture as a way to demonstrate their humanity and show that the racist/sexist sentiments towards them were unfounded. By behaving in a culturally accepted manner, Black clubwomen sought to challenge the prevailing stereotypes of them by simply acting more Victorian than whites.

This was a strategic political decision, to be sure. Though deeply rooted in conservative class and sexual politics, it was an attempt to craft a distinct gendered space for Black men and women. In doing so, Black clubwomen such as Nannie Barrier Williams, Mary Church Terrell, and Lucy Craft Laney used the Black female body as a site for social construction within an embodied discourse (Cooper 2017), meaning the Black female body became the main tool in articulating, policing, theorizing, and advancing respectability politics. Ideas about gender and race were mapped on to Black women's bodies, as well as what it means to properly perform racialized gender.

In this chapter, I demonstrate how Black women political elites are concerned with respectability politics. Some may argue that this is an overstated concern given today's more liberal sexual and gendered politics. However, the Black women candidates and elected officials in my study demonstrate that Black communities, in particular, remain deeply committed to respectability politics. Black women political elites display their adherence to respectable norms through their hair style choices. The demonstration of respectable styling and grooming choices signal that Black women political elites do not fall within one of the four prevailing race/gender stereotypes – the Mammy, Sapphire, the Black Lady, and the Jezebel (Hill Collins 1990) – that continue to stigmatize this group. I show that Black women political elites are conscious of these community norms, historical stereotypes, and their current role in dictating Black women's sociopolitical positioning.

Why Hair Matters

Black women's hair and hairstyle choices are a salient political issue because of the cultural, symbolic, and economic meaning attached to their hair. Hair is linked to symbolic meanings that are at once gendered and classed (Gill 2010). The versatility of Black hair has drawn curiosity and awe from non-Blacks, causing many to ask questions about these women's hair. Conversely, the tight coils and kinks of some Black hair have been viewed as a curse both within and outside of Africana communities (Candelario 2007; Lindsey 2017). Hair has social meanings that are often obscured in discussions of personal choice and self-expression. Conversations that take Black hairstyles as merely a form of expressing one's identity are deeply misguided and devoid of a sociohistorical understanding of the centrality of hair in both the lives of Black women and American culture (Mercer 2005). Along with Black music, food, and culture, hair is a central component of Africana life.

In particular, within electoral politics, Black women's hair has political ramifications. Johnson Carew (2012) and Brown (2014) have documented that Black women political elites are evaluated differently than their race or gender counterparts because of their appearance. Intersectional experiences and stereotypes drive not only Black women's political experience but also their evaluations by voters and constituents. Indeed, respectability politics demands that Black women alter their self-presentation in ways that reject white stereotypes by embodying morality and de-emphasizing sexuality (Cooper 2017; Higginbotham 1993). It is important to note that Black women in general, and scholars in particular, have been both challenging and reaffirming (dis)respectability as a site for Black women's sociopolitical mobility (Cooper 2017). Centring Black women political elites themselves gives us unique entry into understanding how the myriad of perceptions of Black women's hair – that have often been framed in a negative way – find themselves an issue for electoral politics.

Data and Methods

As prototypical intersectional subjects – doubly marginalized by race and gender and whose narratives are used to expose the under-theorized categorization of identity[1] – Black women candidates and elected officials warrant rigorous study, specifically with respect to how they experience and manage race and gender in American politics. The need to look at intra-group differences within a single case study is guided by shortcomings within the extant literature on Black women in American politics. In this chapter, I move beyond cross-group analysis among women or minority men to look within Black women candidates and political elites as a group, to examine how the distinct and/or analogous narratives of the salience of hair impact their political experiences as well as their understanding of race/gender in America.

One-on-one, in-person interviews were conducted between 2014 and 2017. The data for this study come from twelve in-depth, semi-structured, and opened interviews that I conducted with Black women political elites in Maryland, the District of Columbia, Virginia, Illinois, and Missouri. Interviews lasted between forty-five and ninety minutes, and all were on the record. These interviews were recorded and transcribed and organized into themes.[2] These states were selected because I had access to this population: I had built professional relationships with these candidates and lawmakers during my previous academic research projects.[3] All the women in the study were asked, "Please tell me about how you decided to wear your hair" and "Do you think that your hair plays a role in politics broadly defined?" These questions serve as the bases for the analysis of this paper. However, the larger interview protocol asked questions about the woman's political priorities, how her appearance may or may not affect her political experiences, and her understanding of how race/gender influences political behaviour.

In what follows, I present the narratives of Black women political elites to better understand the politics of appearance by focusing on hair as a site of respectability politics. Basing my analysis within the social context of race/gender in America and within the structures of electoral politics, I critically assess the experiences and views of Black women political elites regarding the salience of hair as an intersectional project. By giving a thick description of these women's narratives I provide deeper insight into how the politics of appearance is fluid, contextual, and largely based on sociopolitical factors that are deeply embedded in the symbolic meanings of Black women's hair both inside and outside of formal politics.

Straight Hair = Respectability

Several of the women in my study explicitly noted that Black constituents and communities view having straight hair as the gold standard for Black women political elites. However, they pushed back against this view in nuanced and dynamic ways. Often, they did this in covert ways, such as only straightening their hair with heat for campaign events or while in session. Others indicated that they knew the expectations of having straight hair but that this was not the motivating factor in their personal styling decisions. Instead, their more conservative look was based in their profession or personal taste. Others shared that they are aware of societal tropes of Black women and use personal styling as a way to counteract these stereotypical imagines. While each woman's personal strategies and internal calculations regarding how she wears her hair may vary, what remains the same is their common calculations of respectability politics within electoral politics.

Take, for example, the narrative of Diane Harris, who was a candidate for a seat in the Illinois House of Representatives in the winter of 2014 when we first spoke. Harris is a Republican who has run unsuccessfully several times to represent majority-minority districts in the Chicago-land area. When asked about her hair choices, Harris describes how her hair is often pulled back in a bun because she does not have the resources to pay a beautician to keep up with routine maintenance of chemically relaxed hair. For Harris, her conservative political values are reflected in her personal styling decisions. However, because she is unable to afford regular hair appointments, the reality of her personal style is largely dictated by her inability to maintain relaxed hair. Yet her analysis of how possible constituents view her hair reveals the ways that partisans, but mostly racialized groups, make inferences about Black women political elites based on their hair. Harris commented:

> Republicans don't know what's going on with my hair. African American voters, I know they look at what a person looks like. And I say that

because I've been there, I know. As far as Republicans, I know that they will look, but I don't think that's more of an emphasis as much as African American Democrats. They [Republicans] may wonder how much I'm spending and who's money I'm spending. But I don't think that the focus [on my hair] would be more critical as it is on the Democratic side. I'm sure you know what I mean [reference to the author as a Black woman]. We were raised that we should look our best and be our best. And if we're going to be representing people, that is what is expected. To look our best and to be our best. It's expensive and time consuming. The others [whites] might not have to. But you can't please everybody.

Here candidate Harris juxtaposes how whites and Blacks, and by consequence Republicans and Democrats, view looking good and doing one's best. These sentiments are based in respectability politics (Higginbotham 1993) in which Black women are evaluated by their actions, style choices, and lifestyles. An aspect of respectability politics is the policing of Black women, by other Black women, to comport to the social values and norms of middle- to upper-class white women and society. Rather than challenging the dominant values of mainstream culture, appearance, and behaviour, this form of respectability politics reassigns blame from the oppressors to the oppressed. Candidate Harris's comments reify these norms of respectability, which may give her inroads with Republicans, but she is aware of how appearance matters among Blacks and how Black women should navigate societal norms. Related to electoral politics, respectability politics demonstrates candidate Harris's understanding of Black voters and that their perceived values of propriety and morality are reflected in the politics of appearance. However, she is not contesting racism and sexism nor the societal structures that recreate these oppressions. Rather, she is highlighting the differences between Blacks, whom she sees as Democrats, and Republicans, whom she sees as whites.

Unlike candidate Harris, delegate Aisha Braveboy campaigned in and was elected to serve a majority-minority constituency yet still prefers a conservative look. At the time of our interview, delegate Braveboy was in the midst of an unsuccessful bid to be Maryland's attorney general. She was currently representing a suburban Washington, DC, district in the Maryland House of Delegates. She is a member of Generation X, is dark skinned, and wears her hair in a straight close-cropped cut. For her, the politics of appearance has distinct electoral consequences. She noted: "How you decide to present yourself matters. Because we know that voters, you could be saying all the right things, but they can't get past what you look like, the dress you have on, how you combed your hair. How you present yourself matters." To further elucidate, she shared: "I'm pretty conservative, and I think that most voters, regardless of whether I'm a woman or a man, I think most voters feel more comfortable with people who [present themselves in a more conservative manner]. So yes, a more conservative look. Plus, I'm a lawyer. We don't go into courtrooms with rock star hair or anything like that." Delegate Braveboy's presentation style is coupled with her own personal and professional preferences that are more conservative leaning as well as her assessment of what voters prefer. She believes that non-conservative self-presentation of candidates acts as noise that interrupts how voters perceive one's messages.

Unlike delegate Braveboy and candidate Harris, who were seeking to represent majority-minority communities, school board member C.J. Brown ran for election in West Lafayette, IN, which has an overwhelmingly white population. In contrast to Braveboy and Harris, Brown does not have straightened hair; however, she received pushback on her personal styling decisions from other Black women. She described the possibility of some voters ascribing negative stereotypes to her solely because of her race, gender, and natural hair. Additionally, she mentioned that respectability politics played a role in initial reactions to her decision to stop chemically relaxing her hair:

> When I went natural, I got flak from old ladies and church sistas. [They'd ask], "why are you wearing your hair nappy like that?" This was back in 1971. The sisters in the church were the ones that gave me the most grief. These ladies, they were into the creamy crack. They didn't want no naps on their heads. And [they thought] that we shouldn't either. And when I talk about the church sisters, I'm talking about the old ones, the ones that helped raise me. So, they were the ones sucking through their teeth and whatnot. But my peers were different. Oh yea, we were all wearing, letting our hair grow out … But I was quick to say [to the church sisters], "why are you wearing your hair like that? Because I don't think we need to adhere to European standards of beauty."

Brown's embrace of her natural hair and questioning of European beauty standards was a by-product of the time. As Tanisha Ford (2015) argues, Black women used their hair and personal style as a form of resistance during the Black Power era and beyond. By celebrating her identity through natural hair, Brown pushed her church sisters to rethink beauty culture as a symbol of both gender and political liberation. The initial decision to go natural in the early 1970s was rooted in the cultural/political practice of the time. Brown's narrative demonstrates that she was aware that this hairstyle might have political repercussions.

Lastly, Missouri state senator Jamilah Nasheed, who represents a district in St. Louis, decided to straighten her naturally kinky-curly hair while on the campaign trail. She connected her personal aesthetic to going mainstream so that voters could pay full attention to her policies rather than what she looked like. Nasheed also connected her appearance to legacies of racism and gender-based discrimination in which Black women needed to look more Eurocentric to be considered beautiful. She noted:

> Your image is nonverbal. You are talking to people even when you are not talking. And they are going to listen to you, not literally listen to you, but listen to you and pay attention to you based on your appearance. They prejudge you way before you open your mouth. So, you have to have this mainstream image so to speak … A lot of African Americans are not confident in their own skin. And they want to be accepted. So, they change their dialect when they are around non–African Americans. Their posture, their hair. They allow for people – not all Black folks, but many – allow for people to define who they are versus them defining themselves. This is troubling. Because what was defined as "beauty" within the African American community, with the first fifty elected officials, you had to almost look like a white person.

For Nasheed, beauty norms for Black women are part and parcel of racialized/gendered stereotyping. Their self-presentation is viewed through a lens of otherness, and in order to be fully heard and acknowledged as a viable candidate, a Black woman running for office must confirm to Eurocentric beauty norms – even if she's running in a majority Black district.

Discussion and Conclusions

The acknowledgment of respectability politics is more than a tacit understanding of the impact of policing Black women's bodies, but rather shows an engagement with (dis)respectability in ways that are organic for each woman in this study. The three women highlighted here demonstrate that they are aware the Black communities assess them based on their personal hair styling choices. Indeed, these careful calculations of self-presentation are reflected, albeit in varying ways, by the other six women in my study.

Furthermore, these women note that straight hair is a way that Black women can engage with controlling stereotypes about Black womanhood. They all believe that having straight hair enables voters to see

Black women candidates and elected officials as viable candidates. But these women are primarily having these conversations in Black communities and assessing their looks as racial/gendered markers of otherness. These indicators point to the continued salience of respectability politics.

The dual processes of racing-gendering (Hawkesworth 2003) and women's beauty norms may lead Black congresswomen to alter their self-presentations in order to appear more feminine and with softer racially distinct features. Because hair, both texture and style, is a political heuristic, Black women lawmakers may forgo Afro-centric styles in order to achieve their legislative goals in a white-male-dominated institution. However, because the election of these women to these legislative bodies is largely controlled by Black communities, it is necessary to increase awareness of how these communities seemingly police the bodies of Black women political elites. In sum, we see the continued impact of historical attitudes towards Black women's bodies played out on modern electoral stages.

NOTES

1 Black feminists have long advanced the claim that multiple identities – such as race, gender, class, and sexual orientation – are mutually reinforcing and interlocking, thus calling on feminist scholars to complicate the view of a "universal woman" (e.g., Crenshaw 1989; Davis 1981; Higginbotham 1993; Nash 2008; Smith 1983).

2 With the assistance of an undergraduate research assistant, the transcripts were coded using an open-ended method. The undergraduate research assistant pulled quotes for me to more deeply analyse based on a set of broad codes. I then performed a more fine-grained analysis on the highlighted quotes and developed a list of secondary themes that were more detailed than the original coding scheme. From there, I thematically organized quotes to reveal overlapping and divergent narratives. All coding was done in Microsoft Word and required a detailed reading of each transcript. The selected quotes were highlighted for ease of searchability and comparison with both the broad and detailed codebook. Lastly, because this method of hand coding required a deep attention to the data, I was able to analyse the data while I simultaneously coded. This technique is common in interpretivist methods. Indeed, interpretivist analysis is holistic and contextual. As such, the researcher code does not isolate statements made about hair from other responses given by the Black women in this study as I attempted to understand the perspectives the women used

to make sense of hair as a sociopolitical phenomenon. This rigorous, systematic, and transparent approach to data collection and analysis serves as an interpretivist benchmark for validity and significance testing, since the simultaneous analysis and coding allows a researcher to capture the phenomenon better by correcting for potential flaws earlier in the process.

3 Because subjects were selected for their accessibility, the data are not representative of all Black women serving in elected offices or running as candidates for electoral office.

7 Women in the Plenary: Verbal Participation in the Argentine Congress

TIFFANY D. BARNES AND VICTORIA BEALL

In recent years, women across the world have gained access to legislatures in record numbers. Nonetheless, once in office, women face formal and informal barriers to power that limit their influence in the chamber. Despite these limitations, women have incentives and obligations to participate in the policymaking process. In this chapter we investigate two propositions: first, whether women navigate the legislative process differently than men to overcome these power imbalances and, second, whether formal and informal barriers to women's influence further reinforce gendered power dynamics, limiting women's influence over policymaking.

We posit that in an effort to overcome their limited access to power, women may be more likely than men to adopt distinct tactics to circumvent roadblocks and wield influence (Barnes 2016). In particular, women may pursue legislative activities where their behaviour cannot be easily checked or constrained by party leadership. Participating in plenary discussions may represent an opportunity for women to influence the policymaking process absent the formal constraints of party leadership.

Alternatively, even if women want to exert influence by engaging in plenary discussions, exclusion from formal and informal legislative power may further exacerbate gender power imbalances. When formal rules governing plenary discussion disproportionately benefit party leadership, women may have fewer formal opportunities to speak. Moreover, the gender dynamics of male-dominated institutions may discourage women from wielding speech as an effective tool of political influence. We examine original data on legislative speech from the Argentine Chamber of Deputies to evaluate whether women appear more frequently on the chamber floor, or if the formal and informal rules that limit women's access to power perpetuate gender power imbalances on the floor.

Women's Access to Legislative Power

Despite their gaining access to legislative office in record numbers since the adoption of gender quotas, women's experiences once in office vary dramatically from those of their male colleagues (Barnes 2016; Heath et al. 2005; O'Brien 2015). Women's experience in the chamber is frequently characterized by their limited access to formal and informal avenues of power.

Indeed, women worldwide are under-represented in the most influential political posts (Bashevkin 2010; Kerevel 2019; Tremblay 2012). Women are less likely to be appointed to the most powerful committees (Barnes 2014; Heath et al. 2005; Kerevel and Atkeson 2013), and when they do gain access, they are far less likely to chair these committees (Barnes 2016; Schwindt-Bayer 2010). Beyond this, they rarely ascend to the most powerful party leadership positions (Barnes and Jones 2018; Morgan and Hinojosa 2018; O'Brien 2015; O'Neill and Stewart 2009).

Women in male-dominated political institutions also confront informal barriers that limit their ability to wield influence in the policymaking process. To begin with, women legislators face gendered stereotypes about their propensity to lead that often call women's power into question and undermine women's influence (Alexander and Andersen 1993; Funk, Hinojosa, and Piscopo 2017). Women are frequently assumed to be less competent, especially when working on stereotypically masculine policy domains such as finance, economics, and defence (Barnes and O'Brien 2018; Holman, Merolla, and Zechmeister 2011). Further, women lack access to elite networks and circles of power that govern political advancement (Franceschet and Piscopo 2014). This exclusion results in a gendered power deficit, with women being "cut off from important leadership discussions, having limited access to timely strategic information, and [not being] consulted for advice" (Barnes 2016, 32).

Navigating Gendered Power Deficits

Even in the face of limitations to their political power, women legislators (like all legislators) have an obligation to advocate for their constituents, represent their political party, and participate in the policymaking process. And given that women bring different policy preferences and priorities to the fore (Beall and Barnes 2020; Funk and Philips 2019; Schwindt-Bayer 2010), their participation is vital for representation. Certainly, there are a number of legislative activities – such as verbal participation on the floor, collaboration, and bill introduction – that allow rank-and-file members to wield influence.

Given women's limited access to formal and informal power, we may expect to observe that women work harder on other types of legislative activities to exert power.

In this vein, Barnes (2016) argues that women collaborate more than men because they are marginalized in ways that limit their influence on the policymaking process; collaborating with other women is a means of exerting more influence on that process. Similarly, Holman and Mahoney (2018) find that women in U.S. state legislatures are more likely than men to collaborate to advance their policy interests. Evidence from the U.S. Congress likewise suggests that women in the minority party introduce more bills than minority men and are more effective at advancing their legislation (Volden, Wiseman, and Wittmer 2013).

Whereas previous research demonstrates that women engage in collaboration and bill introduction to overcome their gendered-power imbalances, scholars have focused less attention on how women participate in plenary discussions to overcome these imbalances. Notably, Pearson and Dancey (2011) examined women's legislative speech-making in the U.S. Congress and found that congresswomen speak more on the House floor in part due to challenges they face in the chamber. Beyond the United States, little work has evaluated whether women participate in plenary discussions to overcome inequalities in influence.

Wielding Influence on the Chamber Floor

Participating on the plenary floor represents a low-cost opportunity for legislators to accomplish a variety of tasks, signalling important information to their co-partisans and party leaders, the opposition, current and future collaborators, and their constituents (Martin and Vanberg 2008; Proksch and Slapin 2015). Plenary discussions are an ideal time for legislators to communicate with a variety of key audiences necessary for effective legislating and re-election (Schwarz et al. 2015). With respect to women in particular, participating on the plenary floor gives them the opportunity to communicate expertise over stereotypically masculine policy domains (Pearson and Dancey 2011), to advocate for policies that disproportionately affect the lives of women (Catalano 2009; Clayton, Josefsson, and Wang 2017; Osborn and Mendez 2010; Piscopo 2011), and to signal the importance of legislation to their male colleagues (Dietrich, Hayes, and O'Brien, 2019).

Given that participating in legislative discussions represents a meaningful and low-cost tool, women may utilize speech to exert more influence. With women's under-representation in key positions of power, participating in floor discussions represents an alternative opportunity to wield political influence that is formally unconstrained by party leadership. As a result, women may speak more than men, who have access to conventional sources of power and influence.

Gendered Power Imbalances Perpetuate Women's Limited Influence

Although we anticipate that women may work harder than men, speaking more frequently on the chamber floor to overcome power deficits, there is also reason to believe that gendered power imbalances may work to further diminish women's influence in the chamber, and specifically during legislative speech-making. That is, even if women want to use plenary discussions to attain influence, they may not be able to because formal chamber rules are designed to concentrate power into the hands of legislative leadership and informal legislative dynamics may further curtail their influence.

With respect to formal rules, in the Argentine Congress, for example, the rules that govern how much legislators can talk during the plenary session give disproportionate access to party leaders. Since women are not well represented among the party leadership, if party leaders take full advantage of their leadership privilege and if parties try to present a unified position on the floor by informally controlling or monitoring what their party members say, women may participate on the floor less than men.

In addition to formal chamber rules, informal legislative gender power imbalances may limit women's ability to influence the policy-making process through floor participation. In majority-male (and even mixed-gendered) settings – such as the plenary – men are more likely than women to dominate the discussion (Karpowitz and Mendelberg 2014). As men are less likely to view women as adept policymakers or to welcome input from women who take initiative (Barnes 2016; Rosenthal 1998), women may be discouraged from participating on the floor where men are in the majority. Additionally, given that women tend to be more conflict avoidant than men, they may shy away from participating in legislative discussions, particularly in the context of highly conflictual or competitive debates (Mendleberg, Karpowitz, and Goedert 2014). Further, in the United States and Canada women politicians, especially those holding high-profile posts, are more often the targets of hostile social media posts (Rheault, Rayment, and Musulan 2019). Negative backlash on social media may discourage women from pursuing highly visible activity such as speaking on the plenary. Combined, these informal legislative dynamics may work to hinder women's access and willingness to take the plenary floor to influence the policymaking process.

Women's Participation on the Chamber Floor:
Evidence from the Argentine Plenary

To assess whether women are more active on the floor or whether gendered power imbalances further limit women's influence we turn to the Argentine National Chamber of Deputies. Argentina stands out among the world's democracies for having over two decades of experience with legislative gender quotas. As a result of well-designed gender quotas, women have since 2002 consistently held more than 30 per cent of seats in the Chamber of Deputies. Despite dramatic increases in their numeric representation, women remain institutionally disadvantaged in the Argentine government, as they are disproportionately under-represented in critical party (Barnes and Jones 2018) and chamber (Schwindt-Bayer 2010) leadership positions, have limited access to influential networks (Barnes and Holman 2020; Franceschet and Piscopo 2014), and face informal barriers to influence (Barnes 2016).

Further, although all legislators are permitted to speak on the floor, Argentine rules disproportionately empower legislators in party leadership. Whereas rank-and-file members are permitted to speak twice for five minutes each time, leaders of small party blocks (one to ten deputies) are permitted to speak for seven minutes and leaders from larger party blocks (more than ten deputies) are allowed to speak for ten minutes. Combined, the institutionalization of women's numeric representation, women's limited access to formal and informal political power, and legislative rules that grant all members access to the floor – but disproportionately empower party leaders – represent an ideal setting to investigate how women navigate the legislative arena to exert their political influence on the plenary.

To test our empirical expectations, we collected speech data for each legislative term of the Argentine National Congress between 2013 and 2017 for the Chamber of Deputies. The Congress provides floor transcripts for each plenary session in the Chamber of Deputies understudy. The transcripts were collected using the R software package *rvest* (Wickham 2014) and processed using the *quanteda* package (Benoit et al. 2018). The data were processed so that each observation represents an instance where a legislator spoke on the plenary floor. We included the sentence count and the word count for each observation.

Figure 7.1 plots the share of floor appearances who are women (black columns) compared to the share of deputies in the chamber who are women (grey columns). A few important trends are apparent from this figure. First, overall, men take the floor more frequently than women. Specifically, when a legislator verbally participates during the plenary

Figure 7.1. Percentage of Women in Floor Appearances vs. Percentage of Women in Congress

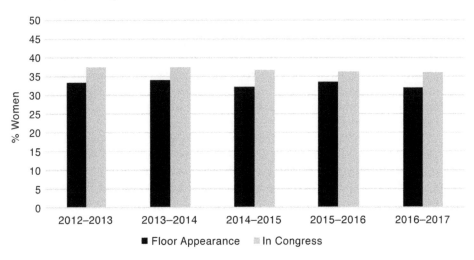

session, the speaker is a man about 67 per cent of the time and a woman about 33 per cent of the time. Second, and equally important, women's share of verbal participation is below their share of legislative seats, meaning that they are under-represented not only during verbal floor participation overall but also relative to the share of seats they hold.

Although these trends suggest that women are not enjoying as many opportunities as men to talk on the floor, Figure 7.1 does not tell the entire story. It is possible that women take the floor less frequently, but when they do they take full advantage of the time allotted to them such that they talk more.

To assess whether men and women talk more when they take the floor, we compared the average number of sentences and number of words used while speaking on the floor. On average, legislators use about 17.4 sentences (and 416 words) when speaking. That said, there are important differences in men's and women's speech patterns.

Figures 7.2 and 7.3 plot the average number of sentences and words (respectively) that men and women use when they appear on the plenary for each term understudy. Whereas men use an average of 17.02 sentences (403.76 words) each time they take the floor, women use an average of 15.53 sentences (369.53 words). When looking across the legislative terms, we observed statistically significant differences between men and women's verbal activity for each term except for the 2016–17 term (the 134th

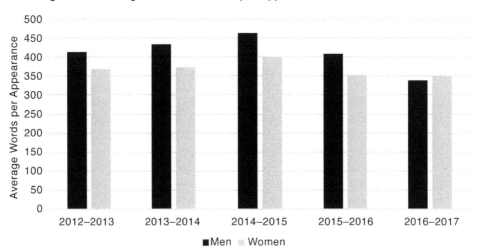

Figure 7.2. Average Number of Sentences per Appearance, Women vs. Men

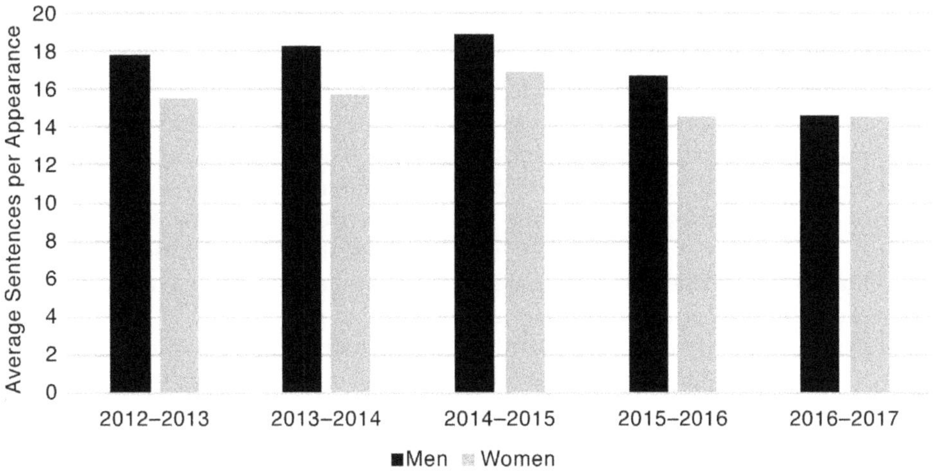

Figure 7.3. Average Number of Words per Appearance, Women vs. Men

Congress), where men and women spoke the same amount when they appeared on the floor. Despite this equality in the 134th Congress, however, women are still under-represented overall and relative to their seat share during floor appearances. Combined, these data suggest that women are exerting less influence than their male colleagues on the plenary.

Conclusion

Women face limited access to formal and informal power in the legislature and in politics more generally. Despite these limitations, women legislators have obligations to represent their political party and constituents, to engage in the legislative process, and to articulate their unique policy preferences and priorities (Beall and Barnes 2020; Clayton and Zeterberg 2019; Funk and Philips 2019). Utilizing an original dataset of plenary discussions from the Chamber of Deputies in the National Argentine Congress (2012–17), we examine whether women leverage their opportunities to participate on the chamber floor to wield political influence, or whether women's exclusion from power reinforces gendered power dynamics, resulting in women participating less than men. We find that not only are women under-represented in their seat share in the chamber, but they also speak less frequently, and use fewer sentences and words when they do speak, across four of the five legislative terms in our dataset. Still, there is more work to be done to explain gender patterns of verbal participation in the Argentine Congress.

Future research should examine the extent to which women's participation on the plenary can be explained by their formal access to power (i.e., their under-representation in party leadership) or if informal power imbalances also work to limit women's participation. Further, it is possible that women do work harder than their male counterparts and are therefore more prepared; as a result, they may be less likely to ramble when taking the floor. We cannot account for this in this aggregate analysis. Future research could examine if there are differences in how men and women prepare for legislative sessions, as well as in the use of non-specific language, and whether these factors explain women's lower participation in plenary discourse.

Finally, it is important to consider how these results generalize to other chambers. In Canada, for example, despite rising numbers of women legislators, parties are less likely to elect women as their leaders (O'Neill and Stewart 2009) and women have unequal access to other positions of power (Bashvekin 2010; Tremblay 2012). Given this gendered power deficit, our research suggests that it is important to understand how formal and informal rules work either to facilitate women's access to influence via participation on the floor or to reinforce gender inequalities in the plenary.

8 Women as Party Leaders

DIANA Z. O'BRIEN

Party leaders are the most important political figures in modern democracies. They are influential actors within their parties, and they shape their organizations' vote, office, and policy-seeking aims. And the most prestigious government position available to the party when in office is typically reserved for the party leader, including the post of prime minister. Women's sustained exclusion from party leadership represents a major challenge to full gender equality in politics.

In this chapter, I begin by asking when and where women become party leaders. My cross-national, over-time analysis shows that green/environmental parties are especially likely to select women leaders, but there are no other clear trends with respect to party ideology. Instead, women's access to these posts is shaped by gendered political opportunity structures, which may be evolving over time. Turning to the implications of women's access to power, I ask whether female- and male-led parties present different policy agendas. I find no differences on either the left-right dimension or on attention to social justice issues, welfare state growth, and education expansion. I discuss why this may be the case and interrogate the representational obligations of (women) party leaders as compared to legislators. I conclude by outlining two strategies – increasing the number of women elites and empowering intra-party women's organizations – that could encourage leaders, both men and women, to focus greater attention on women's representation.

When and Where Do Women Lead?

Party leadership has long been male dominated. Data from 358 parties in 35 democracies between 1976 and 2016[1] show that of the 1,557 party-election year observations, 234 (15 per cent) are female-led organizations. Unfortunately, these numbers have largely failed to improve over time. When the data are restricted to observations since 2000, 165 of 970 party-election years had female leaders (17 per cent). Focusing on the most recent period (post-2010), women's leadership rate is still only 18 per cent.

Where do women come to power? There is variation in women's presence in leadership positions across countries. Some states are high performers. Denmark, in particular, outpaces virtually every other country. A majority of its parties have had at least one woman leader. Indeed, at one point during Helle Thorning-Schmidt's tenure as prime minister, each of the three governing coalition parties was headed by a woman. Others underperform. There are fewer women leaders, for example, in Central and Eastern European countries. Canada is on par with most other parliamentary democracies (Scandinavian countries excepted). As in most other states, the glass ceiling has been shattered in some parties, whereas others have yet to break with the male-dominated status quo.

Which kinds of parties select women leaders? Here, there is a clear trend with respect to party ideology – green parties surpass all other organizations with respect to women's leadership. A number of green parties mandate that the leadership post be shared by female and male co-leaders. The greens in England and Wales, Germany, New Zealand, and Sweden all opt to split the position. Even green parties that eschew the co-leader model are more likely than other parties to have been female led. Importantly, this finding holds even when accounting for parties' seat share and government status. This suggests that it is not simply these parties' niche position that explains women's presence in leadership, but rather a deeper commitment to gender egalitarian values.

Beyond green parties, there are no meaningful differences in other party families' propensities to select women leaders. In contrast to the greater numbers of women in their legislative delegations (O'Brien 2018), socialist and social democratic parties are not more likely to be female led than their right-leaning counterparts. Indeed, 48 per cent of the instances of women's leadership in the dataset occur in non-left organizations (e.g., not green, communist, or socialist/social democratic parties). Some of the most high-profile leaders of the modern era, including Germany's Angela Merkel, Britain's Theresa May, and Marine Le Pen of France, lead right-wing parties, while some important left-leaning organizations – including the British and Dutch Labour Parties – have yet to break with their male-dominated status quo. Müller-Rommel and Vercesi (2017) even show that across ten European Union member states, female prime ministers are more likely to emerge from centre-right parties.

Although the selection of women as party leaders varies across countries and party-families, these two factors are more useful as explanations for women's presence in legislatures. They are less persuasive as predictors of women's ascension to positions of political leadership. What then explains women's access to power? Existing work suggests that prospective female leaders face gendered political opportunity structures. Particularly with respect to the initial selection of female leaders at the national level, parties' political performances matter. Women are more likely than men to be selected to lead parties that are in crisis or decline (Beckwith 2015; O'Neill and Stewart 2009). Focusing on Canada, Trimble and Arscott (2003) argue that the most common pathway to power for female party leaders is to take control of "electorally decimated and moribund parties" (77). Bashevkin (2009) notes that no Canadian woman had won a leadership contest in a competitive party. O'Brien (2015) demonstrates that those trends hold beyond the Canadian case. An analysis of 71 national-level political parties in 11 parliamentary democracies shows that women are most likely to initially come to power when the position is least desirable – that is, in minor opposition parties and those that are losing seat share. Beckwith (2015) suggests that party crises – including election loss, political or economic upheaval, and party and personal scandals – often create opportunities for women's leadership by removing experienced male incumbents and deterring more junior men from standing for the post.

Despite the importance of this work on political performance, it is not clear that the same gendered political opportunity structures hold in all cases. First, we should be cautious in applying this logic to presidential systems. Though women in parliamentary regimes are most likely to initially ascend to power in weakened parties, female presidents in Latin America have gained office by succeeding popular male incumbents from the same party (O'Brien and Reyes-Housholder 2020). Second, even within parliamentary systems, we do not know whether party performance has similar effects at the subnational level. Newer scholarship by Thomas (2018), for example, finds that performance explains the ascension of only four of eight female Canadian premiers (the head of government of a province or territory). Third, it is possible that the effects of performance wane once women have broken the glass ceiling. If parties have previously selected a female leader, women no longer provide a novelty bonus. As women's presence in office becomes more common, moreover, we hope that women will be able to access leadership posts in parties that are not in crises.

As more parties break with the male-dominated status quo, we must shift from asking how women shatter the glass ceiling to considering how we can normalize women's access to power. That is, how can we guarantee women's continued inclusion as viable candidates in leadership contests? Though scholarship on this topic is lacking, existing work does suggest that women's presence in other positions within the party likely matters. In particular, there is a correlation between the number of women legislators and women's access to leadership posts (O'Brien 2015; O'Brien and Rickne 2016). Legislators both constitute the supply pool for leaders and are also typically involved in leadership selection. Bolstering women's presence among the party's legislative delegation thus increases the supply of – and demand for – women leaders. We should work to ensure that there are large numbers of women in the parliamentary delegation so that there are viable women candidates who can seize upon opportunities – crises or otherwise – to compete for the leadership post.

Do Female Leaders Produce Different Policies?

Women's access to power within political parties is a matter of fairness. Women are half the population, and in many countries constitute an even larger percentage of the electorate. In a just world, we would expect women to make up half of all viable contenders for leadership posts. Though women's presence in these positions is vital in and of itself, as the most important politicians within their parties, it is also reasonable to examine the broader influence of female party leaders, particularly vis-á-vis policy outcomes.

To date, most work on the effects of women's leadership examines citizens' attitudes towards women leaders and female-led parties. Case study analyses from established parliamentary democracies suggest that leader gender influences female voters' propensity to support the leader and her party (Banducci and Karp 2000; Denemark, Ward, and Bean 2012; Kosiara-Pedersen and Hansen 2015). Survey data from Canada and New Zealand indicate that respondents perceive that female leaders have distinct issue priorities (Gidengil, Everitt, and Banducci 2009). And a cross-national analysis demonstrates that female-led organizations are viewed as more centrist than their male-led counterparts (O'Brien 2019). Related to voters' perceptions of (fe)male-led parties, scholars have also explored how media coverage of male- and female-led organizations varies (Gidengil and Everitt 2000, 2003; Greene and Lühiste 2018), a phenomenon that Linda Trimble explores in chapter 3 of this volume.

In contrast to the growing body of work on female leaders and audience effects, fewer studies assess the policy consequences of women's access to power. This is surprising for two reasons. First, party leaders are typically the single most important policy actors within their organizations, so it is reasonable to ask whether women's inclusion in these posts yields distinct policy outcomes. Second, there is a large body of work suggesting that women's unique life experiences will lead (at least some) women in power to prioritize and promote different policies than their male counterparts. Indeed, much of the scholarship on the election of female legislators supports this claim. Given that leaders have greater agenda access than backbench parliamentarians, will women's presence in the post yield similar, or even greater, policy effects?

As an initial assessment of the policy consequences of selecting a woman leader, I compare the policy platforms of male- and female-led parties. These policy statements, which parties draft prior to elections, outline the legislative priorities that the organization hopes to enact should they win. They serve both as campaign documents designed to sway the electorate and as blueprints for behaviour once in office. Indeed, pledge fulfilment rates are relatively high in advanced industrialized democracies (Thomson et al. 2017).

I use data from the Comparative Manifestos Project (CMP/MAPOR) to measure parties' policy priorities. Coders match up quasi-sentences from each political party's pre-election policy manifesto with a policy category (e.g., defence, law and order, welfare). The percentage of references in each category represents a measure of the party's priorities. For this analysis, I consider parties' overarching left-right location (RILE score[2]) as well as three issues that Kittilson (2011) identifies as particularly associated with women's policy representation: social justice, welfare state expansion, and education. The social justice measure captures parties' efforts to advocate for the fair treatment of all people, end discrimination, and provide special protections for underprivileged and historically marginalized groups (including women). The welfare state expansion variable includes favourable mentions of the introduction, maintenance, or expansion of social security programs. Finally, the education measure captures policies aimed at expanding and/or improving educational provisions at all levels.

My main explanatory variable of interest is party leader gender. This measure is taken from the time series cross-sectional data introduced above. The regression model also includes several other variables whose exclusion might otherwise bias the results, including a lagged dependent variable, CMP party family measure, an indicator variable that denotes governing coalition membership, and party seat share in the legislature as a measure of party size.

The results of the analysis are found in Table 8.1. The first outcome variable (Model 1) is the overall left-right position of the party. Consistent

Table 8.1. Linear Model Predicting Political Parties' Manifesto Positions

	Model 1: Left-Right	Model 2: Social Justice	Model 3: Welfare	Model 4: Education
Intercept	−6.85*	3.27*	3.96*	2.42*
	(1.67)	(0.44)	(0.57)	(0.36)
Female leader	−1.13	0.29	0.50	−0.14
	(1.11)	(0.27)	(0.36)	(0.24)
Lagged DV	0.60*	0.60*	0.58*	0.54*
	(0.02)	(0.02)	(0.02)	(0.02)
Seat share	−3.64	−1.69*	−0.15	0.95
	(3.39)	(0.81)	(1.10)	(0.73)
Cabinet	0.47	0.24	0.39	−0.36
	(0.92)	(0.22)	(0.30)	(0.20)
Communists	−2.28	−0.10	0.30	0.15
	(1.96)	(0.47)	(0.64)	(0.42)
Social Democrats	2.27	−0.22	0.39	0.16
	(1.91)	(0.46)	(0.63)	(0.41)
Liberals	9.95*	−1.67*	−1.27*	0.35
	(1.92)	(0.46)	(0.61)	(0.40)
Christian Democrats	7.30*	−1.36*	0.19	0.06
	(1.98)	(0.47)	(0.63)	(0.42)
Conservatives	10.97*	−1.61*	−0.22	0.40
	(2.15)	(0.51)	(0.67)	(0.44)
Nationalists	13.46*	−1.10	−1.25	−0.56
	(2.52)	(0.59)	(0.79)	(0.52)
Agrarians	6.20*	−1.31*	−0.12	0.25
	(2.28)	(0.55)	(0.74)	(0.48)
Ethnic Parties	2.24	−1.77*	0.40	−0.40
	(2.45)	(0.60)	(0.80)	(0.52)
Special Issue Parties	9.79*	−1.84*	−0.65	0.10
	(2.53)	(0.60)	(0.80)	(0.53)
Alliances	1.72	−1.92	0.08	−0.23
	(13.59)	(3.25)	(4.43)	(2.91)
N	1,197	1,197	1,197	1,197
R^2	0.58	0.45	0.37	0.32
Resid. Sd	13.49	3.23	4.40	2.89

Notes: For party family, baseline category is green/ecology parties. Standard errors in parentheses.

* Indicates significance at $p < 0.05$.

with Greene and O'Brien (2016) and O'Brien (2019), the results reveal no differences in the average left- right positions of the policy statements of male- and female-headed parties.[3] Models 2, 3, and 4 examine variation in attention to social justice issues, welfare state growth, and education expansion respectively.

After accounting for parties' pre-existing commitments to these policy areas, we once again observe null results. Models considering the interaction between leader gender and party family yield similar findings.[4] Whereas women's presence in parties' parliamentary delegations is associated with more left-leaning agendas (Greene and O'Brien 2016) and more attention to social justice issues (Kittilson 2011), these trends do not hold for party leaders. Female-led organizations are simply not dedicating more attention to these policy arenas than male-led parties.

What Can We Ask from Female Leaders?

The leader is the single most powerful individual within her political party. Her actions have wide-ranging implications, and her influence surpasses that of any one legislator (and in some instances, all legislators combined). Those invested in women's representation hope for (women) leaders who will advance women's descriptive, substantive, and symbolic representation. We want leaders who will bring women into leadership posts within the party and, when possible, the government; advocate for policies that enhance women's well-being; and transform beliefs about appropriate gender roles and women's ability to govern. Yet, at least with respect to policy priorities, evidence suggests that female leaders may not have these transformative effects.

Can we expect female leaders to be critical actors for women? Unfortunately, the realities of leadership (de)selection – coupled with the constraints facing (women) party leaders – erect barriers to representation. To begin with, parties are unlikely to select leaders who they perceive will deviate too far from the aims of the selectorate, whether that be elected representatives, party activists, the rank-and-file membership, or a combination of these actors. Thus, the women who are viable contenders for these posts are likely to closely resemble their male competitors. This is especially true given that the archetypal leader is not simply "male in appearance and gender" but also "masculine in character traits" (Sjoberg 2014, 73). Female leaders may thus find themselves wielding power in "gender-specific environment[s] molded by 'masculinist' norms and expectations" (Sykes 2014, 691). Such environments are not conducive to advancing the status of women. Indeed, research from Latin America indicates that the presence of a female party leader does not affect female nomination rates (Funk, Hinojosa, and Piscopo 2017, 2019). Leaders in parliamentary systems, moreover, must also constantly manage prospective challengers who threaten to unseat them (Bynander and 't Hart, 2007). Even if they wish to work on behalf of women, the threat of losing the post can disincentivize this behaviour, particularly if it will be framed as pursuing "identity politics."

It is not only these constraints, however, that are at issue. We also need to interrogate the representational demands that we place on female party leaders, particularly as compared to female parliamentarians. The legislative branch is explicitly tasked with representing the will of the people, and legislators provide the only direct link between citizens and the state. Given that women make up half (or more) of legislators' constituents, representatives (both men and women) have a responsibility to act on their behalf. Because women are a historically under-represented group, this obligation often falls to descriptive representatives.

Party leaders, in contrast, do not face the same representational imperatives. Their obligation is to their party, not the broader citizenry. In their capacity as leader, they work to advance the parties' policy-, vote-, and office-seeking aims. There is no clear moral imperative to represent women in particular. Rather, the goal is to promote the party as an institution. Though we want leaders of both sexes to promote women's well-being, it is not clear that female leaders in particular have a special obligation to do so.

How Can We Incentivize Leaders to Act for Women?

If we accept that female leaders cannot necessarily be expected to act on behalf of women, where do we go from here? Moving forward, we are best served by asking how we can ensure that leaders – both men and women – are incentivized to advance women's descriptive, substantive, and symbolic representation. I suggest a two-fold approach: feminizing the party elite and empowering women (and women's organizations) in intra-party politics.

First, leaders are likely to be more responsive to women (and women's concerns) as women's presence in the legislative delegation and cabinet grows. Irrespective of leader gender, gender parity should have positive effects. With more female political elites, we have more women to advocate on behalf of women with the leader. Women legislators and cabinet members also provide leaders with policymaking expertise, thereby enhancing their capacity to represent women. And women's increased presence among elites should make it easier for them to hold the leader accountable on these issues. Women's inclusion among legislators and cabinet officials may also be especially important for female leaders. Their presence normalizes and feminizes power, so that women leaders do not have to avoid "women's issues" for fear of provoking backlash. Evidence from Latin America suggests that female leaders are more likely to legislate on behalf of women when they have elite feminists within their networks (Reyes-Housholder 2019).

A second tactic for ensuring that parties generally, and party leaders in particular, attend to women's interests is to confer more control over intra-party politics to women's rights activists. This includes empowering women, particularly women's organizations within the party, in the leadership selection process. Even if party leaders do not hold "female-friendly" sentiments, offering women some say over leadership selection would incentivize candidates for these positions to commit to representing women's interests. That is, having to rely, at least in part, on women's organizations in order to attain and retain power should lead to greater responsiveness to this constituency. Many parties already have internal women's organizations. Yet the composition and strength of these groups varies (Kittilson 2006; Morgan and Hinojosa 2018). Ensuring that these organizations are controlled by members who are both committed to promoting women's interests and also invested with significant influence within the party should convince party leaders to attend to women's concerns.

NOTES

1 These data were originally assembled for a project examining citizens' beliefs about female- and male-led parties (O'Brien 2019). These attitudes are measured on election surveys, so the unit of analysis is country-election year. These years typically correspond to national elections, though some surveys were fielded around European Parliament elections.

2 The RILE score is calculated as follows. First, the proportions of the party platform covered by the "left" and "right" sets of categories are determined separately. This is accomplished by summing the references to the thirteen left-wing and thirteen right-wing categories. Then, the "left" proportion is subtracted from the "right" proportion. This results in a measure that could in principle range from −100 (the manifesto is entirely devoted to left-wing categories) to +100 (the manifesto is entirely devoted to right-wing categories).

3 These results are robust to an alternative measure using the logit scale suggested by Lowe et al. (2011).

4 There are no meaningful differences across party families with respect to education spending. On social justice issues, there is a significant difference between male- and female-headed green parties, but no differences among men and women leaders for other party families. For welfare state expansion, there are statistically significant differences for social democratic and conservative parties, but no differences for other party families. The lack of consistent results, and concerns about multiple comparisons, suggest that male- and female-led parties are more similar than not.

9 A Question of Ethics? Addressing Sexual Harassment in the Legislatures of the United States, the United Kingdom, and Canada

TRACEY RANEY AND CHERYL COLLIER

Global awareness of the problem of sexual harassment has grown exponentially since #MeToo, and this includes legislative workplaces. Since fall 2017, male legislators in several countries have resigned (either voluntarily or involuntarily), been stripped of their party affiliations, or demoted in their parliamentary duties in response to public allegations of sexual misconduct made against them.[1] Despite these recent events, it is important to remember that sexual harassment has a long history inside political legislatures (Lovenduski 2014; Collier and Raney 2018b). The problem has furthermore persisted even though most representative democracies have had long-standing ethics infrastructures in place, which include various rules, policies, and codes that supposedly regulate the behaviours of those who work in and for legislatures. Ethics rules have presumably been established in order to hold elected and appointed public officials to a higher, yet expected, standard of performance (Saint-Martin 2003).[2] Recent passage of anti-harassment rules in some legislatures arguably constitutes a public acknowledgement (if implicit) that each has failed to address this problem historically, and that new measures are required to regain the public's trust in the #MeToo era.

In this chapter we assess the gendered implications of established and new ethics rules in the lower houses of the United States, the United Kingdom, and Canada.[3] Our argument is twofold: first, we posit that sexual harassment has historically not been considered a serious breach of legislative ethics protocols. Past ethics rules have been largely gender-blind and have contributed to a climate where sexism and sexual harassment are permissible. Second, we argue that recently adopted anti–sexual harassment rules in all three countries contain gender blind-spots. Although these new rules may appear to usher in real change, they are not likely to be enough to tackle the root cause of gendered abuses of power: a male-dominated institutional culture. Consequently, the re-establishment of the public's trust and confidence in these legislatures during the #MeToo era remains in doubt.

Below we briefly review recent anti–sexual harassment provisions and analyse existing ethics rules. Using a feminist lens, we then apply three democratic principles (transparency, oversight, and legitimacy) to recent measures, revealing their gendered inadequacies.

Recent Anti–Sexual Harassment Measures

Over the last five years, the US House of Representatives and the British and Canadian Houses of Commons have either updated older or created entirely new anti-harassment rules. In the US, this includes a December 2018 revamp of quarter-century-old legislation (the Congressional Accountability Act of 1995) that oversees the dispute-resolution process for sexual harassment (and other) claims in the congressional workplace (United States Congress 2017–18). The revised legislation includes a more streamlined claim-filing time frame and removes existing requirements for mandatory counselling, mediation, and a "cooling off" period for claimants before proceeding with a case. It also provides claimants with a "confidential advisor" and ensures congressional members must now reimburse the Treasury for certain awards and settlements.[4] Prior to the new law, all awards or settlements related to sexual harassment cases involving members were paid out with public funds.

In July 2018, the British House of Commons adopted the new Independent Complaints and Grievance Scheme that covers bullying, harassment, and sexual misconduct. It includes a new Parliament-wide behaviour code embedded in its MP Code of Conduct, a clearer claims process with timelines, a new Independent Sexual Misconduct Service to advise and support claimants, mandatory training for staff, and workshops for MPs. The possibility of an initial independent investigation into claims overseen by the independent parliamentary commissioner for standards is also new (United Kingdom Parliament 2018).

In 2014, in the wake of sexual harassment/assault allegations made against two male Liberal MPs, the Canadian House of Commons drafted a policy covering staff. The House of Commons Policy on Preventing and Addressing Harassment includes a definition of sexual harassment and covers this under better-defined and expanded procedures for non-sexual harassment claims. In 2015, the House of Commons Procedures and House Affairs Committee (PROC) created the Code of Conduct for Members of the House of Commons: Sexual Harassment that covers

MP-to-MP sexual harassment cases, and appended it to the House's Standing Orders. The code requires new MPs to sign an anti–sexual harassment pledge, provides optional training on sexual harassment prevention (changed to mandatory training after #MeToo), and outlines sexual harassment complaint reporting and resolution processes. In 2018, the Liberal government passed Bill C-65, An Act to Amend the Canada Labour Code (harassment and Violence), the Parliamentary Employment and Staff Relations Act and the Budget Implementation Act, 2017, to bring all federal public service employees (as well as volunteers and interns) under one single, improved policy. Parliamentary staff covered under the 2014 House of Commons Policy on Preventing and Addressing Harassment will also be covered under Bill C-65, although proposed regulations on how the 2014 policy may or may not be altered by C-65 are not yet known.[5]

Gendering Legislative Ethical Infrastructures

The fact that all three countries have sought to address this problem at all is, perhaps symbolically, a positive development. But these actions should also sound the alarm about why sexual harassment has been permitted to occur where ethical protocols governing members' behaviours have been in place for some time.[6] Feminist political science research suggests that this "paradox" is likely due to the broader sexist culture embedded within political institutions that has long permitted gendered and racialized abuses of power to occur (Inter-Parliamentary Union 2016; Collier and Raney 2018a).

Table 9.1 provides an overview of some of the main ethical rules and policies adopted in each of the three countries. In the US House of Representatives, long-standing ethics rules include a half-century-old Official Code of Conduct for Members that prohibits various ethical violations (e.g., limits on outside income and financial disclosure requirements), but until 2018 did not reference sexual harassment. In 2008, Congress established an independent Office of Congressional Ethics to review ethics violations. The Congressional Accountability Act of 1995 (mentioned earlier) included specific anti-harassment provisions and created a new independent office (the Office of Compliance; now the Office of Congressional Workplace Rights) to oversee such cases, but these procedures were confusing and cumbersome to employees, and were not well regarded.

The British House of Commons' ethical infrastructure is similarly extensive and includes a Code of Conduct for members created in 1995, which also did not reference sexual harassment. That same year, an

Table 9.1. Comparison of Legislative Ethical Infrastructures, 1999–2020*

United States	United Kingdom	Canada
Code of Ethics for Government Service (1958)	*Standing Orders & Erskine May: Parliamentary Practice* guide (historical)	*Standing Orders & House of Commons Procedure and Practice* guide (historical)
First legislative ethics committee (1967)	Committee on Standards in Public Life (1994)	Parliament of Canada Act (1985); amended in 2004 to create ethics commissioner
Code of Official Conduct (1968)	MP Code of Conduct & parliamentary commissioner for standards (1995)	Conflict of Interest Code for Members (2004)
Ethics Reform Act of 1989	"Valuing Others" policy (2007)	Conflict of Interest Act (2006)
Congressional Accountability Act and Office of Compliance (1995)	Independent parliamentary standards authority (2009)	Conflict of interest and ethics commissioner (2007)
Office of Congressional Ethics (2008)	"Respect" Policy (2011; amended in 2014)	House of Commons Policy on Preventing and Addressing Harassment (2014)
Congressional Accountability Act of 1995 Reform Act (2018)	Independent Complaints and Grievance Scheme and new behaviour code (2018)	Code of Conduct for Members of the House of Commons: Sexual Harassment (2015)

* Non-exhaustive. Relevant to lower houses only.

independent office for the parliamentary commissioner for standards was created to oversee some provisions in the MP Code of Conduct, but not those that related to MPs' "purely private or personal lives." A Committee on Standards in Public Life, a Select Committee on Standards, and an Independent Parliamentary Standards Authority committee that regulates MPs' salaries and expenses all exist to monitor MPs' ethical behaviour. A "Valuing Others" policy (2007) and a "Respect" policy (2011; revised in 2014), were created to address discrimination and harassment in Westminster. As in the US, staffers and employees were sceptical about their effectiveness, given their lack of independence and the extreme length of time a case would take to be heard, contributing to a lack of trust in both policies (Cox Report 2018, 98–105). In 2019, over 68,000 people signed an online petition demanding that

British MPs adopt a new code of conduct that would prohibit the usage of violent or dehumanizing language and name-calling (Change.org 2019). To date, Parliament has made no indication it intends to amend its code accordingly.

Despite not having a generalized code of conduct, the Canadian House of Commons has adopted rules that govern members' behaviours, many of which are found in the Houses' standing orders, including the Conflict of Interest Code for Members of the House of Commons (2004). Additionally, rules of conduct are found in the Parliament of Canada Act (1985), the Criminal Code, and the Conflict of Interest Act (2006). Members can also find reference to these acts as well as to general responsibilities and behavioural expectations in the *House of Commons Procedure and Practice* guide (Bosc and Gagnon 2017). None addresses sexual harassment.

As of 2007, ethics and conflict of interest rules are enforced by an independent conflict of interest and ethics commissioner. The commissioner, however, has no jurisdiction over sexual harassment claims – which are the purview of the party whips and/or the chief human resources officer in the House, as well as the PROC committee. The Office of the Public Sector Integrity Commissioner governs ethical conduct of public sector employees, but also cedes governance over sexual harassment claims to the chief human resources officer/ whips.

Legislative Ethics in the #MeToo Era

Despite the fact that women have been speaking out about sexual harassment long before #MeToo, public allegations against Hollywood producer Harvey Weinstein drew worldwide attention to this issue. Women politicians in all three countries – including US Representative Jackie Speier and Senator Kristen Gillibrand, Canadian MP Michelle Rempel, British MP Jess Phillips, and many others – utilized the global media spotlight brought by #MeToo to speak out on the continued prevalence of sexism and sexual harassment in politics, making it difficult for legislators to claim that existing ethics rules were sufficient to address this problem. These and other women voiced the perspective that *gendered abuses of power* have been largely ignored in existing ethical infrastructures, leaving intact sexist cultures in each legislature. Their calls for action have resulted in a suite of recent policies and rules adopted to address gendered abuses of power. Below we identify a few of the gender blind-spots in these recent measures, making future cultural change doubtful. Through a feminist lens, we apply three democratic principles to these new rules: transparency, independence, and legitimacy; each is arguably essential to reclaiming institutional accountability and rebuilding public trust following political scandals (Buchanan 2002; David-Barrett 2015; Bovend'Eert 2018).

The *transparency* measures in the anti-harassment rules are mixed across the three countries. On balance, the US Congress has the strongest transparency provisions of all three countries. In the House of Representatives, pre-existing rules require the Office of Compliance to publish an annual report regarding payments of awards and settlements on sexual harassment or retaliatory behaviours, but these were not well publicized, nor did Congress regularly review them. The office is further obligated to publish annual statistics on the number of eligible employees who contact the office, how many complaints are filed, and any resulting action taken. The 2018 rule changes expand these disclosure provisions, and the office must also now publicize the names of members involved in a harassment or retaliation case when an award or settlement has been reached.

The British House of Commons is less transparent. Its new rules state that the parliamentary commissioner for standards (PCS) must weigh the need for public disclosure against that of the need to protect members from potentially negative "reputational" impacts (United Kingdom Parliament 2018, 23). This applies to substantiated claims of sexual misconduct. The UK Parliament went one step further in 2018 and clawed back existing disclosure requirements for MPs who are being investigated for ethical breaches broadly. Previously, the PCS was permitted to publish the names of MPs who were under investigation for possible conduct breaches. As per the provisions of the new Independent Complaints and Grievance Scheme (ICGS), the PCS is now able to publish only "statistical information about complaints received" (United Kingdom Parliament 2019, 190).

The Canadian House of Commons has the weakest transparency requirements of all three countries. While the staffing policy publishes statistical information in an annual report (e.g., the total number of claims received), there are no reporting requirements in the MP-to-MP code of conduct. This means the Canadian public will never know how many complaints have been filed against an MP, or whether any MPs have been punished for code violations. The only instance when an MP may be named is if, at the end of a very long claims process, the PROC committee agrees to do so.

In all three cases, *independent oversight* over these anti-harassment rules either does not exist or exists only as part of the grievance and sanctioning processes. In the US, claims involving members or senior staff as respondents (i.e., alleged perpetrators) will be given independent hearings, but the final decision-making body is the House Ethics Committee, comprised of politicians (United States Office of Congressional Workplace Rights 2019). In the United Kingdom, independent oversight is more developed. While the independent PCS will retain the authority to impose less serious sanctions, on 23 June 2020 the House agreed to establish an Independent Expert Panel (IEP) to consider more serious sanctions and appeals of all ICGS cases, replacing the role of the Committee on Standards. The IEP is to consist of eight members, none of whom may be a member or former member of either House. At the same time, in cases where the IEP recommends that a member be suspended or expelled, the House retains its authority to approve (or disapprove) of these recommendations through a motion in the chamber. Although the creation of the IEP is an excellent step towards independent oversight, British politicians will remain the final arbiters on punishments for the most serious ICGS cases. In Canada, in the case of the MP-to-MP code, the PROC committee is the final arbiter, while in the event of a staffer being harassed by an MP, any corrective action is imposed by the requisite party whip.[7] The net effect of these weak oversight provisions is that politicians in all three countries continue to "mark their own homework" and are self-policing sexual harassment cases made against their colleagues and fellow partisans (Leversridge 2019).

The composition of legislative committees with direct oversight over cases involving members further raises *democratic legitimacy* questions.[8] Clayton et al. (2018) suggest that gender parity in decision-making bodies helps legitimize decision outcomes and fosters institutional trust amongst the public. The illegitimacy of all-male, or male-dominated, panels in adjudicating cases of sexual misconduct has been demonstrated, for example, in the US Senate confirmation hearings for Brett Kavanaugh's appointment to the US Supreme Court in fall 2018, and twenty-seven years earlier when Anita Hill testified before the same committee regarding her experiences of being sexually harassed by then-nominee Clarence Thomas.

Table 9.2 shows the gendered composition of these legislative committees over the last twenty years. With the exception of the current UK Standards Committee, none has achieved gender parity and only two women have ever served as chair, presiding over just .05 per cent of all committee sittings (three out of sixty-one years).[9]

In the midst of the 2014 scandal discussed earlier, the Canadian PROC committee had just one female member and struck an ad hoc subcommittee with better gender balance (five women, two men), presumably in recognition of the dubious optics of male-dominated

Table 9.2. Composition of Committees with Final Oversight over Sexual Harassment Claims Involving Members, 1999–2020

	United States	United Kingdom	Canada
Committee	House Committee on Ethics	House Committee on Standards	Procedure and House Affairs
Current % female members	30 (3 of 10)	50 (7 of 14)*	33 (4 of 12)
Highest % female members	40	50*	36
Lowest % of female members	0	0	10
Number of female chairs	1	1	0
Total no. years under female chairship	2	1	0

Note: Current as of 4 January 2020.

*Four women are lay members.

adjudication over these issues. The systematic over-representation of men on decision-making committees raises serious legitimacy questions, as those who stand to benefit the most in cases related to sexual harassment – male politicians – remain in charge.[10]

Conclusion

In this chapter we have shown how existing ethics rules have largely ignored gendered abuses of power as *ethical problems* in politics historically. In addressing this problem, the Canadian House of Commons appears to have the weakest approach of all three countries, where secrecy, partisanship, and a male-dominated committee remain central. By contrast, the British House of Commons has adopted stronger, albeit still insufficient, anti-harassment rules, particularly with the creation of an Independent Expert Panel. In a #MeToo era that demands public accountability on this issue, recent sexual harassment measures are unlikely to restore public trust in all three countries. While it could be argued that having some rules in place is better than none, our concern is that these new provisions may be used by some political leaders to justify further inaction. More change is clearly required to uproot the sexist cultures within which these new ethical rules remain embedded.

NOTES

1 These include US representatives Joe Barton, Blake Farenthold, Trent Franks, Ruben Kihuen, Pat Meehan, and Tim Murphy; UK ministers Michael Fallon and Damian Green and MP Charlie Elphicke; Canadian minister Kent Hehr and MPs Tony Clement, Darshan Kang, and Aaron Weir.

2 Many countries' ethics standards followed the US post-Watergate scandal.

3 As "early adopters" of sexual harassment rules, these three countries may be used as global benchmarks. Canada's early 2014–15 steps pre-date #MeToo.

4 Reimbursement applies to harassment and retaliatory violations only, and not to discrimination cases.

5 At time of writing, proposed workplace harassment and violence prevention regulations and their impacts on existing harassment regulations across the federal public service were not yet finalized. Bill C-65 has not yet been fully implemented, and the regulations are expected to cost the government over $840 million over ten years to implement across all public service sites Canada-wide. As such (and due to space constraints) we are unable to analyse Bill C-65 here.

6 Scholars have raised concerns about the effectiveness of ethics infrastructures in democratic legislatures; see Menzel 2009.

7 The chief human resources officer may be consulted at any time during the process.

8 In the United Kingdom, the Committee on Standards had oversight until November 2020, when the first Independent Expert Panel was appointed.

9 While the first appointed British Independent Expert Panel comprises five women and three men, gender parity is not a formal requirement for the panel.

10 Although men can be sexually harassed, women are predominantly targeted. Racialized minority and young women are especially vulnerable.

PART THREE

Responses to Women's Electoral Under-Representation

10 Gender Quotas and Beyond: Policy Solutions to Women's Under-Representation in Politics

MAGDA HINOJOSA, MIKI CAUL KITTILSON,
AND ALEXANDRA M. WILLIAMS

In this chapter, we explore the use of gender quotas and gender parity provisions intended to boost women's political representation in order to understand why such policies have worked in some places but not in others. In addition to exploring how formal and informal institutions affect the success of quotas, we also identify other strategies that can be used to increase women's access to political office.

Argentina adopted the world's first legislated gender quota in 1991, requiring that political party lists include a minimum of 30 per cent women. Since then, national gender quotas have spread to over seventy-five countries across the globe (Hughes et al 2016). The diffusion of gender quotas has been well documented (Krook 2009). These far-reaching reforms are largely responsible for the notable increases in women's representation worldwide, yet the effects of quota adoption have been far from uniform.

Because of quotas, Mexico's legislative bodies are now half female, but quotas have had virtually no effect on women's representation in Brazil. The success or failure of a gender quota is dependent not only on the quota law itself, but also on the formal and informal institutions of the electoral system. In the sections that follow, we note the role of formal institutions – such as electoral system type, district magnitude, party magnitude, and other rules – in determining the success or failure of gender quotas, as well as the part that informal rules can play in either fortifying gender quotas or weakening them. We then examine other policy tools for increasing women's political representation.

Crafting Success, Creating Failure: Formal Institutions, Informal Rules, and Gender Quotas

The formal institutions that can determine the success or failure of gender quotas are both internal and external to the quota itself. Much of the success of gender quotas depends on the design of the quota

(Schwindt-Bayer 2009, 22). Some of the earliest work on gender quotas noted that successful quotas needed to include significant thresholds (the percentage of women candidates required), placement mandates (when applied in closed list proportional representation seats), universal application, and enforcement mechanisms (Htun and Jones 2002; Jones 2005).

The quota threshold matters given that it dictates the percentage of female candidates that parties must nominate. A low quota threshold is unlikely to have the effect of a quota with a much higher threshold (e.g., 20 per cent versus 40 per cent threshold). However, the threshold is not the only factor that determines the success of a gender quota. Placement mandates also matter. Initially, quota laws lacked placement mandates, allowing party elites to undermine quotas by slotting women into the most unelectable spots (see Jones 2004). These placement mandates, which can only be used in closed list systems, prevent political parties from pooling female candidates at the bottom of their party lists. The "reach" of quotas also determines success. Quotas applied across all seats will have larger effects than quotas applied to only a subset of seats; parties have been exempt from meeting quotas based on the legislative body, the electoral rules for electing candidates (applying the quotas only to proportional representation seats rather than to plurality seats), and the selection procedures used for selecting candidates (Hinojosa 2012a; Hinojosa and Piscopo 2013). Moreover, where political alternate positions exist (political alternates are substitutes elected to serve in case the titleholder is temporarily or permanently unavailable due to travel, illness, etc.), quota laws must specify that the threshold applies to titleholder positions rather than to the alternate positions. Some early quota laws (for example, in Bolivia) allowed the quota to be met by placing women in alternate positions rather than as titleholders, limiting the effects of gender quotas (Hinojosa and Vijil Gurdian 2012). Finally, effective quota laws include strong mechanisms for enforcing the law and sanctioning parties for non-compliance. Early quotas lacked sanctions (as in Brazil, Honduras, and Venezuela) or utilized inadequate sanctions (as in Argentina, where women would need to sue their own political parties for failure to comply with quotas) (Hinojosa 2012b). In some cases, the penalty for non-compliance with the quota was insufficient. In France, some parties opted to pay a fee rather than meet the quota (Murray 2007). The most efficacious quotas prevent the registration of any candidates if a party's list fails to meet quota stipulations. This is the case in countries such as Argentina, Belgium, and Macedonia.[1]

The loopholes written into gender quotas went beyond setting abysmally low thresholds or a failure to include strong sanctions. The Brazilian case was notorious for its loopholes. The quota, adopted in 1997, allowed parties to run 50 per cent more candidates than there were seats in a district. Unless all possible spots on their lists were filled, parties were not held responsible for meeting the quota (Htun 2005). Parties could nominate as many candidates as there were seats in a district and avoid the quota altogether.

In addition, scholars have noted that institutions external to the quota itself determine if the quota succeeds or not. First, scholars have emphasized that application is more likely to succeed where there is closed list proportional representation (Htun and Jones 2002). While in open list systems, voters can cast preference votes for individual candidates, in closed list proportional representation, voters choose among parties but cannot vote for specific candidates. In open list proportional representation, parties cannot be obligated to use placement mandates and voters could show biases against women candidates. Yet more recent work indicates that open lists are not particularly disadvantageous (Schmidt and Saunders 2004; Jones 2009, 76). Kittilson argues that voters' ability to cast a preference vote meant that the Finnish legislature ended up with greater female representation; parties were not rank-ordering candidates and so they could not place women at the bottom of their lists (2005, 641). Second, having larger multimember electoral districts is also seen as advantageous (Jones 2005). Parties may diversify their lists when they have more spots on their lists to dole out. Third, party magnitude, which refers to the number of candidates elected from a party list in a given electoral district, also matters for increasing women's representation, especially when combined with quotas (Schmidt and Saunders 2004).

It should be noted that while some formal institutions are more likely to generate success than others, this does not mean that the absence of advantageous rules will doom a quota to failure. For example, when electoral districts are considered, it is possible for countries with single-member districts to overcome obstacles to successful quota adherence, such as in France and Mexico (see Franceschet, this volume).

In addition to formal rules that either set quotas up for success or set the stage for failure, informal norms emerged that served to undermine gender quotas. For example, political alternate positions were informally used to limit the impact of gender quotas. Mexican parties undermined quotas by having women resign their positions in favour of their male alternates after the election (Piscopo 2017). In Uruguay, the existence of political alternates allowed parties to break previous political norms and nominate individual women simultaneously to *electable* spots for both lower and upper house positions; when they were (unsurprisingly) elected to both seats, they were forced to cede one to an alternate (Hinojosa 2017).

Quotas have regularly been adopted with notable loopholes or without a full understanding of their incompatibility with the current electoral system. Because of this, quotas have routinely been revised; for example, in Latin America, only one of the twelve countries that adopted a quota during the 1990s failed to revise its quota by 2015 (Piscopo 2016). Increases in women's representation are not simply the result of the adoption of quotas, but rather repeated and concerted efforts to reform these laws so as to eliminate loopholes, to fortify the quota laws, and to increase quota thresholds (Hinojosa and Piscopo 2013). According to Paxton and Hughes, "the increasing effectiveness of quotas cannot be explained by changes in quota rules alone; even candidate quotas without placement mandates or sanctions for noncompliance are increasingly able to reach stated goals over time." They argue that poor quota design can no longer be assumed to prognosticate failure because party elites, influenced in part by quota success in other countries, have accepted that including more women in politics is "normatively appropriate" (Paxton and Hughes 2015, 354).

Beyond Gender Quotas

In addition to the challenges faced in implementing gender quotas in single-member districts, quotas often focus on women as though women are a monolithic group. Hughes (2011) points out that quotas favour women from dominant groups, largely ignoring important intersections of disadvantage. The "single group strategy" pursued under gender quotas can be exclusionary (Krook and Nugent 2016). In Britain, MP Diane Abbott has dubbed Labour's quotas as the "all white women's shortlists" (Krook and Nugent 2016). Gender quotas may perpetuate other forms of inequality in access to elected office. In the section that follows, we discuss other innovative tools to increase the representation of women in politics.

The 1995 Beijing Platform for Action pushed not only for the adoption of gender quotas, but also for the application of a number of other strategies intended to increase women's representation in political positions. Yet the focus – on the part of policymakers and academics alike – over the last three decades has largely been on gender quotas (Krook and Norris 2014).

Scholars have identified a number of other strategies for increasing women's representation, such as awareness-raising campaigns by civil society organizations, private fundraising efforts geared to getting women into office (along the lines of Emily's List in the United States), and party-level interventions to identify and train potential female candidates (Hinojosa 2012b; Krook and Norris 2014). Political parties in Latin America routinely offer training specifically to women; 65 per cent of the largest parties in the region offer training that is reserved for women and one-quarter of parties also allocate funds directly to women's training programs (Roza 2010, 125). In Canada, parties that use search committees to identify potential candidates are more likely to select women candidates than parties using more traditional recruitment methods (Erickson 1993, 76).

Political parties can also adopt internal gender quotas. Britain has avoided adopting national quotas for its single-member district elections. Yet at the party level, the British Labour Party has used an all-women shortlist (AWS) approach, designating some winnable seats as those where the shortlist of potential nominees be composed of women only. As British parties sought to expand their appeal and competed for women's votes, women's organizations convinced Labour leadership that the AWS strategy would appeal to female voters (Perrigo 1996; Kittilson 2006). Indeed, this approach was effective, and the number of women elected from the Labour Party doubled in the 1997 election. Challenges by male party members led to setbacks in implementing this policy; however, the Sex Discrimination Act of 2002, renewed in 2010, does allow parties to use policies to promote equality among elected officials (Krook and Nugent 2016). Labour's use of AWS in subsequent elections has propelled the party well ahead of other British parties in women's representation. In Latin America, parties have regularly adopted internal quotas. But given limited commitment to these types of efforts, such voluntary quotas have largely proved ineffectual (Roza 2010).

While these strategies depend on voluntary organizations and political parties, other initiatives focus on state-directed efforts. In many countries, parties receive public funding; such public funds for parties can be tied to promoting women's participation. In Mali, Niger, Bolivia, and other countries, state funding is based in part on the number of women that these parties elect, while in Croatia and Burkina Faso, parties receive bonus funds if they elect more women to office (Krook and Norris 2014). Governments can not only reduce taxes but also lower election registration fees for parties that meet goals for female candidacies (Women's Environment and Development Organization 2007).

Campaign finance regulations can have important implications for women's ability to enter politics. As Chilean politician Adriana Muñóz explained, "Men have access to circles or networks where money is lent – they are friends with bank managers. But we are not supported this way. For us, it's pretty complicated, this arena of power and money ... Because even if the party accepts you and you are a candidate, how do you get elected if you have no money?" (Franceschet 2005, 89–90). Campaign finance reforms can alter barriers to women's entry into politics (Hinojosa 2012b).

Tying these types of efforts to quotas can be especially effective. For example, the Chilean quota, which was applied for the first time in 2017, works alongside a campaign-financing element. Parties receive a reimbursement of 500 UF (1 UF is currently about US$40) for every woman elected. Additionally, men receive 0.04 UF for each vote they receive, while women receive 0.05 UF, a 0.01 bonus. This firm financial component is intended to make sure that parties invest in female candidates, rather than just meet the numerical threshold required by the quota law. Another example comes from East Timor, where parties that place women in the most electable spots on their candidate lists are rewarded with greater airtime than parties who meet the more minimal quota requirements (Pires 2002, 37). In Mexico, as in other countries of the region, a set percentage of state-provided funding to parties must be allocated to training programs for women (Hinojosa and Piscopo 2013). Such requirements for state-provided funding, if managed through parties, may contribute to diversifying the types of women that enter politics, given that political parties may have ethnic, racial, linguistic, or geographic ties to particular groups.

State-directed efforts can also focus on creating cultural changes within legislatures to make them more friendly to women, which can affect not only the recruitment of women but also their retention. Adopting gender-neutral language when referring to the legislative body, changing the working days of parliaments to align them with school calendars, and making provisions for pregnancy and childcare are changes that have been implemented in other countries in an effort to make legislative bodies into better workplaces for women (Krook and Norris 2014, 13).

These state-directed efforts can simultaneously target other forms of political under-representation. Public funds that are disbursed to parties can be tied not only to the promotion of women's candidacies, but also to that of Indigenous persons. Similarly, campaign-financing stipulations can also be rewritten to address inequities in the representation of other under-represented groups. Making legislatures more women-friendly may also make them more accessible to other under-represented populations.

Gender quotas are not the only policy option available to countries intent on increasing the under-representation of women (and other groups) in their legislative bodies. But, like national quotas, party- and state-directed efforts require commitment. Formal and informal institutions alike can undermine the best-intentioned policies.

NOTE

1 The Gender Quotas Database, now maintained by IDEA International, includes regularly updated information on gender quotas across the world, including detailed information on specific quota regulations by country. The Gender Quotas Database also notes whether parties are barred from registering any candidates if they fail to meet the quota. The database can be found here: https://www.idea.int/data-tools/data/gender-quotas.

11 Effects of Quotas, Reserved Seats, and Electoral Rules on Women Parliamentarians in Asia

NETINA TAN

Asia has seen the rise of many powerful women leaders in recent years. In the 1980s most female leaders, such as Indira Gandhi (1980) and Bena-zir Bhutto (1988), were from South Asia. Now, more are emerging from East and Southeast Asia. After Corazon Aquino (1986) and Megawati Sukarnoputri (1998) became their country's first female presidents in the Philippines and Indonesia, others like Yingluck Shinawatra (2012), Park Geun-hye (2013), and Tsai Ing-wen (2016) also made history after being elected head of state in Thailand, South Korea, and Taiwan. In Myanmar, Aung San Suu Kyi was released after years of house arrest and elected to top state counsellor position in 2016 – making her one of the five female heads of states in Asia.[1]

The success of these elite women leaders belies the fact that the average proportion of female parliamentarians in Asia remains low, at 19 per cent, 5 points below the global average of 24 per cent for 2019 (see Figure 11.1). Apart from Timor-Leste (40 per cent), Taiwan (38 per cent) and Nepal (33 per cent), no country in Asia has achieved the 30 per cent "critical mass" of female parliamentarians – a num-ber seen as the minimum proportion necessary to influence policies in the legislatures (Childs and Krook 2006; Dahlerup 2006). And apart from Taiwanese leader Tsai Ing-wen, most elite women leaders in Asia are also largely from prominent political dynasties, rising to power because of their association with men who were former national leaders (Derichs and Thompson 2013; Thompson 2002). The media attention and prominence of these elite women have obscured the cultural and institutional challenges that everyday women face in moving from grassroots or party politics to key political leader-ship positions.

Instead of focusing on elite leaders, this chapter investigates whether more women are becoming parliamentarians in Asia. It

Figure 11.1. World and Regional Averages of Women in Parliaments

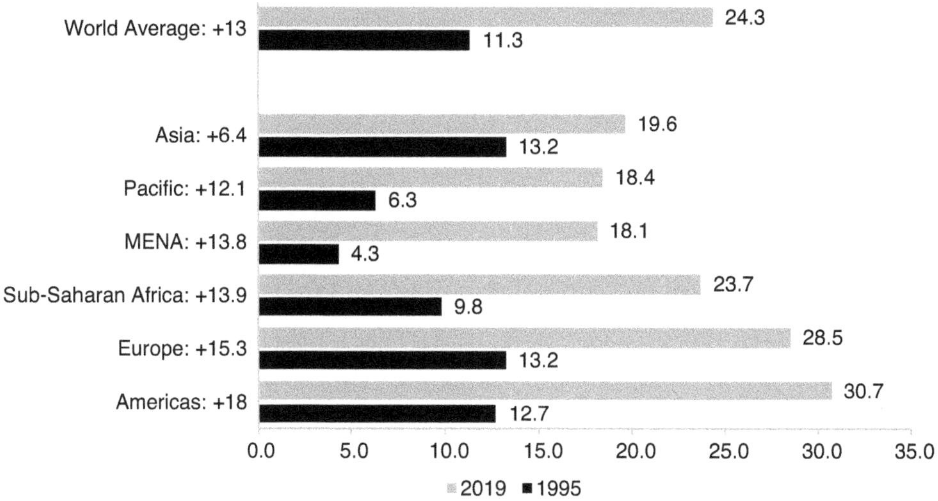

Source: Based on Inter-Parliamentay Union 2019a.

begins by providing an overview of the numeral representation of women in twenty-five parliaments in Asia and comparing the formal quota mechanisms and parity laws to improve women's political participation and representation. Asia is a large continent with diverse socio-economic development levels, religions, ethnicity, colonial backgrounds, electoral systems, and regime types.[2] Here, I focus on East, Southeast, and East Asia, which includes Afghanistan, Bangladesh, Bhutan, Brunei, Cambodia, China, India, Indonesia, Japan, Laos, Malaysia, Maldives, Mongolia, Myanmar, Nepal, North Korea, Pakistan, Philippines, Singapore, South Korea, Sri Lanka, Taiwan, Thailand, Timor-Leste, and Vietnam. Following the quota system developed by Dahlerup (2013, 19–21), I highlight the formal mechanisms such as reserved seats, legal candidate quotas, and party quotas (voluntary and institutionalized) introduced at the state or party levels that guarantee a specific number of seats or percentage for women mandated through constitutional and legislative means (Inter-Parliamentary Union (IPU) 2019b).

Overall, the key finding of this chapter is that formal quota mechanisms have raised the number of women parliamentarians in both electoral and non-electoral regimes in Asia. However, the numbers are uneven across the region and regime types. Party politics remains key to understanding women's access to political power. More study is needed to understand how sociocultural or attitudinal factors affect the "secret garden of politics" – the nomination and selection of women candidates and parliamentarians in traditional patriarchal societies and dynastic, weak party systems (Gallagher and Marsh 1988).

Women's Progress in Asian Parliaments, 2019

Globally, the average percentage of women in parliament has improved by 13 points, from 11.3 per cent in 1995 to 24.3 per cent (IPU 2019a). By comparison, the average number of women parliamentarians in Asia has only improved by 6.4 per cent, to 19.6 per cent by 2019. Despite this, women are still making gains; parliaments across the region improved their overall share of women winning seats in single and lower chambers in the 2018 elections, raising the average to 23.3 per cent for the year. Notable progress was made in the lower houses of Bhutan (+8.5 points), Malaysia (+3.5), China (+1.5), Timor-Leste (+1.5), and Bangladesh (+0.9). This is despite slight setbacks in Pakistan (−0.5) and Cambodia (−5.1), which saw falls in the average number of women parliamentarians in 2018 (IPU 2019b).

Origins and Types of Gender Quotas in Asia

In 2018, elections in more than 130 countries around the world were governed by some type of quota policy introduced at the state or party level (IPU 2019b, 10). A large body of work exists on the types and effects of quota policies in different parts of the world (Dahlerup 2009; Dahlerup et al. 2014; Franceschet and Piscopo 2008; Hinojosa and Franceschet 2012; IPU 2013; Jones 2009; Krook 2009; see also Hinojosa, Kittilson, and Williams, this volume; Franceschet, this volume). Broadly, the recommendations to "fast-track" women in politics include formal mechanisms such as establishing reserve seats and candidate quotas for women to access parliament, institutionalizing gender parity or targets for the party list, or initiating processes for candidate recruitment and nomination. Other informal mechanisms include building capacities of women candidates and representatives through civil society initiatives: designing gender-sensitive parliaments that facilitate women's caucuses implementing family-friendly facilities and mentorship to women (Hart 2012; Norris 2012).

In Asia, most governments share the common goal of achieving gender parity. However, there is no single preferred solution to boost women's political participation. As Table 11.1 shows, eleven out of twenty-five

Table 11.1. Quotas, Regime Types, and Women's Political Representation in Asia

Country	Adoption Date	Quota Type (LH)*	Party Quota	Subregional	Last Election	Women (LH) %	EIU** Regime Type 2018
Timor-Leste	2006	Candidate quotas	No	Reserved seats	2018	40	Flawed democracy
Nepal	2013	Candidate quotas	No	Candidate quotas	2017	33	Flawed democracy
Indonesia	2012	Candidate quotas	No	Candidate quotas	2014	18	Flawed democracy
South Korea	2000	Candidate quotas	Yes	Candidate quotas	2016	17	Flawed democracy
Mongolia	2011	Candidate quotas	No	Candidate quotas	2016	17	Flawed democracy
Taiwan	2005	Reserved seats	No	Reserved seats	2016	38	Flawed democracy
Afghanistan	2004	Reserved seats	No	Reserved seats	2018	24	Authoritarian
China	2007	Reserved seats	Yes	NA	2018	25	Authoritarian
Pakistan	2002	Reserved seats	No	Reserved seats	2018	20	Hybrid regime
Bangladesh	2004	Reserved seats	No	Reserved seats	2018	21	Hybrid regime
Vietnam	2007	Target system	Yes	Target system	2016	27	Authoritarian
Philippines	NA	None	Yes	Reserved seats	2016	30	Flawed democracy
Laos	NA	None	No	NA	2016	28	Authoritarian
Singapore	NA	None	Yes	NA	2015	23	Flawed democracy
North Korea	NA	None	No	NA	2014	16	Authoritarian
Bhutan	NA	None	No	NA	2018	15	Hybrid regime
Cambodia	NA	None	No	NA	2018	20	Authoritarian
Malaysia	NA	None	No	NA	2018	14	Flawed democracy
India	NA	None	No	Reserved seats	2014	13	Flawed democracy
Myanmar	NA	None	No	NA	2015	11	Authoritarian
Japan	NA	None	Yes	NA	2017	10	Flawed democracy
Brunei	NA	None	No	NA	2017	9	Authoritarian
Maldives	NA	None	No	NA	2014	5	NA
Sri Lanka	NA	None	No	NA	2015	5	Flawed democracy
Thailand	NA	None	Yes	NA	2014	5	Hybrid regime

Sources: Based on data from Dahlerup et al. 2014; EIU 2019; Hart 2012; United Nations Development Programme 2010.

* LH = Lower House.   ** EIU = Economist Intelligence Unit.

countries studied have introduced reserved seats, candidate quotas, or parity laws to improve women's representation at the legislative level over the last two decades.[3] Specifically, five countries (Afghanistan, Bangladesh, China, Pakistan, and Taiwan) have reserved seats for women in parliament, while another six (Indonesia, Mongolia, Nepal, South Korea, Timor-Leste, and Vietnam) set quotas or targets for all parties to nominate a proportion of women candidates for legislative elections. Additionally, major parties in seven countries (Philippines, South Korea, China, Vietnam, Thailand, Japan, and Singapore) were recorded to have voluntarily introduced quotas or targets to ensure gender parity in the party list or key party committees. At the subregional level, twelve countries have established targets or seats reserved for women at the local governments or councils.

As the entries under "Adoption Date" in Table 11.1 show, most countries adopted gender quotas after the region's modernization and historical turn towards "majoritarian democracy" in the 2000s. For example, the wave of democratization triggered electoral reforms in South Korea (2000), Taiwan (2005), and Indonesia (2012) that included institutional guarantees for women and, in some cases, ethnic minorities (Horowitz 1985; Reilly and Reynolds 1999; Reynolds 2006). The realization that institutional means are the fastest way to improve women's representation rallied feminist groups in Taiwan, South Korea, and Mongolia to use international agreements like the Convention on the Elimination of All Forms of Discrimination Against Women (CEDAW) to lobby the government for affirmative action (True and Mintrom 2001; True et al. 2013). The desire for international legitimacy may also explain why traditional and patriarchal societies undertook nominal reforms to promote women's political participation in Afghanistan, Pakistan, and Bangladesh (Bush 2011; Htun and Jones 2002, 32–56).

What this research shows is that human development and economic modernization are necessary but insufficient conditions to guarantee women's political representation (Norris 2012; Prihatini 2019). In high-income and affluent countries like Japan and South Korea, women make up only 10.2 per cent and 17 per cent, respectively, of members of parliament. It is curious that contagion effects or strong inter-party competition in Japan, India, and Sri Lanka did not drive major parties to lobby for gender quotas at the national level to attract female voters and expand their support base (Kenny and Mackay 2013). In contrast, Timor-Leste, Nepal, and Afghanistan, three of the poorest countries, with low human development, have quota policies and managed to boost the number of women in parliaments above 25 per cent.

The cases here also show no direct correlation between regime type and women's legislative representation. In fact, authoritarian regimes or one-party states such as Afghanistan (24 per cent), Laos (28 per cent), Vietnam (27 per cent), and China (25 per cent) that do not hold competitive elections have voluntarily imposed quotas or reserved seats to guarantee at least 25 per cent of women parliamentarians in their national legislatures. On average, the number of women parliamentarians in authoritarian and single-party regimes exceeded that in electoral democracies such as Indonesia, South Korea, India, and Japan. Critics may dismiss seat reservations in one-party regimes as "window dressing" (Truex 2016, 42), serving only the symbolic function of inclusion, with gender quotas serving an important strategic role in these regimes. For example, Joshi and Thimothy argue that Vietnam adopted quotas to promote women's political participation as part of its "autocratic adaptation," because co-opted women in the ruling party help maintain regime stability and its dominant position (2018). Similarly, for Singapore's hegemonic party system, my research finds that the ruling party nominates more women in elections out of party pragmatism and strategic calculations: to appeal to younger, progressive voters and maintain a hegemonic position (Tan 2016). The experiences of these semi- or non-competitive regimes suggest that the ruling/dominant party's willingness to support affirmative action for women will make a big difference in their overall political participation.

What Works and What Doesn't?

In Asia, the use of gender quotas and reserved seats at legislatures has raised the number of women parliamentarians. As Figure 11.2 shows, the eleven countries that mandated candidate quotas or reserved seats for women have an average of 25 per cent women parliamentarians. This is five points higher than the fourteen non-quota countries, with an average of 20 per cent of women parliamentarians. Asia's experience corresponds with studies such as IPU's global report that finds thirteen countries that applied 30 per cent legislated quotas have on average 28 per cent women in the lower chambers, a higher level than the average of sixteen countries that did not apply quotas, with 19 per cent of women.[4]

Presently, Timor-Leste (40 per cent) and Taiwan (38.1 per cent) are the two countries in Asia with the highest number of women parliamentarians. It is unsurprising that both have had a mix of gender quota policies in place since 2005 and 2006 (Sun 2005; Huang 2016; Marx 2012). But while Taiwan's experience with the mix of gender quota policies, reserve seats, and party quotas to boost women's representation is widely hailed as a success, the same cannot be said of Timor-Leste.

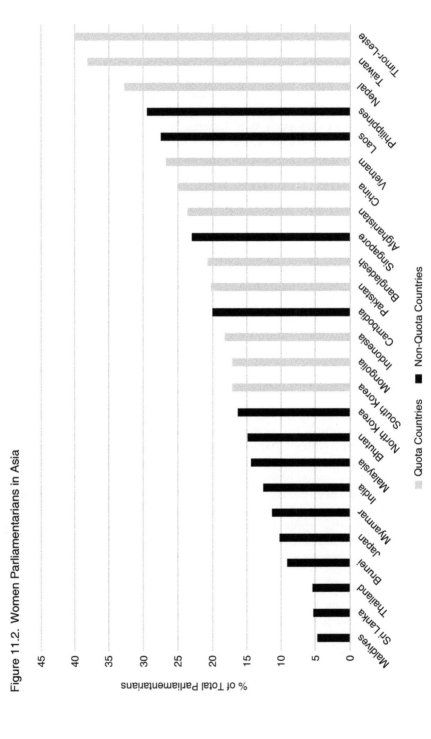

Figure 11.2. Women Parliamentarians in Asia

The interactions between traditional and modern governance in Timor-Leste remain a key challenge for women elected under candidate quotas to make their mark or for those elected under reserved seats at the local level to have any impact in the community (Cummins 2011; Marx 2012; Hutt 2016). Timor-Leste suggests that in highly patriarchal and traditional societies, we need to look beyond numbers to consider how other mechanisms can work to forge an egalitarian political culture.[5]

This comparison of quota policies based on numerical values alone does not tell us whether all quota mechanisms are equally effective. In cases such as Mongolia (17 per cent), South Korea (17 per cent), and Indonesia (18 per cent), simply mandating quotas, without including placement mechanisms or sanctions, has failed to result in major breakthroughs in women's parliamentary representation. There is a wide variation within Asia, and we need to understand how gender relations operate within each particular cultural, social, and economic context in order to explain the wide variance in institutional impact of quotas. In particular, more work is needed to compare and understand the experiences of Islamic women with respect to personal status, marriage, and family relations in quota and non-quota Muslim-dominant countries such as Afghanistan, Bangladesh, Brunei, Indonesia, Malaysia, and Pakistan (Fleschenberg and Derichs 2011; Rai et al. 2013; Prihatini 2019).

Studies have found strong links between particular electoral systems and women's representation (Roberts, Seawright, and Cyr 2012; Rule 1994; Salmond 2006). For example, a 2018 IPU study found that the average share of elected women is notably higher in proportional and mixed systems (26.5 per cent) than in majoritarian systems (20 per cent) (2019b, 1). Likewise for Asia, more proportional electoral systems also appear to favour women. Table 11.2 lists twenty countries that conducted multiparty elections in Asia, eight with majoritarian (first-past-the-post, or FPTP) electoral systems and twelve with more proportional systems, and compares the number of women each elected in the lower house (LH). The table indicates that the more proportional systems (list proportional representation [PR] and parallel systems) work better in boosting women's descriptive representation than do purely plurality-majoritarian (FPTP) ones. The twelve countries with more proportional systems have an average of 22 per cent of women parliamentarians, seven points more than the eight FPTP systems' average of 15 per cent. However, what this brief study does not tell us is how open and closed list PR systems, ranking of candidates on the ballot, size of district magnitude, and threshold requirement interact with the quota mechanisms to affect overall women's representation.

Table 11.2. Electoral Systems and Women's Legislative Representation in Asia

Country	Quota (LH)	Electoral System (LH)	Women (LH) %
India	No	FPTP	13
Bangladesh	Yes	FPTP	21
Mongolia	Yes	FPTP	17
Bhutan	No	FPTP	15
Malaysia	No	FPTP	14
Maldives	No	FPTP	5
Myanmar	No	FPTP	11
Singapore	No	FPTP	23
Cambodia	No	List PR (closed)	20
Timor-Leste	Yes	List PR (closed)	40
Sri Lanka	No	List PR (open)	5
Indonesia	Yes	List PR (open)	18
Thailand	No	MMP	5
Afghanistan	Yes	SNTV	24
Philippines	No	Parallel	30
South Korea	Yes	Parallel	17
Pakistan	Yes	Parallel	20
Taiwan	Yes	Parallel	38
Nepal	Yes	Parallel	33
Japan	No	Parallel	10

Sources: Based on data from International IDEA 2019a, 2019b.

Implications and Conclusion

This chapter has provided an overview of the formal quota mechanisms to improve women's political representation in twenty-five countries in Asia. It finds that quota policies, broadly defined to include candidate quotas and reserved seats adopted by eleven countries at the national levels, have improved women's description representation. But the numbers are uneven across the region and regime types. In terms of electoral systems, the more proportional ones appear to work better with quota policies and favour the election of women.

Party politics is also key to understanding women's access to political power. In Asia, barriers to women's political participation include the dominance of family-run political dynasties in political parties, as well as the strong influence of corruption and money during elections (True et al. 2013, 34). We need to reveal the mechanisms of candidate selection, or the "secret garden of politics" – how formal mechanisms and informal party dynamics affect the selection and supply of women from the local to national level, to be elected as party leaders, ministers, or heads of state. The experience of quotas for women in electoral and non-electoral regimes suggests that the ruling party's willingness to support affirmative action will make a big difference in women's overall political participation.

NOTES

1 Singapore elected its first female Malay president, Halimah Yacob, in 2017. However, the powers of the president are largely ceremonial, and her election was unopposed, under a new "reserved presidency" scheme that was reserved for minority Malays.
2 Depending on how one counts, there can up to forty-eight countries included in "Asia."
3 Vietnam has a "target system" to include ethnic minority, youth, non-party members, or independents to ensure diversity in the political system (United Nations Development Programme 2012, 14).
4 Setting the gender parity objective at 50 per cent in four countries was found to be effective (IPU 2019b, 2).
5 Cultural factors such as "Asian values" or patriarchal structure have been found to deter women's political participation; see Edwards and Roces 2006; Inglehart and Norris 2003; Richter 1990; and Stivens and Sen 1998.

12 Changing Minds: Canadian Perspectives on Gender Quotas and Diversity

CHANTAL MAILLÉ

The adoption of quotas for the election of women is a worldwide trend that is changing the face of national politics in many countries (Hughes 2011). Research shows that such measures are successful. Although electoral gender quotas have emerged as one of the critical political reforms of the last two decades (Krook and Zetterberg 2014), a new wave of research is raising questions about the impact of gender-only quotas on a wide variety of representative processes. For example, a number of authors raise issues about the diversity of women elected under quota regimes (Krook and Zetterberg 2014, 287–8) or apply an intersectional lens to the discussion of political quotas by introducing variables beyond gender, such as ethnicity (Celis and Erzeel 2013).

Although they have been adopted in more than 130 countries, quotas are not universal (Krook 2019). In Canada, for example, initiatives over the last thirty years to counter the problem of low numbers of women elected have strongly emphasized training for political office rather than gender quotas (Maillé 2015). The idea of quotas for women is gaining traction in Canadian politics, but although there seems to be a new symbolic opening for gender quotas at some levels of Canadian political institutions, popular support is still lacking. What about the idea of adopting quotas for improving the representation of other groups within Canadian political institutions? In the first section of this chapter, I refer to two authors who raise questions about gender quotas in relation to current feminist theories and I review research on processes that lead to the adoption of gender quotas. I then look at support for different types of quotas in Canada. Next, I analyse an informal yet successful campaign for gender quotas in Quebec. In my conclusion, I make two observations: (1) more research is needed to explain why there is still resistance to certain types of quotas in the Canadian context, and (2) campaigns for gender quotas can also create openings to introduce diversity into the conversation.

Diversity and Gender Quotas

Jessica Huber observes, on the subject of women, quotas, and intersectionality: "Evidence that supports the positive impact of gender quotas in political representation is mounting, and the debate has shifted from 'do they work?' to 'what else is needed?'" (2017, n.p.). There is agreement in scholarship and practice that gender quotas require enforcement mechanisms, incentives, and accompanying action and activities to produce gender equality in political leadership (Huber 2017). Huber identifies a new challenge in today's discussion of quotas: the treatment of women as a monolith. She writes, "The rise in discussions about intersectional feminism … is a global trend, perhaps most visible as a deliberate inclusion strategy … Women have unique experiences because of their race, class, religion, disability, sexual orientation and gender identity. How does this diversity play a role in implementing gender quotas?" (n.p.).

Hughes (2011) looks at how quotas affect minority women. She identifies the conditions under which gender quotas and minority quotas might improve the political representation of minority women through a worldwide analysis comparing the election of women from more than three hundred racial, ethnic, and religious groups across eighty-one countries. According to Hughes, policies designed to promote the political representation of women and of minority groups interact to produce diverse but predictable outcomes for minority women. She concludes that the quota policies currently in effect rarely challenge majority men's dominance of national legislatures.

One question Hughes raises is which type of quota is best for promoting representation of marginalized groups:

> Empirical research on quotas … tends to ignore minorities and minority women … Research on quotas has left at least three important questions unanswered. First, do quotas effectively increase the political representation of minority females relative to their majority female and minority male counterparts? Second, which policies – party gender quotas, national gender quotas, or minority quotas – tend to benefit minority women the most? Third, do minority women benefit or suffer from the simultaneous presence of these policies? (Hughes 2011, 606)

She concludes that gender and minority quotas tend to benefit primarily majority women and minority men. Minority women do benefit from national gender quotas or minority quotas to a lesser degree, but majority women appear to be the only beneficiaries of party gender quotas. The picture changes substantially, however, when these policies are combined. The few countries with tandem quotas have dramatically higher levels of minority women's legislative representation than do countries with any other institutional configuration of quotas.

Processes Leading to the Adoption of Quotas

Another important question that relates to the adoption of quotas in politics has to do with the process that leads to their adoption. Who initiates the process? How do quota campaigns get started? Krook (2010) identifies two key elements: women in civil society and political parties. She also highlights the importance of context: quota campaigns are successful to the extent that quotas mesh with pre-existing political dynamics. In their 2006 study, Krook, Lovenduski, and Squires identify additional elements: usually, quota proposals originate with women's groups inside political parties, but these efforts culminate in quota adoption only when elites perceive such policies as an effective way to compete favourably with other parties for the support of female voters. The authors also note that how the notion of equality is understood and applied in a country will influence the discussion on quotas. They suggest that representations of equality are related to citizenship models and identify Canada, like the United States, as having a liberal citizenship model that involves a philosophical commitment to individuals, favours equal opportunities, attributes responsibility for unequal outcomes to individuals (merit), and views prospects of change in terms of individual initiative.

Canada and Quotas

The fact that there are no gender quotas for women in Canadian politics has to do with the fact that none of the elements identified in the previous section as possible starting points for gender quota campaigns have ever mobilized around this claim in this specific context. In the October 2019 election, without gender quotas, the number of women elected to the Canadian Parliament rose by three percentage points, to 28.9 per cent (98 women/338 seats). Canadian initiatives over the last thirty years aimed at countering the problem of low numbers of elected women were characterized by a strong emphasis on women's training for political office and a lack of mobilization in favour of legal quotas. Both women's groups and women involved in the promotion of women in politics did not support the strategy of legal quotas and privileged women's individual characteristics (such as personality traits, socialization, gender roles, and professional paths) as the key factor in explaining women's under-representation in electoral politics instead of focusing on structures and systemic discrimination (Maillé 2015). Among factors proposed to explain the absence of mobilization for gender quotas in Canadian electoral politics, Young (2013) identifies features of Canadian political culture, such as the notion that political parties are private entities and the belief in merit over affirmative action: "We have inherited the British notion that political parties are private entities that should not be subject to extensive state regulation ... Second, even though the Canadian Charter of Rights and Freedoms explicitly allows for positive discrimination, affirmative action measures tend to collide with a deeply held belief that merit should trump all other considerations in the hiring of employees, including politicians" (263).

In 2015, the newly elected prime minister, Justin Trudeau, appointed a parity cabinet, with women holding 50 per cent of ministerial seats. When asked why he prioritized gender equality when recruiting ministers, he answered, "Because it's 2015" (Chartrand 2015). The principle of a cabinet with an equal number of women and men became a permanent commitment for the Liberals during the 2019 electoral campaign. This example implies that the idea of quotas is current in Canadian politics, even if not directly translated into measures at the candidate level. Another form of quotas that has been constitutive of Canadian politics concerns territory; Bashevkin has suggested using Canada's geographic quotas as a guide for building the demand for gender representation: "What about introducing rules that insist on gender representation – to parallel existing provisions that entrench geographic or territorial quotas in our system?" (2009, 151). Again, regional representation has always been at the centre of selection to Canadian cabinets, providing another instance of how issues of diversity and quotas have been reflected in some aspects of Canada's electoral system. "In the end, those who disagree with such quotas [for women] bear the burden of demonstrating that the equitable representation of women in government is unmeritorious – a position that is simply not supported by evidence" (Franceschet, Beckwith, and Annesley, 2015). In the view of Franceschet, Beckwith, and Annesley, critics of quotas have framed the debate in a way that sets up an irreconcilable tension between the principle of merit and the goal of diversity.

What about quotas for other groups? A survey conducted in 2016 by Environics Institute and the Institute on Governance found that a majority of Canadians are open to designating seats for the country's Indigenous peoples to boost their representation in Parliament and on the Supreme Court (May 2016). Another study conducted on existing affirmative action programs in the Canadian context provides insight on how quotas are perceived. These programs are aimed at redressing past inequities and promoting the hiring of five designated groups: women, visible minorities, racial minorities, Indigenous peoples, and persons with disabilities. The survey indicates that no one is in favour of discriminating against marginalized groups; nevertheless, a large majority of respondents support meritocracy and resist affirmative action (Ng 2016).

In 2019, the government of Canada conducted hearings on measures that could be implemented to help improve the representation of women in electoral politics in Canada. Various opinions were presented on quotas. In its final report, the committee made no recommendations about quotas but listed as an observation the following idea: "The Committee encourages registered parties to set voluntary quotas for the percentage of female candidates they field in federal elections and to publicly report on their efforts to meet these quotas after every federal general election" (House of Commons, Canada 2019, 45).

The 2018 Election in Quebec

In Quebec, for years, feminist interventions on the problem of low numbers of elected women in politics identified clearly the gender gap in elected officials but failed to examine the race and class characteristics of political elites. The prevailing actions developed by women's groups were based on strategies such as training programs designed specifically for generic women. Despite decades of training programs, there were fewer women in provincial elected office just before the start of the 2018 election than there had been in 2003. Things changed in the October 2018 provincial election: Quebec elected 41.6 per cent women (52 women/125 seats). Although no legal quotas for women were implemented for that election, there was a strong movement in favour of the adoption of such quotas in the background of the 2018 Quebec election, which became an opportunity to introduce diversity to the gender quotas campaign.

In 2015, the Conseil du Statut de la femme (CSF), an advisory body to the government of Quebec, published *Les femmes en politique: En route vers la parité*. The study's authors looked at the impact of measures that had been implemented over the previous twenty years in Quebec to increase the numbers of elected women and concluded that these measures had been insufficient and therefore quotas were necessary. One specific recommendation was to adopt an obligation for political parties to recruit at least 40 per cent women candidates, with financial penalties for parties that did not meet the objective. The CSF also expressed a concern for diversity with the introduction of quotas based on gender only (CSF 2015, 106).

The ideas brought forth by the CSF were supported by the women's group Groupe Femmes, Politique et Démocratie (GFPD), the most influential group in Quebec on women and politics. In a position paper presented in 2015, GFPD stated that the adoption of quotas was essential on a temporary basis (cited in GFPD 2019). In a book published in 2015, journalist Pascale Navarro, a spokesperson for GFPD, argued for parity in Quebec's National Assembly. On 8 March 2018, GFPD launched the campaign #paritépourdebon, asking for measures to guarantee the joint representation of women and men. In May 2018, GFPD proposed a bill calling for parity in Quebec politics and specifically asking for an amendment to the Election Act that would force all political parties to ensure that women make up 40 to 60 per cent of all candidates. The GFPD proposal would have required every political party to field a minimum of 40 per cent female candidates, a proportion that would rise to 45 per cent in the subsequent election.

During the 2018 Quebec election campaign, the question of quotas for women received a good deal of attention. In *Le Devoir*, a highly influential daily newspaper, a *"vigie parité"* (parity watch) was created, providing weekly reports on the progression of percentages of female candidates selected for each party. On 11 September 2018, *Le Devoir* journalist Guillaume Bourgault-Côté reported that the final count for that election was 47.9 per cent female candidates. Though there were no legal quotas for the 2018 election, all four main parties exceeded the 40 per cent target. Overall, the pressure was built through specific interventions made by the CSF and GFPD. Even the leading political party, Coalition Avenir Québec, which is more conservative on women's issues, went along, recruiting 48 per cent women candidates, which is part of the explanation for this significant jump in the proportion of elected women. Interestingly, the public conversation around quotas for women in politics created an opportunity to introduce the issue of diversity into the discussion, and Institut NéoQuébec kept a record of percentages of candidates from visible minorities. Québec solidaire had the highest percentage, with 17 per cent racialized female candidates, against 14.6 per cent for Coalition Avenir Québec, 7.1 per cent for Parti québécois, and 5.4 per cent for Parti liberal du Québec (Institut NéoQuébec 2018). In an article published in *Le Devoir*, sociologist Myrlande Pierre (2017), referring to the movement for a parity bill initiated by GFPD, suggested including measures to promote diversity: "How could we, in 2016, envision reaching parity in power structures without systematically integrating the principle of diversity? I'm asking the question to all progressive Quebec feminists" (translation mine).

Conclusion

In December 2018, *Maclean's* magazine published an editorial titled "It's in the Air: Canada Should Elect a Gender-Balanced Parliament in 2019." The author made reference to the need for change in the House of Commons: "Nearly a century after Agnes MacPhail was the first woman elected to the House of Commons, only about a quarter of seats are held by women. It's time for that to change." I suggest that the mainstreaming of the demand for gender-balanced representation in the House of Commons means that there is a new opportunity. There is evidence of growing social pressure to have a more diversified body of elected representatives. The proportion of women elected in the 2019 federal election provides an additional argument for the implementation of quotas. Without such measures, the progress in numbers of women elected could remain slow and unpredictable for another century.

The example of Quebec and its informal campaign for gender quotas in the most recent provincial election is inspiring because it shows that it is possible to build support for gender quotas by combining the strengths of women's movements with other public voices, without a formal legal framework. Another observation for the Quebec case is that when opportunities are offered to women, there is no shortage of candidates and all the traditional explanations for having fewer women candidates are overturned. Finally, Quebec's events confirm that campaigns for gender quotas can create openings to introduce diversity into the conversation.

13 Gender Quotas and Women's Political Representation: Lessons for Canada

SUSAN FRANCESCHET

This chapter tackles debates about gender quotas as a solution to the problem of women's under-representation in Canada's federal parliament. Drawing on international evidence about gender quota design in different kinds of political systems, I show that arguments against quotas in Canada are based on flawed claims about a mismatch between what makes quotas effective and Canada's political realities. The chapter concludes that there are no compelling reasons why gender quotas would not work in Canada. Instead, there are ample reasons why Canada should follow the lead of other countries and adopt gender quotas to improve women's access to electoral politics.

Although a relatively recent phenomenon, gender quotas have become enormously popular, appearing in some form in more than 130 countries worldwide (Hughes et al. 2019). Recent studies find that gender quotas are the primary source of cross-national differences in women's representation around the world. Examining a range of factors in 153 countries, Tripp and Kang (2008, 355) conclude that gender quotas have a greater impact than other institutional factors on the presence of women in elected office. In their global study of gender quotas and women's representation, Paxton and Hughes (2015, 355) note that "quotas may be a more useful mechanism to jumpstart women's legislative representation than adopting a new [proportional representation] electoral system," concluding that adopting a quota policy could boost women's presence by 8.5 per cent.

Should Canada Adopt Gender Quotas?

Canada made headlines around the world after the 2015 federal election when newly elected prime minister Justin Trudeau formed the country's first-ever federal cabinet with gender parity.[1] But women's share of

Table 13.1. Women's Representation in Canadian House of Commons and Global Rankings

Year	Women in House of Commons (%)	Global Ranking
2000	20.6	20th
2005	21.1	34th
2010	22.1	50th
2019	26.9	62nd

Source: Inter-Parliamentary Union archives, http://archive.ipu.org/wmn-e/world-arc.htm. Accessed 23 March 2019.

posts in federal cabinets has long outpaced women's share of seats in the House of Commons, where by all accounts progress has been glacially slow (Thomas and Young 2014). In a world where many countries are taking bold measures like gender quotas, Canada is falling further and further behind in global rankings (see Table 13.1). In 2000, Canada ranked twentieth worldwide in terms of women's parliamentary representation, but prior to the 2019 elections, Canada dropped to sixty-second place even though the proportion of women in the House of Commons grew in that period from 20.6 per cent to 26.9 per cent. Despite compelling evidence from around the world that quotas are an effective mechanism for increasing the number of women in office (see Hinojosa, Kittilson, and Williams, this volume), their adoption has not emerged as a serious solution to women's under-representation in the Canadian federal parliament.

Those who advocate gender quotas as a means to increase women's presence in the House of Commons typically encounter three objections: (1) quotas are ineffective in countries with single-member district electoral systems; (2) centrally imposed quotas clash with the principle of local autonomy in candidate selection; and (3) quotas undermine the principle of merit in candidate selection, thereby reducing the quality of elected officials. Below, I show why each of these objections is based on flawed arguments and runs counter to evidence from countries around the world.

Quotas and Single-Member Plurality Electoral Systems

Canada is among more than sixty countries around the world with a single-member district (SMD) electoral system, where political parties can nominate just one candidate in each district. The conventional wisdom is that electoral rules based on proportional representation (PR) are more quota friendly because policies can include placement mandates that prevent parties from placing women near the bottom of party lists where they are not likely to be elected. Applying quotas successfully in single-member districts is more difficult. Those believing quotas would be ineffective in Canada argue that parties who do not want to displace incumbent men will simply place women candidates in districts the party is unlikely to win. In effect, parties could comply fully with the quota requirement and fail to increase significantly the share of women elected. Most federal parties in Canada appear to do this already: a study published in 2013 showed that women were more likely than men to run in hard-to-win districts (Thomas and Bodet 2013). An analysis of where candidates were placed in the 2019 elections likewise found that forty-eight men candidates ran in party strongholds compared to just fourteen women (Oulett and Shiab 2019).

Looking at quota implementation in France and Mexico demonstrates how the challenge of getting parties to run women in districts they can win might be overcome. France elects members of its National Assembly using a single-member majority electoral system. A parity law adopted in 2000 initially seemed ineffective, with women's representation growing from 10.9 per cent in 1999 to just 18.2 per cent by 2008. Parity's ineffectiveness at the national level was largely blamed on the SMD electoral system, especially since quota requirements were proving successful at the local level where councillors were elected using proportional representation. At the national level, however, parties not only fielded significantly fewer women candidates than the law required, but they tended to place them in unwinnable districts (Murray 2012).

Things have changed in France, however. Between 2011 and 2017, women's share of seats in the National Assembly jumped from 26.9 per cent to 39 per cent, a spectacular increase in a relatively short time. Part of the explanation may be the declining fortunes of the main party on the right, which always resisted displacing men in favour of women. Another explanation is that the newer and smaller parties comply with parity rules because they are less able to absorb the financial penalties that the law imposes for non-compliance than are the large parties. But research also finds that norms and perceptions of democratic legitimacy matter greatly and shape party behaviour. Ideas about the importance of gender diversity are changing, with growing support for women's role in public life over time. Indeed, quotas have diffused beyond the political realm to business and civil society organizations (Lépinard 2016). Voters increasingly view diverse representative assemblies as more legitimate, a belief that is confirmed when gender quotas are adopted as law. In these cases, party behaviour changes too, making parties less likely to comply minimally with the law by placing women in unwinnable districts.

Evidence from Mexico likewise challenges the myth that quotas are ineffective in single-member districts. Mexico uses a mixed system, electing three hundred members of the Chamber of Deputies through single-member districts and the other two hundred through proportional representation with closed-party lists. Mexico first adopted a 30 per cent quota law in 2003, raising the threshold to 40 per cent in 2009. But women's representation remained short of the target, in large part because parties placed women in losing districts (Hinojosa and Piscopo 2018). Organized women lobbied for stricter provisions, ultimately winning a constitutional requirement for parity in 2014. They were not successful, however, in getting what they really wanted: having the law establish three categories of electoral districts – safe, competitive, and losing – and requiring that women comprise half of all candidates in each type. Instead, the law simply prohibited parties from placing women "exclusively" in districts where the party had performed most poorly in the last elections (Piscopo 2017, 148).

The law's wording did not permit Mexico's National Electoral Institute (INE) to apply sanctions on parties so long as not *all* women were placed in losing districts. Instead, the INE worked with the gender observatory created by women's groups to publicize parties' placement of women candidates (Piscopo 2017). Concerns about public shaming led parties to comply not just with the letter of the law, but with the spirit of the parity rule: parties did not relegate women to losing districts. In fact, women's share of seats increased from 37 per cent in 2012 to 42.4 per cent in 2015 and almost hit parity in 2017 when women won 48.2 per cent of seats. Mexico's success in increasing women's legislative representation shows that quotas can indeed be effective even with single-member district electoral rules.

Quotas and Decentralized Candidate Selection

Local autonomy in candidate selection is a sacred principle in Canadian politics (Medeiros, Forest, and Erl 2019). Unfortunately, decentralized nomination is also associated with lower proportions of women candidates (Hinojosa 2012). According to Pruysers and Cross (2016, 792), "local autonomy can create a coordination problem as hundreds of individuals and atomized associations choose their candidates in isolation without a broader discussion of diversity or what is occurring in other districts." Skeptics often acknowledge that improving gender balance is a desirable goal, but it cannot be realized while maintaining local control over candidate nominations. Such objections not only underestimate the role that central parties have always played in candidate selection, they also ignore evidence from other countries where local autonomy co-exists alongside of mechanisms to increase the selection of women candidates.

Canada is not alone in experiencing tensions between local autonomy and national party goals. Ireland finally addressed women's under-representation in parliament through a 30 per cent national electoral quota in 2012. Ireland uses a PR system with a single-transferable vote. But, like Canada, there is a strong tradition of localism, with candidates selected by local rather than national party selectors (Brennan and Buckley 2017; Culhane 2017). National parties sometimes issue direc-tives to local selectors to nominate women, but such impositions are rarely welcome. Men's dominance of local networks and the previously slow pace of change in Ireland did not inspire confidence that parties would respect the new quota law. Perhaps surprisingly, women's share of candidacies doubled, growing from 15.2 per cent in 2011 to 29.6 per cent for the 2016 elections (Brennan and Buckley 2017, 18). Parties com-plied with the quota because they couldn't afford not to: failure to com-ply would lead to a party's losing fully half of its state funding (Buckley, Galligan, and McGing 2016).

Local autonomy in candidate selection is an important tradition in the United Kingdom as well. While lacking a national electoral quota, the UK Labour Party began using a quota policy known as all-women-shortlists (AWS) in 1993. The policy mandates that in half of the vacant seats the party is likely to win, only women be considered for nomina-tion (Nugent and Krook 2016). All-women-shortlists represent a com-promise between the national party's objective of improving gender balance among candidates while also respecting the local party's auton-omy to select its candidates without interference from the central party. While the goal is to have constituencies volunteer to have an AWS, if there are not enough volunteers, some constituencies will have an AWS imposed by the central party, based on several factors, including pat-terns of women's representation in that region (Cutts, Childs, and Field-house 2008, 578–9). Such imposition is often unwelcome, as evidenced by a high-profile case in 2005. In that election, an AWS candidate was defeated in a long-held Labour seat by a strident opponent of Labour's quota policy who ran as an independent. The loss provoked claims that imposing AWS on local constituencies was risky and cost the party votes (Cutts, Childs, and Fieldhouse 2008, 578–9).

Ample evidence shows that the loss of an AWS candidate in a pre-sumably safe Labour seat was not indicative of a larger backlash against the central party's imposition of gender quotas. Several studies con-clude that candidates selected through AWS were no more or less likely to lose than other candidates in both 2005 and 2010 (Cutts, Childs, and Fieldhouse 2008; Cutts and Widdop 2013; Nugent and Krook 2016).

As in Ireland and the United Kingdom, in Canada too there is a clear tension between central party goals and local autonomy in candidate selection. But it is not uncommon for normative principles to compete, and in this case, there is no reason why maintaining local control of candidate selection ought to be prioritized over improving the diversity of representative bodies.

Quotas and Candidate Qualifications

Possibly the most commonly voiced objection to gender quotas is that selecting candidates on the basis of sex rather than qualifications undermines the principle of merit, which, in turn, threatens the quality of our political class. Fortunately, gender and politics scholars have undertaken several studies, producing extensive evidence from countries around the world to refute such objections. Sweden's Social Democrats adopted gender quotas for local elections in 1993, in an effort to improve women's representation. Exploring the impact of the quota on the competence of municipal politicians, researchers concluded that the quality of elected councillors *improved* rather than declined (Besley et al. 2017). Quotas reduce the number of spots available for men, which has the effect of increasing competition among men for those spots. The result is that gender quotas not only serve the goal of improving the diversity of voices in parliament, they also "disrupt some of the political forces that maintain the dominance of a mediocre male elite" (Besley et al. 2017, 2240).

Several other studies confirm that arguments about sacrificing quality by pursuing gender equality are not grounded in facts. Murray's (2010) study of French parliamentarians after adoption of the parity law finds "quota women" to be no less effective in parliament than their male colleagues. Murray found that women elected to the National Assembly were just as active in parliamentary tasks as were men. In Argentina, where a quota law was adopted in 1991, Franceschet and Piscopo (2012) found that women in congress exceeded men's qualifications in some areas, like education, and had similar levels of political experience as men. Nugent and Krook, looking at all MPs in the United Kingdom over the last five parliaments, find that women elected through quotas had "*higher* levels of political experience than their Labour colleagues" in all but the 2010 election (2016, 118, emphasis in original). And in Italy, researchers found that women elected after the adoption of a quota law had similar or better qualifications than elected men (Weeks and Baldez 2014).

In sum, there is no evidence to support the charge that quotas lead to the selection of under-qualified candidates. In fact, the imposition of quotas contributes to improved quality by compelling party selectors to expand the eligibility pool to include women (Murray 2014).

Drawing Conclusions from International Experiences with Gender Quotas

Looking at international experiences provides several lessons for Canada. First and foremost, the evidence shows that quotas work. They are powerful tools to boost women's representation. Canada should therefore adopt gender quotas to improve the slow pace of change in the federal parliament.

Second, international experiences suggest that some creativity is needed to ensure that quotas will work effectively in Canada's single-member district electoral system. Both France and Mexico show the importance of having a strong electoral observatory that monitors parties' compliance with rules requiring gender balance in candidate selection. The strategy proposed by Mexican feminists, namely, categorizing districts into safe, competitive, and losing, and making sure that women and men are evenly placed across them, is a clear and relatively uncomplicated solution to overcome any perceived incompatibility between quotas and SMD. It is also important for equality advocates in civil society and the media to keep up the pressure on political parties to provide women with the same opportunities as men to run in winnable districts. Increasing the number of women candidates on its own will not increase the number of women elected unless parties abandon their current strategies of favouring men in their stronghold ridings.

Third, the sacredness of local autonomy in candidate selection should not stand in the way of another desirable normative principle, improving gender balance in Parliament. In light of growing public support for women's presence in public office, expectations of local resistance to strategies like all-women-shortlists or central party directives for certain districts to nominate women may in fact be overstated. Evidence from both Ireland and the United Kingdom supports the idea that local resistance can be overcome in order to apply quotas effectively.

Finally, we must put to rest once and for all arguments that pit gender quotas against merit. Such arguments are better viewed as a rhetorical strategy to maintain a status quo that benefits the powerful, namely, men incumbents and aspirants. Evidence from several countries shows that women elected with quotas are either just as qualified as their male colleagues, or sometimes even more qualified. Quotas require selectors to include qualified women and prevent selectors from overselecting candidates from just one half of the population (see Murray 2014).

NOTE

1 Parity cabinets had been formed previously at the provincial level in Quebec in 2007 and 2008 and in Alberta in 2015.

PART FOUR

New Research Directions

14 Making the Case for Women's Representation: What, Who, and Why

KELLY DITTMAR

Interrogating the causes for and implications of women's political under-representation is nothing new in the field of women and politics; in fact, the study of gender and political representation is itself rooted in both problematizing and addressing the disparities in political power between women and men. But making the case for women's political inclusion must be done with caution about the traps that gender scholars often call on others to avoid. First, women are not monolithic in their identities, beliefs, or approaches to politics and policymaking. Still, scholars and advocates for gender equity are pushed to make a singular case for why and how women's political representation matters. Second, elected leaders are not the only actors shaping the culture, processes, and outcomes of political institutions. Expanding our sites for evaluating representation levels and outcomes is key to accurately assessing the realities and implications of gender disparities in political representation across levels and types of office. Finally, in working to make an affirmative case for increasing women's political representation, scholars and advocates can easily, if not intentionally, reinforce a double standard for inclusion for women. More specifically, the burden of proof has often fallen on women and people of colour to justify disruption of the status quo in descriptive representation instead of falling on white men to justify its maintenance.

In this chapter, I push for greater interrogation and avoidance of these traps in research and advocacy on women's political representation, reviewing the content of, oversights in, and audiences for the case for women's representation.

What Is the Case for Increasing Women's Political Representation?

A fundamental argument for promoting gender parity in political leadership relies on democratic tenets of fairness and legitimacy (Mansbridge 1999; Phillips 1998). More specifically, increasing women's

representation is not only important to remedying existing inequality of influence, but also strengthens the legitimacy – both real and
perceived – of a governing body that is tasked with representing the full
diversity of its constituents. Evidence of women's distinct representational impact is not necessary in making this case for women's political
inclusion, as gender is included among the many axes of diversity that
are described as enhancing democracy. This argument suggests that
the benefits of variance in perspective and experience will be broad,
diverse, and sometimes unanticipated or difficult to isolate.[1]

The reluctance of many to accept a case for women's political representation based on broad principles of fairness and legitimacy has
encouraged scholars and advocates to identify more direct measures
of women's political influence. Work on the symbolic representation of
women candidates and office holders has offered some evidence that
greater representation of women on ballots and among elected leaders has a positive impact on feelings of political efficacy and levels of
political engagement among individuals from politically marginalized
groups, especially women (Atkeson 2003; Atkeson and Carrillo 2007;
Reingold and Harrell 2010). In research that my colleagues and I have
recently done on representation in the US Congress, congresswomen
included their influence as role models as one indicator of how their
presence has altered political institutions (Dittmar, Sanbonmatsu, and
Carroll 2018). As Representative Terri Sewell (D-AL) told us, "If I spark
the imagination of one woman who wouldn't have otherwise thought of
themselves as a policy maker, I am hopefully creating a pipeline of other
women who will join the ranks of the elected" (191). By demonstrating
that women's political leadership is possible, women candidates and
office holders challenge beliefs that political institutions are inaccessible
to women (or, more broadly, to historically excluded groups), and contest perceptions that women's capabilities are incompatible with office
holding.[2] To women considering candidacy, the presence of women in
political leadership may more directly combat doubts over their fitness
for candidacy or office holding and foster greater optimism about their
potential for electoral success.

Measuring the symbolic impact of women's political representation
is possible but difficult, especially in the degree to which we are able
to quantify and isolate citizens' exposure to women leaders as a factor influencing their beliefs or behaviours. Scholars have tried to offer
more concrete findings of women's impact by identifying gender differences in measures of legislative behaviour, including the magnitude
and policy focus of bill sponsorship, floor speeches, and roll call votes,
as well as indicators of legislative effectiveness. In doing so, they have

contributed to a case for women's political representation that relies on the idea that women bring something different – and, in some cases, better – than men to political institutions. The most cited findings on women's substantive representation point to women office holders' prioritization of issues that disproportionately affect women, children, and families; their likelihood of doing more work than their male counterparts on behalf of their constituents; and women's heightened levels of legislative effectiveness (Anzia and Berry 2011; Lazarus and Steigerwalt 2018; Osborn 2012; Swers 2002; Volden, Wiseman, and Wittmer 2013). There is also some evidence that women's entry as political principals might enhance institutional representativeness vis-à-vis staff in professionalized legislatures (Wilson and Carlos 2014).

My co-authors and I have argued that identifying the substantive benefits of women's representation requires more nuanced measures of impact, including those that move beyond publicly available measures of output to consider the ways in which women's distinct and diverse perspectives and experiences influence not only policy outcomes, but also policy processes and deliberation (Dittmar, Sanbonmatsu, and Carroll 2018). In discussing her work to address sexual assault in the military and on college campuses, Senator Kirsten Gillibrand (D-NY) told us, "I think it is easier for a female member to imagine what it's like to be victimized, to be disbelieved, disregarded and retaliated against" (154). That understanding informs how women define the policy problem and develop policy solutions. Substantive impact can also be measured in institutional terms, as we did by identifying ways in which congresswomen disrupt institutional structures, rules, norms, and expectations as they conduct their congressional work. An overt example included congresswomen securing their own restroom off of the US House chamber; its absence prior to the twenty-first century reflected the reality of an institution literally built by and for men. Less explicitly, women office holders told us that their results-oriented approach to legislating distinguishes them from their male counterparts and alters the way business is done in Congress. Crediting this impact to women's motivation to run and serve, Representative Anna Eshoo (D-CA) explained, "I don't think women come here to be somebody. I think we come here to get things done" (197).

Beyond expanding the sites for measuring women's political impact, we have also argued for greater nuance in evaluating gender differences in office holder behaviour. In our research on women in Congress, we focused on partisanship and race as key identities that (with gender) simultaneously shape members' perspectives, priorities, and behaviours. Accepting the multilayered identities with which women come to their representational roles yields more complex and less universal, but arguably more accurate, conclusions about the impact of women on legislative institutions, processes, and outcomes.

Who Counts in Our Assessments of Women's Political Representation?

Our academic and practical debates over women's political inclusion have focused disproportionately on women's representation in elected and appointed positions, lifting these positions up as the primary roles responsible for translating public views and priorities into policy outcomes. However, limiting our assessments of women's influence in political institutions to political principals ignores the representational influence of other institutional actors. Comparative scholarship on politics and gender has identified the importance of assessing the role and influence of feminists in governmental bureaucracies, suggesting that feminist women have the potential to shape and prioritize outcomes that promote gender equality (see, for example, Chappell 2002). In the United States, some research on legislative staff – those working directly for elected legislators – has noted that staff perform representative functions in policy deliberation and navigation of the legislative process (Malbin 1980). At the least, a strong case can be made for viewing representation in professionalized legislatures as mediated by legislative staff (Bell and Rosenthal 2003).

In my own research on gender, race, and congressional staff in the United States, I have argued that assessing the representativeness of our legislative bodies necessitates consideration of the gender and racial diversity (or lack thereof) among staff (Dittmar 2018). Making visible the disparities in presence and power among both male and female staffers as well as white and racial and ethnic minority staffers is the first step to rethinking the scope of our measures and definition of representation. The next step is considering the implications of these disparities for institutional culture, legislative processes, and policy agendas, debates, and outcomes. Even more than with elected office holders, isolating the impact of legislative staffers is difficult. Staffers' behaviour and influence is often invisible by design; they commonly adhere to norms of loyalty and deference to their principal by characterizing their own positions and contributions as indistinguishable from that of their boss.

Still, there are multiple avenues by which to evaluate the potential influence of staff diversity on institutions and policy. For example, we asked congresswomen directly about the role of their staff. They were quick to tout the critical role staffers play in expanding office capacity, but also revealed the influence of staff on legislative strategies and priorities. US Senator Patty Murray (D-WA) explained, "I don't hire people who just say yes. I hire people who help me think" (Dittmar 2018, 10).[3] Some congresswomen offered examples of staff's direct influence on policy, with one senator crediting a staff member for her commitment to legislation addressing youth homelessness. The staffer, a former runaway and homeless youth, shared her story with Senator Susan Collins (R-ME); "It was hearing her story that made me really interested in delving more deeply into this," Collins told us, adding, "But for the personal experience of a staffer, I'm not sure I would have had my awareness heightened to the point where I've made it a priority" (11).

Direct insights from staffers provide additional evidence of their intervening role in congressional representation. In my recent work, I have drawn upon the concept of racialized professionalism to consider the ways in which women congressional staff might engage in gendered professionalism – defined broadly as gender-informed professional behaviour with recognition of the intersections of gender, race, and other interlocking forces – that informs staff intervention and influence.[4] For example, a woman congressional staffer explained, "Having women and staff who are parents, who think about childcare, who think about healthcare for women, who think about maternity leave, who think about sexual assault – all of these things are useful." She continued, "Staff are incredibly influential on their bosses and provide that context when their bosses may not have it" (Dittmar 2018, 24–5). Likewise, a former committee staffer described the value of having tribal women staffers like her at the table when the Congress was debating reauthorization of the Violence Against Women Act (VAWA) in 2013, which sought to cover Native women on reservations for the first time. She told me, "You can learn issues. You can read about issues. [But] … the experience factor of living in a community that you are representing, of being a female when you are talking about violence against women, it adds an extra layer to the conversation" (26).

Why Do We Have to Make a Case for Women's Political Representation?

Just as we consider how to expand and refine the case for women's political representation, addressing both the multiple sites for women's influence and the multiple layers of identity that shape it, we must also reflect on why, to whom, and how this case is made.

When appealing to the public, particularly voters, scholars and advocates alike are incentivized to present an if/then case for increasing women's political representation: if more women are elected to office, x and y will happen. In making this affirmative case for women's empowerment – one that goes beyond increasing the legitimacy of representative institutions, it is easy to fall into the trap that women as a group need to bring something distinct, and often better, to governing in order to justify their inclusion. In contrast, white men have rarely, if ever, been asked to justify the maintenance of their dominance as political office holders. Moreover, they are not tasked with making the case for their political inclusion on the basis of what their gender and/or race identities will bring to legislative institutions.

Relatedly, in an effort to isolate the distinct impact of women, scholars and advocates too often present conclusions as universalities to make a more persuasive case for what difference it will make to elect more women to office. The truth is that research findings on the relationship between women's descriptive and substantive (or even symbolic) representation come with many caveats and too infrequently evaluate women in their diversity instead of in their totality. By discussing commonalities in findings as universalities in expectations, we risk burdening the women office holders we are seeking to boost. For example, if a woman's representational priorities and behaviours prove more similar than different from men's, she may be criticized for not doing enough to bring something new or distinct to a legislature. Likewise, if a woman's representational priorities and behaviours prove divergent from other women's – both in office and in the electorate – she may be regarded with skepticism instead of valued for the fullness of her diversity. We see this often in the United States across party lines, whereby Republican women are accused of *mis*representing women when the reality is that they represent *different* women (and men) in their approach to governance.

The case for increasing women's political representation is also made more directly to potential women candidates, which is important to overcoming well-documented – and gendered – hurdles to candidate emergence and recruitment. In this volume, Dolan, Shah, and Stripp explain that even among the women who *did* run for office in the 2018 US elections, self-doubt, lack of party support, and concerns about money and family responsibilities played a role in their decision-making calculus. Other research demonstrates that women make the decision to run for office differently than their male counterparts, relying more than those male counterparts on both encouragement and evidence that the benefits of running and serving will outweigh the costs (Carroll and Sanbonmatsu 2013; Lawless and Fox 2010; Shames 2017). Illuminating women's potential for influence on policy agendas, debates, and outcomes is key to shifting the balance towards the benefits of participation. Drawing upon existing research on the impact of women in office, scholars and advocates often emphasize the need for women to run to be sure that their unique perspectives and experiences *as women* are present in the policy process. Likewise, and drawing from prospect theory, they emphasize the threat to policy outcomes when women are absent from the legislative process. But in making this case to prospective women candidates, universal claims of women's representational influence are not only unnecessary, but potentially problematic. Instead, reframing the case for women's representation in a way that embraces the diversity of women's perspectives, experiences, and influence will help to combat the constraint they may feel (or others may place on them) upon taking office and making good on the promises made and expectations raised about their service. Moreover, when the potential sites for women's (or men's) impact are presented as broad instead of narrow, the case made to women for running and serving might be even more persuasive.

Conclusion

While those of us seeking to increase women's political representation may have legitimate critiques about the extra burden on women to justify their inclusion, the reality is that we must continue to make the case for women's representation – to voters, to practitioners, and to prospective women candidates. In this chapter, I have suggested that we – as scholars and advocates – be thoughtful in *how* we make that case and *who* we include as representatives. First, in expanding our sites for identifying impact and embracing multiplicity over universality of women's influence, we can best avoid traps that reduce women to a monolith and amplify singular models for women's representation. And second, making a comprehensive case for women's political representation necessitates that we advocate diversity among and empowerment of all actors that contribute to institutions' representative functions, which – at least in professionalized governing bodies – includes staff. These suggestions capitalize on the important work done for decades by scholars and advocates, with an eye to the need for an evolved approach to this conversation in the midst of an evolving reality for women's political representation worldwide.

NOTES

1 See Mansbridge (1999) on "uncrystallized interests" and descriptive representation.
2 See Mansbridge (1999) on the "construction of social meaning" and descriptive representation.
3 Interviews quoted in this section were conducted as part of the CAWP Study of Women in the 114th Congress.
4 For the concept of racialized professionalism, see Watkins-Hayes (2009).

15 Women in Parliament: From Presence to Impact

MALLIGA OCH

Twenty years ago, women made up only 13 per cent of parliamentarians worldwide (Inter-Parliamentary Union (IPU) 1999). Today, the number stands at 24.1 per cent (IPU 2019a). While progress has been made, it has been incremental and slow. Further, women's presence in parliament is highly variable, from women-majority parliaments in Rwanda, Cuba, and Bolivia to women being completely absent in the parliaments of Yemen, Vanuatu, Papua New Guinea, and Micronesia (IPU 2019b). Arguments for the inclusion of women in politics have been made not only on the basis of justice and fairness – that is, women represent over half of the population so they should be represented in parliament – but also based on the idea that the presence of women (descriptive representation) will lead to women-friendly policy outcomes (substantive representation of women). There is plenty of evidence that women indeed represent women's interests;[1] yet the exact mechanism that translates women's presence in parliament into tangible policy outcomes that improve gender equality overall is less clear. In this chapter, I argue that no single factor can guarantee the translation from presence to impact. Instead, we need to consider the policy-making process in its entirety and identify the critical junctures where *critical actors* need to exert pressure to ensure policy success. Specifically, I argue that women need to command political and institutional resources in the policy-making process to have policy impact.

Critical mass theory is certainly the most well-known mechanism that links the descriptive with the substantive representation of women. Critical mass theory argues that women need to reach a specific numerical threshold – most commonly put at 30 per cent – in parliament. Once women constitute a critical mass, the story goes, parliament will pass women-friendly policies (Dahlerup 1988; Kanter 1977). If one works as an advocate for women in politics, it is hard to avoid the term "critical mass": international organizations and women's groups frequently cite critical mass theory when making their case for more women in politics. However, the validity of the critical mass argument is highly contested in the literature. For one, there is little agreement on where this critical mass is located – studies put it as low as 15 per cent and as high as 40 per cent women in the legislature. Further, evidence for the argument has been mixed – some have found a link between critical mass and women-friendly policies while other have not.[2] As a result, women and politics scholars, in contrast to practitioners, have largely shifted away from the critical mass argument, abandoning the underlying assumption that the presence of women *automatically* translates to women-friendly policy outcomes.

If the presence of women alone does not translate into policy impact, what other factors are necessary for women to have a tangible effect on policy? To answer this question, women and politics scholars have explored a host of other factors, including but not limited to the impact of women's movements, femocrats (feminist actors within the bureaucracy), women's agencies and caucuses, women in cabinets or governments, women in political parties, and, of course, women leaders.[3] Others have pointed to the importance of strategic partnerships between women's agencies, femocrats, and feminist experts.[4] While each of these studies has tried to elucidate the precise mechanism that translates women's presence in politics into tangible policy outcomes, they all start from the same problematic assumption as does critical mass theory: they focus on one factor (or in some instances a combination of factors) that is thought to promote policy impact without considering the policy-making process in a holistic manner.

From Presence to Impact

Contrary to the critical mass argument, the critical actor approach focuses on how specific actors – both men and women – realize the substantive representation of women. Critical actors are "legislators who *initiate policy proposals* on their own and/or embolden others to take steps to promote policies for women regardless of the number of female representatives" (Childs and Krook 2009, 528). Past research has confirmed the existence and importance of critical actors: in the Scottish and Welsh parliament, the same small group of women accounted for most of the women-friendly initiatives in the legislature and committees, and in Australia critical actors played an important role in allowing RU 486, more commonly known as Mifepristone or the abortion pill, to be sold (Chaney 2006, 2012; Sawer 2012).

The presence of critical actors, however, is not enough to secure policy success. In any political system, critical actors need to secure the support of political decision makers to pass their preferred policies. Put differently, critical actors will have a greater chance of passing their preferred policy if they have access to political and institutional resources or if they have the ability to influence those actors that do. Thus, it is crucial to examine the different roles that critical actors can play in any political system and the different levels of political and institutional resources that come with them. Overall, critical actors can perform two different roles: gatekeepers and insiders. Both roles afford critical actors the political and institutional resources necessary to influence the policy making process.

Gatekeepers

The most vital institutional role of a critical actor is that of a veto player, defined as "individuals or collective actors whose agreement is necessary for a change of the status-quo" (Tsebelis 2002, 19). For policy change to occur, unanimous consent to the new policy by all veto players is necessary (Tsebelis 1995, 1999). Thus, the more veto players exist, the more difficult it is to bring about policy change. However, not all veto players are created equal. Primary veto players have agenda-setting powers, and their policy preferences will influence what is considered for legislation. For example, in the German system, the minister responsible for a specific policy area will be a primary veto player, as he or she is tasked with developing any policy proposals and chaperoning them through the policy process. In these instances, critical actors should be thought of as *primary gatekeepers*, as their consent is necessary to initiate any policy proposal. Whenever critical actors are primary gatekeepers, they are in the most opportune position to push for women-friendly policies, as they are responsible for initiating legislation. In practice, this means that critical actors can introduce legislation that they themselves have drafted and that, as a result, can be as broad in scope and strong in language as the critical actor deems necessary.

Secondary veto players are those actors or entities (such as the parliament) whose consent is necessary to pass any policy but who do not have agenda-setting powers. For example, secondary veto players can include committee chairs (particularly in political systems where committee chairs decide whether a bill is allowed for a vote on the floor) or executive leaders (prime ministers or presidents), whose consent to a policy is always necessary whether before a policy can be proposed or when a policy needs to be signed to become law. In instances where critical actors occupy a secondary veto player position, critical actors should be considered *secondary gatekeepers*, as their consent is necessary for a bill to become law. In practice, this means that critical actors in secondary gatekeeper positions can ensure that a women-friendly bill moves through the policy-making process, protecting a bill from oppositional forces that might want to delay, weaken, or kill the bill.

Insiders

Even when critical actors are not primary or secondary gatekeepers, they still have ample opportunities to command political and institutional power in the policy-making process. During the drafting stage a host of actors (for example, party factions, party leaders, members of parliament, bureaucrats, heads of women agencies or caucuses) provide feedback and request changes to the drafting of bills. Whenever critical actors are part of the internal consultation process, we should consider them *insiders*. The same holds true for the legislative process when the bill moves to the committee stage and is discussed by parliament. Again, when critical actors are committee members or representatives, they can be considered *insiders*. While their consent to a policy is not required, insiders nevertheless possess political and institutional resources that can protect policy proposals from being weakened or stymied in the policy process. For example, when critical actors are members of the committee responsible for debating a woman-friendly bill, they can protect the bill from committee changes that might weaken the bill's scope or language or keep pressure on the committee chair to bring the bill up for a vote.

Of course, policy opponents can also be veto players or insiders. Thus, the position of policy opponents compared to critical actors matters tremendously for any policy outcomes. Whenever opponents are primary or secondary gatekeepers, the substantive representation of women will be impossible. For example, when Germany discussed a corporate board quota in 2013, the responsible minister was an outspoken quota opponent, and thus a quota policy proposal was never introduced (Och 2015). In contrast, when opponents are insiders they are less able to stop a policy. However, they can still shape the language and scope, as they are formally consulted in the policy-making process. In these instances, we can expect the final bill's language to be weaker and more restricted in scope. For example, the final 2015 bill on corporate board quotas in Germany was successfully restricted in scope by quota opponents who were important insiders: the quota target was lowered from 40 per cent to 30 per cent, and only public listed companies rather than all German companies were subject to the legally mandated corporate board quotas (Och 2018).

Consider another example: in 2006, the Merkel government embarked on a massive parental leave reform under the leadership of Ursula von der Leyen, minister for family, women, seniors, and youth. Von der Leyen was an outspoken advocate for introducing greater equality in care responsibilities in the home and as such was a critical actor; as the responsible minister, she was also a primary gatekeeper. To achieve a more equitable distribution of care responsibilities, von der Leyen incorporated the so-called partner month into the new parental leave scheme. Von der Leyen argued that fathers needed a gentle yet forceful push to take over more care responsibilities in the home. Accordingly, her bill proposed a 10+2 model where families would get twelve months of paid parental leave only if the father stays at home for at least two months. This proposal enraged the conservative faction of the party, particularly several conservative state governors. Because state governments are traditionally consulted during the bill-drafting stage, partner month opponents were insiders during the policy-making process. They used their insider status to weaken the bill by insisting on a bonus model where all families receive twelve months of paid leave but receive an additional two months of paid leave if the father stays home for two months. However, opponents were not the only insiders. There were plenty of other critical actors who were insiders as well, both as committee members and during the drafting stage. They used their political and institutional resources as insiders to counter opponents' attempts to kill the partner month policy. This example not only shows how important it is for critical actors to occupy primary gatekeeper positions, as it allows them to enter policy discussion from a much stronger position than would otherwise be possible, but also shows that insider roles afford critical actors the institutional and political power to safeguard policies. Without critical actors in insider roles, opponents might have been successful in quashing the partner month policy altogether.

Conclusion

If we believe that women are more likely to bring forward policies that are in the best interest of women, we cannot stop at electing more women. Having more women in politics is an intrinsic value: democratic fairness should at its most basic mean that men *and* women are equally represented in politics. Yet efforts to get more women into politics based on the belief that the descriptive and substantive representations of women are automatically linked are misguided. Instead, what is more important is that women who, as critical actors, advocate and initiate policy proposals to advance women's interests are placed in positions of power where they have access to the necessary political and institutional resources to initiate policy and influence policy outcomes. As we have seen from the discussion above, critical actors will be most influential if they are *primary gatekeepers* (agenda-setting power), *secondary gatekeepers* (policy consent is necessary), or *insiders* (consulted when bill language and scope are drafted). At the same time, it matters what kind of roles policy opponents occupy.

Which precise positions these gatekeepers or insiders occupy will vary across political systems and policy fields. Thus, we need to identify critical actors and the locations of gatekeepers and insiders anew for each case. Further, we need to do the same for those individuals opposing the substantive representation of women, since it is not the presence of critical actors alone but the constellation of critical actors and opponents that determines the likelihood that substantive representation of women can be achieved. In the end, it is about access to power rather than plain numbers if we want women to have any meaningful policy impact.

Acknowledgment

I would like to thank Sarah Childs for her thoughtful comments on this project and her constant words of encouragement.

NOTES

1 See for example Thomas 1991; Taylor-Robinson and Heath 2003; Chaney 2008; Piscopo 2011; Swers 2005; Reingold 2008.
2 See for example Grey 2006; Studlar and McAllister 2002; Childs and Krook 2006; Childs and Krook 2008.
3 See for example Celis et al. 2008; Beckwith and Cowell-Meyers 2007; Weldon 2002; Gouws 1996; Stoffel 2008; Sawer 2012; Mazur 2002; Jalalzai 2013; Atchison and Down 2009.
4 See for example Lang 2009, 2014; Woodward 2004.

16 Too Feminine to Be a Leader? Systematic Implicit Biases against Women Politicians

SHAN-JAN SARAH LIU

The political presence of women has advanced over the last few decades, albeit slowly. However, women are still less likely to run or be recruited for political candidacy. Women, even when elected, are also held to different standards than their male counterparts. Drawing from extant scholarship on stereotypes and implicit biases, this chapter evaluates the impact of stereotyping women, especially women with multiple marginalized identities, as a systematic barrier to parity in political institutions. It argues that gender norms must be eliminated in order to improve the status and influence of women in positions of political leadership. It also offers policy recommendations for providing a space for women in political institutions.

Introduction

Recent years have witnessed improvement on women's political status. The current percentage of women in national legislatures across the world has doubled since 1997. However, even in countries where there seems to be relatively more gender parity in political institutions, women still face barriers that their male counterparts do not.

This chapter expands upon past work on the systematic challenges that confront women political leaders (e.g., Liu 2019). It argues that stereotypes and implicit biases prevent women from being a part of the political process – especially women with multiple marginalized identities. It also argues that we need to pay attention to how we view the (under)representation of women in politics, in general, to understand the impact of female leadership. The chapter concludes by offering some recommendations for reaching inclusion and equality for women in political institutions.

Implicit Biases and Women's Success in Politics

Despite women's increased presence in some political positions, differences still persist in the experiences of female and male politicians. One major difference is the way voters perceive female and male candidates. For example, voters may associate female candidates with feminine traits, such as approachability, which is not necessarily a qualification for a leader, and associate male candidates with masculine traits, such as dominance, which is considered crucial for leadership. As both women and men are expected to perform their femininity and masculinity, respectively, based on the sex assigned to them at birth, it is not surprising that voters would assign politicians gendered attributes. Such characterization of politicians based on their identities in turn helps voters evaluate how competent they may be and how worthy they are of support, especially when political information is not readily accessible or transparent. People, therefore, may rely upon these commonly assigned characteristics – stereotypes – to form their impressions of male and female candidates, especially when they have limited time and energy to devote to political affairs (for an overview of the literature on these issues, see Bauer 2019).

Stereotypes of Women Politicians

Voters are not the only ones that assume gendered traits and competency of politicians. The media also differentiate their coverage by using stereotypes to portray male and female politicians (Major 2008).

The media trivialize women's political presence by using women's aesthetics as a discursive strategy to convey their dissonance from what a leader looks like – heterosexual, white, and male (Trimble 2017). For example, a Canadian member of parliament (MP), Rona Ambrose, received much publicity focused on her beauty rather than her capabilities as MP in representing her constituents. Soon after she became the environment minister in 2006, she appeared on the cover of *Maclean's* magazine (13 March 2006), which ran an article inside focused on her attractiveness rather than her work as a minister. Even a later article in the *Globe and Mail* that detailed the sexism she faced as a female leader was headlined "Rona Ambrose Has Been Left to Smile Pretty for the Cameras" (Simpson 2006). The media have also scrutinized former NDP leader Alexa McDonough for wearing the same dress on more than one occasion. She was featured on the cover of a magazine with the headline "Alexa McDonough, Call Your Dry-Cleaner" (Goodyear-Grant 2013). These examples show that by emphasizing and scrutinizing women politicians' looks and wardrobe, the media divert the focus from the substance of what women leaders offer. Consequently, the media diminish women's efforts and accomplishments, prompting the audience to perceive female leaders in a stereotypical way (Bauer 2015).

The media further reinforce the abnormality of women's political presence by pointing out their sex more than their male counterparts. Women candidates receive more coverage about their sex and minority candidates receive more coverage about their race than do white men running for political office (Major 2008). In the US elections in 1999 and 2008, Elizabeth Dole, Claire McCaskill, Hillary Clinton, and Sarah Palin all received more news coverage than their male opponents. While exposure seems beneficial, it also indicates how novel it is for women to be the front runners (Meeks 2012). At the same time, the media making maleness the default sex of reported political actors excludes women in the political arena. Such normalization of men's presence leads people to assume that politicians in the news are men when their sex is not revealed or cued. Furthermore, the perceptions and depictions of minority candidates as atypical politicians imply that Blacks, Latinx, and women candidates are outsiders (Gordon 2005).

The media further tend to align female candidates with feminine issues and male candidates with masculine issues, reinforcing the gender divide by suggesting that women are only capable of dealing with soft or less relevant issues, such as education, as opposed to hard or more relevant issues, such as the economy (Major 2008). Cassese and Holman (2018), for example, find that campaigns that attack candidates based on their feminine traits hurt women's chances of winning more than men's. When using feminine stereotypes to characterize female candidates and masculine stereotypes to characterize male candidates, the media belittle the value of women in the political arena and reinforce the role incongruity between being a woman and being a leader (Bauer 2019). Such stereotypical trait attribution varies, however, depending on the level of office that women seek. The media begin to masculinize women candidates as they run for higher office, allowing women to assert power but also suggesting that women must act tough in order to be considered viable candidates. Such masculinization of female candidates seeking powerful positions also comes at a cost – voters become less comfortable and grow more sceptical towards masculinized women. Yet when men run as men, they are seen as authentic and are rarely criticized (Meeks 2012).

Although many studies show that stereotypes are a central part of the media's portrayals of and voters' evaluations of candidates, some studies also show a more muted effect of gender stereotyping. Dolan (2014) shows that the political party of the woman candidate shapes the role of stereotypes in candidate evaluations and vote choice. Bauer (2015) also suggests that stereotyping must be activated by the media in influencing voters' support for female candidates.

Stereotypes and Intersectional Identities

While women politicians are subject to stereotyping, it especially affects candidates with intersectional identities (Carew 2016; Cassese 2019). For example, when Allison Brewer, an openly lesbian leader of the New Brunswick New Democratic Party, first campaigned for her candidacy, the media emphasized her queerness. It was not until a year later, during the provincial election campaign, that the media slowly began to portray her as a regular female politician instead of a lesbian one (Everitt and Camp 2009).

Gay and lesbian candidates send different signals about their competency to voters. Voters tend to assign negative characteristics to gay male candidates and associate lesbian candidates with compassion and ability to deal with feminine issues, such as education (Doan and Haider-Markel 2010). Potential voters also view transgender candidates with even stronger disgust and aversion than they would gay, lesbian, or female black candidates (Haider-Markel et al. 2017). The differences in how voters use stereotypes to evaluate LGBT candidates also suggest that they are likely to use stereotypes to make political decisions, possibly leading to the difficulty LGBT candidates experience in gaining voter support and hence to the under-representation of LGBT politicians.

Not only is the media discourse heteronormative, it is also racialized. On average, white congresswomen in the United States receive more news coverage than Latina and African American congresswomen. At the same time, minority women politicians are subject to more negative coverage focused on their race and ethnicity than white women (Gershon 2012). Even when the media did not vary significantly in their discussions of the viability of white and minority candidates in the 2008 Canadian federal election, the qualifications of white candidates were still portrayed more positively than were those of minority candidates (Tolley 2016).

In addition to gender being an indicator of candidates' traits and competence, voters also judge politicians' positions on issues based on their intersectional identities. For instance, Black and women candidates are perceived as more liberal than white and men candidates (McDermott 1998), rendering it unlikely that conservative voters would support Black women candidates.

Why Do Stereotypes Matter?

Stereotyping can have serious implications as these biases seep into decisions that affect the recruitment and nomination of women for candidacy. Although conforming to stereotypical behaviour may not necessarily hurt women candidates' electoral chances (Brooks 2013), the media's and voters' gendered assumptions are problematic, not just for women but also for the political future of the world. Women politicians' performances are not truly evaluated based on their capabilities and achievements, suggesting that voters do not elect the most suitable candidates for the job.

First, not only do implicit biases mean that women candidates start out at disadvantage, they also suggest that women have hard decisions to make as they develop their political careers. If a woman politician acts tough, she comes off as aggressive and dangerous and gets ridiculed for not being a "real woman." Conversely, if she runs a campaign that is fitting to her gender stereotypes, like Sarah Palin did by embracing her super-femininity in the 2008 US presidential election, she is aggressively sexualized (Heldman and Wade 2011). Women can either conform to stereotypes or masculinize themselves by campaigning on topics that are similar to those of their male opponents (Dolan 2005). Either way, the strategic calculation of whether to conform to stereotypes or alter behaviour is invisible and extra labour that female candidates take on.

Second, as the media continue to dehumanize and humiliate women, it is only natural that women feel discouraged and discount running for public office. When women are exposed to messages that scrutinize women candidates, they might well think twice before putting themselves under such a spotlight.

Third, when the media continue to trivialize women politicians' accomplishments, they paint a picture that women are not powerful. Such images send a signal to women, and especially girls, that they are not equipped to do what men do in the political arena. For instance, journalists' choices in using either feminine-coded or masculine-coded descriptive languages to describe female and male candidates influence how people view the leadership of women and men. This effect is especially strong on female voters – women are more likely to rate women candidates who are described with feminine adjectives lower than those who are described with masculine adjectives (Garrett and Stecula 2018). Women also internalize society's critiques for being ambitious, which may compel them to wonder where they fit in the political culture and thus continue to conform to gender norms. Such conformation starts at a young age: Lawless, Fox, and Fox (2015) show that women already express lower levels of political ambition than their male counterparts at a young age. At the same time, when women do not have political ambitions or are fearful of expressing political ambitions, they get blamed for their own under-representation (Dittmar 2020). And blaming women for their low political confidence and interest further decreases Asian women's political ambition (Holman and Schneider 2018). In other words, not only does gender stereotyping cause women to question themselves, but it also actively and systematically excludes women from the political process.

Moving Forward

The first step towards enhancing women's political representation through eliminating stereotypes and implicit biases is to reconsider the way we discuss the under-representation of women. We need to see the under-representation of women as a systematic issue, instead of an individual choice women make to not run. In doing so, we also need to pay attention to how intersectionality shapes women politicians' experiences. As discussed above, racialized and LGBTQ candidates face challenges even more severe than those faced by heterosexual and white women candidates. There is some – although little – research being conducted on candidate evaluations of disability and mental health of candidates (Reher 2021). In addition, future analyses should consider how the identities of non-Christian women, migrant women, working-class women, and others intersect in voters' perceptions and the media's portrayals of them. Finally, in addition to attaining gender parity at political institutions, we need to also aim for gender equality. It is not enough to just want more women in politics; we want more women and men in politics who represent the interests of the marginalized. We need to do more than just diversify the political arena – we also need to make sure that it is an inclusive place for women, especially women facing intersectional oppressions.

Second, it is important to highlight that women's political representation varies significantly across political parties, types and levels of office seats, and geographical regions. As discussed, voters are not the only group to harbour gender-related stereotypes, stereotypes that may also affect the selection of candidates. To counteract these biases, necessary measures should be adopted, implemented, and reinforced to facilitate women's access to candidacy and positions of leadership.

Third, if mathematics, literature, and physical education are required courses, why is gender studies not? School curriculums should offer classes that teach both girls and boys about gender equality. Such education not only helps lessen gender stereotypes at an early age, but also helps close the gender gap in political opportunities. It also does not hold girls and women accountable for their potential lack of political interest, confidence, and ambition, but helps them discover their power and achieve their potential. Moreover, it shifts the discourse surrounding boys' and men's role and responsibility, assigning them a role in achieving gender parity and equality in political institutions.

When the idea that women too can be political leaders is normalized, presence of women in the decision-making process will increase. The political presence of women will also then lead to inclusive representation and further transform the way people see female leaders.

17 Women in Politics: Beyond the Heterosexual Fantasy

MANON TREMBLAY

Women's participation in politics, whether as voters, political party activists, or elected officials, has generated a considerable amount of research in the last few decades, particularly since the World Conference on Women in 1995. More recently, the election of openly LGBTQ candidates in federal, provincial/territorial, and municipal politics has made me aware of the fact – and I posit in this chapter – that sexualities and gender identity and expression remain invisible in studies on women in politics, and I suspect that this is because heterosexuality as a hegemonic lens obscures our thinking. In fact, my argument here is that studies on women and politics do not question in any way the sexual orientation or the gender identity and expression of women involved in politics, assuming by default that they are heterosexual and cisgender. This obscurantism may be due to the fact that sex, gender, and sexualities are so closely related that, culturally, they are all thrown into the bag of "nature's discourse" and their specificities are erased, a process that Butler describes through the notion of heterosexual matrix: "That grid of cultural intelligibility through which bodies, genders, and desires are naturalized ... A hegemonic discursive/epistemic model of gender intelligibility that assumes that for bodies to cohere and make sense there must be a stable sex expressed through a stable gender (masculine expresses male, feminine expresses female) that is oppositionally and hierarchically defined through the compulsory practice of heterosexuality" (1990, 194).

This blindness to sexualities and to gender identity and expression in our work seems regrettable for two reasons. The first is methodological in nature: sex is simply not gender (Bittner and Goodyear-Grant 2017b; see also Bittner and Goodyear-Grant 2017a), and depriving ourselves of gender as an analytical tool can only impoverish our work. The second is ideological: ignoring sexualities and gender identity and expression and acting as if women politicians are heterosexual and cisgender by default only maintains the hegemonic status of heterosexuality, thus perpetuating what I call heterosexual fantasy. Worse: simply keeping sexuality quiet (that is, silencing the fact that it is possible not to be heterosexual or cisgender and to be in politics) contributes to perpetuating the hegemonic status of heterosexuality. However, diverse sexualities and gender identity and expression may have something else to tell us if we examine them more critically.

In order to explore this idea – that is, that sexualities and gender identities and expressions remain invisible in studies on women in politics, and that this blindness cannot help but have consequences for the heuristic scope of our work – first, I will present some theoretical principles that inspire my reflections. Second, I will examine a matter that we all know about, the pathway to parliamentary representation, first by considering its heteronormative background, then by arguing that new heuristic opportunities lie within it if it is interrogated in light of a broader understanding of sexualities and gender identities and expressions. Finally, I will make some observations on the ways forward for the "women in politics" research field.

Theoretical Reflections

"The private is political" has been a flagship slogan of second-wave feminism. Yet it seems to me that we have not fully integrated this idea into our analyses of women in politics. Indeed, the private, or the space of the sexual, is political – that is, it is characterized by power relations. To the extent that the sexual has been thought of primarily as heterosexual, it follows that the private is political because it is a space of hierarchical heterosexual power relations, in which women are on the bottom. Several authors, including Butler (1990), Dworkin (1974), Ingraham (1994), MacKinnon (1989), Rich (1981), and Weeks (2007), see heterosexuality as the primary organizing principle of gender relations – gender is, by definition, hierarchical. As Jackson puts it, "Heterosexuality, however, should not be thought of as simply a form of sexual expression. It is not only a key site of intersection between gender and sexuality, but also one that reveals the interconnections between sexual and non-sexual aspects of social life" (2006, 107). In other words, private heterosexual power relations inform and legitimize non-sexual relationships between women and men in public life. This transfer from the private to the social is operationalized through what Ingraham calls the "heterosexual imaginary" – a "way of thinking which conceals the operation of heterosexuality in structuring gender and closes off any critical analysis of heterosexuality as an organizing institution. The effect of this depiction of reality is that heterosexuality circulates as taken for granted, naturally occurring, and unquestioned" (1994, 203–4). I would rather use the notion of "heterosexual fantasy," because heterosexuality is based on the fantasy of sex/gender difference (Wittig 1980). This difference operates with binaries: male/female; heterosexual/LGBTQ+; normal/abnormal. As a fantasy performance, heterosexuality involves the sexual and the non-sexual in a creative, subversive dialogue, or even a certain amount of amazement about the significance of sex/gender difference.

Heterosexuality, as a dominant norm, is ubiquitous to the point of being invisible. This is what Ludwig (2011) calls the heteronormative hegemony. This notion allows us to comprehend certain facts that, in themselves, are rather surprising: for instance, how can we explain that a container of milk displays a picture of a woman and a man smiling blissfully if it is not – in addition to their shared taste for milk, I guess – that milk is a source of well-being and pleasure, just like heterosexuality? When will my favourite milk company show two (or three, or more – but that's another debate) lesbians smiling blissfully at each other on the container? What I'm saying is that heterosexual fantasy also requires exclusions: anything that might destabilize the hegemonic position of heteronormativity is invisible, not by overexposure (by which I mean so pervasive that it is unseen, taken for granted, considered natural) but by underexposure. It is the world of intentional ignorance, of the unspoken, or, most boldly, of "exceptions to the rule." Our work on women in politics has fallen into this trap, although we (researchers on women in politics) aren't the only ones. According to Ingraham, "Feminist studies of marriage, family, and sexual violence ... invariably depend upon the heterosexual imaginary deployed in a variety of heteronormative assumptions" (1994, 204). How we think about women in politics not only draws on and reproduces heterosexual fantasy, but has blinded us to the straightforward principle of the diversity of sexualities and of gender identities and expressions. I am convinced that our work would benefit from opening up to this diversity.

Path to Parliamentary Representation

Having argued that those who study women in politics remain blind to sexualities and gender identities and expressions (or, in other words, assume that political women are heterosexual and cisgender) and that this omission impoverishes them, in this section I examine the "funnel model of the candidate selection process." As space is limited, I look only at the recruitment and selection stages, focusing on two ideas: (1) how our understanding of these steps is based on and reproduces heterosexual fantasy; and (2) how a more critical and inclusive view of sexualities and gender identities and expressions can expand this knowledge.

Candidate Supply

This step focuses on the capacity for someone to be a candidate, because her or his political, economic, and sociocultural background is seen as significant by political selectorates. Of course, things are not so clearly delineated insofar as a would-be candidate's perceptions are also shaped by her or his interpretation of political parties' demands for candidates. That being said, nearly every study of women in politics in Canada (including mine) has shown that family responsibilities impede women's political ambitions. This is a good example of heteronormative assumptions: we assume that all women are in heterosexual couples and families, and we don't problematize heterosexuality by seeking to uncover its impact on undermining women's political ambitions. It is as if all women were struggling with family responsibilities, that this was their inevitable karma! Yet Brodie (1985, 79) suggests that women's traditional roles as wives, mothers, and housewives have been discursively constructed as impediments to women's political involvement. In other words, our own work contributes to sustaining heterosexual fantasy and perpetuating the gender regime. We need, I think, to examine critically and qualify the "family responsibilities explanation."

In this respect, what happens if our analysis includes a more critical reading of sexualities and gender identities and expressions? What I mean is that the heterofamily should be not naturalized but reinterpreted in political terms – that is, as a set of heterosexual power relations. Some of the most famous radical feminists of the 1970s (Christine Delphy, Shulamith Finestone, Colette Guillaumin, Kate Millett, and others) saw the core of women's oppression in the heteropatriarchal family (my expression to synthesize their thoughts). But this observation is not confined to the Museum of Feminism! Martha C. Nussbaum says much the same thing in her *Sex and Social Justice*: "The desire to control women's reproductive functioning and to maintain control over their sexuality has been a major impetus behind various restrictions on women's public role" (1999, 17). Is it possible that heterosexual fantasy (that is, the romanticization of the heterofamily lifestyle) is an ideological and materialistic device for controlling women's sexuality that is responsible, at least in part, for their under-representation in politics?

True, this reading – which is my own and may be offensive to some people – is less romantic than arguing that women sacrifice or delay their political ambitions in the name of maternal love.

Candidate Demand

This step concerns the willingness of party selectorates to choose women candidates. Again, all our work shows that this is a crucial cause of women's under-representation in politics: if there is a shortage of women legislators, it is because parties prefer respectable WASP (white, Anglo-Saxon, Protestant) candidates, who, of course, are also male, cisgender, and heterosexual (Ashe and Stewart 2012; Norris and Lovenduski 1989). That being said, since the largest number of LGBTQ candidates for legislative elections in Canada run for office under the New Democratic Party (NDP) banner (Everitt 2015; Everitt and Camp 2014, Everitt, Tremblay, and Wagner 2019), one might surmise that the profile of the respectable male, cisgender, and heterosexual WASP is less of a requirement in left-wing than in right-wing parties. However, more work is needed to substantiate this hypothesis (but see Ashe 2020). Selection of candidates is thus thought of in terms of gender difference and hierarchical relationships: men are dominant in the political space and women are dominated, echoing the interconnection that Jackson (2006) sees between sexual and non-sexual, masculinity (dominant) and femininity (dominated).

The heterosexual fantasy as a foundational principle of society seemed to me to reach its climax in the concept of parity. A key argument of the *paritaristes* was that because sex difference is a universal marker of the human being, the universal republican citizen should reflect this difference. Besides bluntly negating the fact that there are people who don't fit the socio-medical definition of female/woman versus male/man or who self-identify as genderqueer and/or gender nonconforming, this heteronormative assumption draws its strength from a so-called truth of nature: Mother Nature put women and men on Earth, and therefore there can be no genuine universalism without reflecting the sex binarity. A Canadian illustration of this heterosexual assumption was the suggestion to implement binomial parity representation for the Nunavut Legislative Assembly: in December 1995, the Nunavut Planning Commission proposed to the federal government that it create ridings with two representatives, one woman and one man. Parity brands political representation with the hot iron of sex difference.

How can we think of representation beyond gender differences – and therefore heterosexual fantasy? A starting point may reside in the adoption of a broader conception of sexualities and gender identities and expressions.

Concluding Thoughts

My goal in this chapter has not been to discredit our work in any way, but to consider what a more inclusive reading of sexualities and gender identities and expressions can engender in terms of new meanings. Here's an example.

In the special issue of the *Canadian Journal of Political Science* titled "Finding Feminism(s) in Canadian Political Science Scholarship," Amanda Bittner and Elizabeth Goodyear-Grant (2017a) published an article that illustrates how using a broader conception of sexualities and gender identities and expressions can enhance our knowledge of women's political participation. Although gender is a useful concept for understanding political attitudes and behaviours, Bittner and Goodyear-Grant show that gender identity and its saliency (that is, women for whom gender is a significant component of their identity) may be more relevant in explaining some of the gaps between women and men. Similar findings have been made about feminist consciousness: gender gaps are due less to sex/gender per se than to feminist consciousness (Conover 1988) or, in the case of LGBTQ people, to lesbian feminist consciousness (Hertzog 1996).

Above, I criticized parity because it seems to me to be terribly heteronormative, but what model should be substituted for it? A proposal by the NDP seems to offer a promising approach to political representation in that it moves beyond heterosexual fantasy to be inclusive of the diversity of sexualities and gender identities and expressions. During its congress in Edmonton in 2016, the NDP adopted the following resolution designed to encourage more diverse representation of genders (including women) in Canadian federal politics: "Increase funding, through a ballot box premium, for political parties with at least 50 per cent of candidates who identify as a gender other than male; increase funding, through a second ballot box premium, of political parties that elect a deputation of at least 40 per cent of people who identify as a gender other than male" (New Democratic Party 2016). This is a proposal that destabilizes the woman/man binary at the heart of heterosexual fantasy. Yet, though bold and innovative, it seems imperfect, as the largest portion of the cake may in fact go to self-identified cisgender and heterosexual men and the rest may be left over for those who aren't.

Two members of legislative assemblies are challenging gender as conventionally understood. Estefania Cortes-Vargas, who was a member for Strathcona-Sherwood Park of the Alberta Legislative Assembly from 2015 to 2019, self-defines as genderqueer/gender nonconforming (Markussof 2015). Hansard's way of titling members as Ms. or Mr. did not suit Cortes-Vargas, with the result that she was identified in Hansard as "Member." By doing this, Cortes-Vargas destabilized one of the most powerful and insidious devices to hammer home our gender: Ms., Mr.

Manon Massé is a member of the Assemblée nationale du Québec. She defines herself as a woman, a lesbian, and transgender. She proudly displays a moustache, which she interprets as a statement of her pride in who she is (Lussier 2012). Our studies, in line with the heterosexual fantasy, have uncovered that appearance is a diktat for women politicians. Massé's moustache challenges and enriches our knowledge about women in politics because it forces us to recognize that females born and raised as girls do not have a monopoly on femininity, that femininity may not be as coherent and simplistic as we thought it was, and that challenging femininity does not necessarily curb a political career. But there is more: as a lesbian woman who expresses her trans identity, Manon Massé is a counter-hegemonic role model who not only sends a message of hope to, and is a source of pride for, all people who do not fit into the gender straitjacket, but shifts the still too common perception of trans people from ridiculous to respectable.

To conclude, I suggest that one of the ways forward for the "women in politics" field is to embrace a broader understanding of what a woman is in terms of sexuality and gender identity and expression. It can only lead to better studies.

18 New Backlash? New Barriers? Assessing Women's Contemporary Public Engagement*

SYLVIA BASHEVKIN

Since the late 1970s, gender and politics scholars have devoted considerable attention to barriers facing women in politics. Much of the comparative as well as Canadian literature is preoccupied with obstacles at the point of nomination, particularly in political parties of the right and centre that – unlike their counterparts on the left – have tended to reject the adoption of internal gender quotas (Brodie 1985; Bashevkin 1985; Lovenduski 1986; Van Hightower 1977). Researchers have also trained a spotlight on the media coverage of women candidates (see for instance Trimble, this volume). They find reporting is often skewed towards the physical appearance, speaking style, and family status of female elites rather than their substantive policy positions and capacity to undertake public service (Bashevkin 2009, chaps. 2 and 4).

While these problems are important, they constitute only one part of the story. Nomination troubles and media trivializations shape the experiences of women who have already responded to a willingness and indeed appetite among some citizens to promote equality in public engagement (Cheng and Tavits 2011).[1] To their credit, women candidates and decision makers have chosen to put themselves forward, often because they were encouraged to do so by others in their local communities, and stand ready to serve.

* This chapter is an expanded version of a paper presented at the "Women in Politics, Women in Leadership" conference held at the Munk School of Global Affairs and Public Policy at the University of Toronto in March 2019. I am grateful to the Insight Grants program of the Social Sciences and Humanities Research Council of Canada for funding the research on which this chapter is based.

The sustained academic focus on nomination difficulties and media coverage obscures other, potentially more significant challenges facing women in public life. The obstacles to which I refer come into play long before the start of formal recruitment and nomination processes that affect an individual's upward mobility in politics, and well in advance of when journalists notice a specific candidate or legislator. My core thesis is that while a scholarly and public consensus tends to assume opportunities for women's political involvement have widened over time, important empirical trends point in the opposite direction. My chapter draws on Canadian as well as international data to propose that significant, arguably heightened limitations constrain engagement. In particular, I examine frequently ignored indicators, including declining numbers of female first ministers in Canada, increased threats directed at high-profile actors, evidence of limited patience with women leaders among elites in their own parties, and challenges posed by the rise of digital media.

First Ministers

Data on first ministers provide among the most striking measures of the limitations that continue to shape women's participation. Canada has had one female prime minister since 1867. Kim Campbell was in office for a matter of months in 1993, which is more than a quarter of a century before this writing. At the subnational level, the peak level to this point of women premiers was reached in early 2014, when five of the ten provinces, holding more than 31.1 million Canadians among a population of 35.5 million (or roughly 88 per cent), were governed by a female premier.

Since the 2019 defeat of Rachel Notley's NDP government in Alberta, that number has returned to zero provinces and territories with a female premier. The last time Canada faced the situation of no woman in a top political executive role occurred prior to the fall of 2008, when Eva Aariak was sworn in as the second premier of Nunavut. If we consider the presence of women first ministers as an indicator of access to power, therefore, it seems reasonable to conclude that the clock has been turned back more than ten years. Any contemporary photograph of first ministers meeting to discuss the state of Canada's federation therefore looks much as such groupings did in the era before Aariak's ascension, and in particular before 1991, when trailblazers such as Rita Johnston became premier of British Columbia and Nellie Cournoyea became premier of the Northwest Territories (Bashevkin 2019a, 277).

From the perspectives of symbolic and descriptive representation, the absence of women leaders stands as a signal failure of democratic politics in Canada. The photo taken of the premiers' gathering in Regina in summer 2019 reflected in a single snapshot who engages at the most senior levels of federal, provincial, and territorial decision-making in Canada. It offered a shorthand version for children as well as adult observers of what the face of power looks like. The presence of men only in a first ministers' meeting contrasts starkly with talk of an open or diverse Canada in which all citizens hold the potential to engage at the highest levels of public responsibility (Taylor and Graveland 2019).

The failure of elected elites as a group to resemble even remotely the distribution of gender in the general population demonstrates a crucial distortion of the representational mirror that we assume binds citizens with leaders in liberal democracies. Moreover, most Canadian prime ministers and premiers are not just men but also white, middle aged, and middle class. This fact speaks to the intersectional dimensions of political representation, where we see how demographic numbers reinforce powerful messages about gender as well as race, age, and social class as determinants of who wields influence.

Threats Facing Leaders

Threats to the personal security of women leaders constitute dangerous hurdles on the path to equitable engagement. International data gathered by the National Democratic Institute (NDI), a non-profit and non-partisan organization based in Washington, DC, were used to develop a global snapshot of violence facing women in politics. Until early 2019, NDI's map of Canada was entirely free and clear, uncluttered by any indication of even a single incident. As of early 2019, the site reported one event in Canada (National Democratic Institute 2019).

Yet a survey of parliamentarians conducted by Melanee Thomas and Lisa Lambert (2017, 148) found Canadian women MPs avoided posting on the Internet the names and photographs of their children because of safety concerns. Research on women who have led provincial and territorial governments concludes that two premiers faced unprecedented levels of hostility – and they were both leaders of progressive governments. Data from the Ontario Provincial Police as well as the Toronto Police Service show Ontario premier Kathleen Wynne was the object of particularly venomous threats because of her sexual orientation and her willingness to champion changes to the province's sex education curriculum (Dawson 2017). A 2017 CBC report on Premier Wynne's Twitter and Facebook feeds presents in detail the grotesque, often highly sexualized messages she received (Crawley 2017). One section of the

CBC story focuses on the contents of more than three dozen abusive messages Wynne received in the week prior to the article's publication.

According to a 2017 CBC report, Alberta premier Rachel Notley was the target of at least eleven death threats during her first three years as provincial leader. The CBC story details the contents of 386 pages of what the Alberta Department of Justice calls "occurrence summaries" that document "an alarming tweet, vulgar email, threat or call aimed at an Alberta politician – most often Premier Rachel Notley" – during her first two and a half years as premier (Trynacity 2018). In her analysis of Notley's term as premier, Melanee Thomas (2019, 263) notes that of the "more than four hundred incidents of inappropriate contact and communication" directed at Notley, "twenty-six were deemed serious enough to forward to police for investigation."

Alberta's Department of Justice compiled a longitudinal record of hostile communications directed at all Alberta premiers who held office between 2003 and 2015. It found that Premier Notley was by far the most threatened premier during that period. Thomas describes the growth over time in threats against women in Alberta politics as "an exponential increase," which is notable in a province where Notley was the second female (after PC leader Alison Redford) but the first New Democrat to become premier.

These patterns shed critical light on the assumption that all is well with the security of women in Canadian public life. That is, the largely untroubled map of Canada on the website of the National Democratic Institute is inconsistent with multiple incidents reported by police and justice departments of serious threats directed against women leaders and, in particular, women leaders of left and centre-left governments.

Impatience with Leaders

A third set of measures can be gleaned from the circumstances of women leaders' departures from public life. Like data on declining numbers of first ministers and the rise of personal security threats, these patterns point towards a far from welcoming atmosphere. In particular, research on women premiers suggests that their own political organizations often include back-room operatives who are impatient with female leaders and effectively remove them from the public stage. The decisions of Catherine Callbeck in PEI, Kathy Dunderdale in Newfoundland and Labrador, and Alison Redford in Alberta to resign from party leadership positions before completing their full terms in office were taken after each of these women had led her party to a majority government victory in a general election. These three leaders were active in varied jurisdictions, time periods, and parties: Callbeck was a Liberal premier during the 1990s, while Dunderdale and Redford led Progressive Conservative governments beginning in 2010 and 2011, respectively.

Analyses of their departures from office indicate a shared pattern whereby influential party insiders along with the political commentators close to them deemed it appropriate to push aside the top woman before she could seek re-election (Banack 2019; Brown, Goodyear-Grant, and Bittner 2019; Desserud and Sutherland 2019). Callbeck bore the brunt of harsh criticism after she delayed calling a provincial election in the spring of 1996; as her personal approval ratings and those of the PEI Liberals continued to decline, she resigned and the party chose a new leader. Widely condemned for her handling of multiple files, including a province-wide electrical blackout that occurred in January 2014, Dunderdale resigned that same month. Redford quit after multiple members of her legislative caucus and the Alberta PC board of directors expressed displeasure with her leadership.

Although he did not succeed in pushing her out of the Ontario premier's office, Liberal insider Greg Sorbara told reporters in early 2017 that it was "extremely unlikely" his party could secure re-election with Wynne as leader (Crawley 2017). The electoral outcomes for provincial parties led by women who faced internal dissent were similar. In the cases of Callbeck, Dunderdale, and Redford, where insiders succeeded in replacing the leader before the next election, as well as Wynne, where a woman premier fended off internal dissent, the subsequent election yielded a majority government for a competing political party.

As an agenda for future research, I urge scholars to consider how these examples of women leaders facing internal mutiny compare with situations that faced unpopular men premiers. Are male elites offered more internal organizational support, including measurably greater latitude in their caucus and party executive, following their stumbles? Given that both Redford and Wynne led unpopular parties to unexpected majority government victories, the willingness of insiders in their own parties to press them to leave public life seems all the more remarkable.[2]

Digital Media Challenges

Finally, it is important to consider the changing communications climate in which public leaders operate. Informal conversations with former political executives suggest the rise of new social media has created an environment that is more visually charged, more hostile towards women, less forgiving, and more polarized. This view contradicts expectations that the seeming democratization of media channels would empower women by providing alternatives to the conventional print, radio, and electronic outlets that long dominated Canada's political landscape, and which frequently proved less than fair-minded in their treatment of women in public life.

How has the arrival of personal websites, blogs, Twitter, Facebook, and other digital opportunities affected women in politics? At one level, these outlets have demonstrably multiplied the channels available to individuals who seek to enhance their profiles and communicate their ideas. At the same time, the scope and number of those streams have reduced the possibility that any single new entrant can exert much influence, while the stress they place on likeability reinforces traditional assumptions that women should operate in ways that demonstrate nurturing, deference, and other non-agentic qualities (see also Liu, this volume). This means that all contemporary politicians operate within an increasingly fragmented and, in some respects, saturated electronic environment in which older notions of spreading a message or broadcasting widely have been replaced by narrow-band statements to people who likely shared the same basic point of view before they logged on. What is considered common knowledge to one web community appears in some cases to be unknown, ignored, or defined as fiction by competing ones, meaning the core concept of shared public space no longer extends beyond a defined boundary of insiders.

From the perspective of women politicians, existing gender differences in access to leisure time may be compounded by the arrival of web-based communication. Time-study research by Statistics Canada has shown that even as levels of formal education and occupational attainment have grown in the general population, women of all ages have continued to enjoy significantly less free time than men. This pattern follows in large part from the fact that females spend more of their waking hours than males on unpaid work: on average, women assume greater responsibility than men for complex tasks, such as caring for family members, which in turn reduces the availability of leisure time (Moyser and Burlock 2018). Therefore, the same limitations that in the past shaped opportunities for women to raise their profiles in the old media landscape, including by writing letters to newspaper editors, likely restrict their ability to participate in web-based discussions of current affairs.

The visual dimension of contemporary communication flows poses an especially significant risk for women seeking positions of public leadership. Opportunities to reach a wider audience via newer visual media multiply chances for opponents of women's upward mobility to trivialize and dissect female bodies along the lines of body image, hair, clothing, family status, and so on. These are hardly new problems given the marginalizing coverage that greeted Agnes Macphail's arrival as the first woman MP in the Canadian House of Commons in 1921 (Bashevkin 2009, 60–1). Macphail's entry to the federal parliament was consigned to the social pages of leading newspapers, known at the time as women's pages. Reporters detailed her hat, gloves, and dress in terms that suggested they were all deficient. During her terms as a federal MP and later Ontario MPP, Macphail was frequently depicted as a humourless single woman or, in the jargon of the period, a spinster.

Over the longer term, any fixation on matters of personal appearance and family circumstances tends to overshadow women's qualifications for public office as well as their policy priorities, meaning the substantive content they bring to civic discussion risks being obscured or silenced. In an environment that permits unprecedented expressions of hostility towards women leaders, the pitfalls posed by social media's emphases on visuals and likeability are far from trivial. One of the only systematic studies of the digital communications environment facing female politicians echoes this view; it concludes that "women who achieve a high status in politics are more likely to receive uncivil messages than their male counterparts" (Rheault, Rayment and Musulan 2019, 6).

Conclusion

This article identifies four significant but frequently overlooked patterns that point towards the reverse of both public and scholarly expectations of (a) more women in leadership positions in Canadian politics, and (b) an increasingly welcoming atmosphere for political women. I have highlighted declining numbers of female first ministers in Canada, increased threats directed at them, evidence of limited patience with women leaders by elites in their own parties, and challenges posed by the rise of digital media. Taken as a group, these phenomena are worthy of close empirical analysis and sustained normative consideration. They cannot and should not be dismissed as the private, insignificant troubles of individual women. Instead, the dynamics I have outlined constitute critical barriers to democratic engagement in Canadian politics.

NOTES

1 The gender of local party presidents, for instance, can play an important role in encouraging or discouraging female nominees. See Cheng and Tavits 2011.

2 On the phenomenon of what I term "imperiled leadership," where a woman is selected to lead a political party that appears doomed to lose the next general election, see Bashevkin 2019c, 5, 9–12.

References

Alexander, Amy C. 2012. "Change in Women's Descriptive Representation and the Belief in Women's Ability to Govern: A Virtuous Cycle." *Politics & Gender* 8(4): 437–64. https://doi.org/10.1017/s1743923x12000487.

Alexander, Amy C., and Farida Jalalzai. 2020. "Symbolic Empowerment and Female Heads of States and Government: A Global, Multilevel Analysis." *Politics, Groups, and Identities* 8(1): 24–43. https://doi.org/10.1080/21565503.2018.1441034.

Alexander, Deborah, and Kristi Andersen. 1993 "Gender as a Factor in the Attribution of Leadership Traits." *Political Research Quarterly* 46(3): 527–45. https://doi.org/10.2307/448946.

Annesley, Claire, Karen Beckwith, and Susan Franceschet. 2019. *Cabinets, Ministers and Gender*. Oxford: Oxford University Press.

Annesley, Claire, and Francesca Gains. 2010. "The Core Executive: Gender, Power and Change." *Political Studies* 58(5): 909–29. https://doi.org/10.1111/j.1467-9248.2010.00824.x.

Anzia, Sarah F., and Christopher R. Berry 2011. "The Jackie (and Jill) Robinson Effect: Why Do Congresswomen Outperform Congressmen?" *American Journal of Political Science* 55(3): 478–93. https://doi.org/10.1111/j.1540-5907.2011.00512.x.

Ashe, Jeanette. 2020. "Canada's Political Parties: Gatekeepers to Parliament." In *The Palgrave Handbook of Gender, Sexuality and Canadian Politics*, edited by Manon Tremblay and Joanna Everitt, 297–316. New York: Palgrave Macmillan.

Ashe, Jeanette, and Kennedy Stewart. 2012. "Legislative Recruitment: Using Diagnostic Testing to Explain Underrepresentation." *Party Politics* 18(5): 687–707. https://doi.org/10.1177/1354068810389635.

Atchison, Amy, and Ian Down. 2009. "Women Cabinet Ministers and Female-Friendly Social Policy." *Poverty & Public Policy* 1(2): 164–86. https://doi.org/10.2202/1944-2858.1007.

Atkeson, Lonna Rae. 2003. "Not All Cues Are Created Equal: The Conditional Impact of Female Candidates on Political Engagement." *Journal of Politics* 65(4): 1040–61. https://doi.org/10.1111/1468-2508.t01-1-00124.

Atkeson, Lonna Rae, and Nancy Carrillo. 2007. "More Is Better: The Influence of Collective Female Descriptive Representation on External Efficacy." *Politics & Gender* 3(1): 79–101. https://doi.org/10.1017/s1743923x0707002x.

Banack, Clark. 2019. "Women and Politics in Alberta under Alison Redford." In Bashevkin 2019b, 225–49.

Banducci, Susan A., and Jeffrey A. Karp. 2000. "Gender, Leadership and Choice in Multiparty Systems." *Political Research Quarterly* 53(4): 815–48. https://doi.org/10.2307/449262.

Barker, Brittany, Gerald Taiaiake Alfred, & Thomas Kerr. 2014. "An Uncaring State? The Overrepresentation of First Nations Children in the Canadian Child Welfare System." *Canadian Medical Association Journal* 186(14): E533–E535 https://doi.org/10.1503/cmaj.131465. Medline:25002560.

Barnes, Tiffany D. 2014. "Women's Representation and Legislative Committee Appointments: The Case of the Argentine Provinces." *Revista Uruguaya de Ciencia Política* 23(2): 135–63.

– 2016. *Gendering Legislative Behavior*. New York: Cambridge University Press.

Barnes, Tiffany D., and Stephanie M. Burchard. 2012. "Engendering Politics: The Impact of Descriptive Representation on Women's Political Engagement in Sub-Saharan Africa." *Comparative Political Studies* 46(7): 767–90. https://doi.org/10.1177/0010414012463884.

Barnes, Tiffany D., and Mirya R. Holman. 2020. "Gender Quotas, Women's Representation, and Legislative Diversity." *Journal of Politics* 82(4): 1271–86.

Barnes, Tiffany D., and Mark P. Jones. 2018. "Women's Representation in Argentine National and Subnational Governments." In *Gender and Representation in Latin America*, edited by Leslie Schwindt-Bayer, 121–39. New York: Oxford University Press.

Barnes, Tiffany D., and Diana Z. O'Brien. 2018. "Defending the Realm: The Appointment of Female Defense Ministers Worldwide." *American Journal of Political Science* 62(2): 355–68. https://doi.org/10.1111/ajps.12337.

Barnes, Tiffany D., and Michelle M. Taylor-Robinson. 2018. "Women Cabinet Ministers in Highly Visible Posts and Empowerment of Women: Are the Two Related?" In *Measuring Women's Political Empowerment across the Globe: Strategies, Challenges, and Future Research*, edited by Amy Alexander, Catherine Bolzendahl, and Farida Jalalzai, 229–55. Cham: Palgrave MacMillan.

Bashevkin, Sylvia B. 1985. *Toeing the Lines: Women and Party Politics in English Canada*. Toronto: University of Toronto Press.

– 2009. *Women, Power, Politics: The Hidden Story of Canada's Unfinished Democracy*. Toronto: Oxford University Press.

– 2010. "When Do Outsiders Break In? Institutional Circumstances of Party Leadership Victories by Women in Canada." *Commonwealth & Comparative Politics* 48(1): 72–90. https://doi.org/10.1080/14662040903444525.

– 2019a. "Doing Politics Differently?" In Bashevkin 2019b, 275–97.

–, ed. 2019b. *Doing Politics Differently? Women Premiers in Canada's Provinces and Territories.* Vancouver: UBC Press.

– 2019c. "Exploring Women's Leadership." In Bashevkin 2019b, 3–30.

Bauer, Gretchen, and Faith Okpotor. 2013. "'Her Excellency': An Exploratory Overview of Women Cabinet Ministers in Africa." *Africa Today* 60(1): 76–97. https://doi.org/10.2979/africatoday.60.1.77.

Bauer, Nichole M. 2015. "Emotional, Sensitive, and Unfit for Office? Gender Stereotype Activation and Support for Female Candidates." *Political Psychology* 36(6): 691–708. https://doi.org/10.1111/pops.12186.

– 2019. "Gender Stereotyping in Political Decision Making." In *Oxford Research Encyclopedia of Politics.* March 26. https://oxfordre.com/politics/view/10.1093/acrefore/9780190228637.001.0001/acrefore-9780190228637-e-772.

Beall, Victoria D., and Tiffany D. Barnes. 2020. "Mapping Right-Wing Women's Policy Priorities in Latin America." *Journal of Women, Politics, and Policy* 41(1): 1–30. https://doi.org/10.1080/1554477x.2020.1701929.

Beckwith, Karen. 2015. "Before Prime Minister: Margaret Thatcher, Angela Merkel, and Gendered Party Leadership Contests." *Politics & Gender* 11(04): 718–45. https://doi.org/10.1017/s1743923x15000409.

Beckwith, Karen, and Kimberly Cowell-Meyers. 2007. "Sheer Numbers: Critical Representation Thresholds and Women's Political Representation." *Perspectives on Politics* 5(3): 553–65. https://doi.org/10.1017/S153759270707154X.

Bell, Linda Cohen, and Cindy Simon Rosenthal. 2003. "From Passive to Active Representation: The Case of Women Congressional Staff." *Journal of Public Administration Research and Theory* 13(1): 65–82. https://www.jstor.org/stable/3525617.

Benoit, Kenneth, Kohei Watanabe, Haiyan Wang, Paul Nulty, Adam Obeng, Stefan Müller, and Akitaka Matsuo. 2018. "Quanteda: An R Package for the Quantitative Analysis of Textual Data." *Journal of Open Source Software*, 3(30), 774. https://doi.org/10.21105/joss.00774.

Besley, Timothy, Olle Folke, Torsten Persson, and Johanna Rickne. 2017. "Gender Quotas and the Crisis of the Mediocre Man: Theory and Evidence from Sweden." *American Economic Review* 107(8): 2202–42. https://doi.org/10.1257/aer.20160080.

Bittner, Amanda, and Elizabeth Goodyear-Grant. 2017a. "Digging Deeper into the Gender Gap: Salience as a Moderating Factor in Political Attitudes."

Canadian Journal of Political Science 50(2): 559 78. https://doi.org/10.1017/s0008423917000270.

– 2017b. "Sex Isn't Gender: Reforming Concepts and Measurements in the Study of Public Opinion." *Political Behavior* 39(4): 1019–41. https://doi.org/10.1007/s11109-017-9391-y.

Black, Jerome H., and Lynda Erickson. 2003. "Women Candidates and Voter Bias: Do Women Politicians Need to Be Better?" *Electoral Studies* 22(1): 81–100. https://doi.org/10.1016/s0261-3794(01)00028-2.

Blais, André, and Elisabeth Gidengil. 1991. *Making Representative Democracy Work: The Views of Canadians.* Vol. 17 of the Research Studies of the Royal Commission on Electoral Reform and Party Financing. Toronto: Dundurn.

Bledsoe, Timothy, and Mary Herring. 1990. "Victims of Circumstances: Women in Pursuit of Political Office." *American Political Science Review* 84(1): 213–23. https://doi.org/10.2307/1963638.

Bombay, Amy, Kimberly Matheson, and Hymie Anisman. 2014. "The Intergenerational Effects of Indian Residential Schools: Implications for the Concept of Historical Trauma." *Transcultural Psychology* 51(3): 320–38. https://doi.org/10.1177/1363461513503380. Medline:24065606.

Bosc, Marc, and André Gagnon. 2017. *House of Commons Procedure and Practice.* 3rd ed. Ottawa: Clerk of the House of Commons.

Bourgault-Côté, G. 2018. "Vigie-parité finale: 47,2 % de candidates." *Le Devoir*, 11 September.

Bourgeois, Robyn. 2015. "Colonial Exploitation: The Canadian State and Trafficking of Indigenous Women and Girls." *UCLA Law Review* 62(6): 1426–63.

– 2017. "Perpetual State of Violence: An Indigenous Feminist Anti-Oppression Inquiry into Missing and Murdered Indigenous Women and Girls." In *Making Space for Indigenous Feminisms,* edited by Joyce Green, 253–73. Halifax: Fernwood.

Bovend'Eert, Paul. 2018. "Public Office and Public Trust: Standards of Conduct in Parliament: A Comparative Analysis of Rules of Conduct in Three Parliaments." *Parliamentary Affairs* 73(2): 1–27. https://doi.org/10.1093/pa/gsy048.

Brennan, Mary, and Fiona Buckley. 2017. "The Irish Legislative Gender Quota." *Administration* 65(2): 15–35. https://doi.org/10.1515/admin-2017-0013.

Brodie, Janine. 1985. *Women and Politics in Canada.* Toronto: McGraw-Hill Ryerson.

Brooks, Deborah Jordan. 2013. *He Runs, She Runs: Why Gender Stereotypes Do Not Harm Women Candidates.* Princeton: Princeton University Press.

Brown, Drew, Elizabeth Goodyear-Grant, and Amanda Bittner. 2019. "In the Wake of Male Charisma: Kathy Dunderdale and the Status of Women in Newfoundland and Labrador Politics." In Bashevkin 2019b, 132–49.

Brown, Nadia. 2014. "'It's More than Hair … That's Why You Should Care': The Politics of Appearance for Black Women State Legislators." *Politics, Groups, and Identities* 2(3): 295–312. https://doi.org/10.1080/21565503.2014.925816.

Buchanan, Allen. 2002. "Political Legitimacy and Democracy." *Ethics* 112(4): 689–719. https://doi.org/10.1086/340313.

Buckley, Fiona, Yvonne Galligan, and Claire McGing. 2016. "Women and the Election: Assessing the Impact of Gender Quotas." In *How Ireland Voted, 2016: The Election That Nobody Won*, edited by Matthew Gallagher and Michael Marsh, 185–205. Cham: Palgrave MacMillan.

Bush, Sarah Sunn. 2011. "International Politics and the Spread of Quotas for Women in Legislatures." *International Organization* 65(1): 103–37. https://doi.org/10.1017/s0020818310000287.

Butler, Judith. 1990. *Gender Trouble: Feminism and the Subversion of Identity*. Abingdon: Routledge.

Bynander, Fredrik, and Paul 't Hart. 2007. "The Politics of Party Leadership Survival and Succession: Australia in Comparative Perspective." *Australian Journal of Political Science* 42(1): 47–72. https://doi.org/10.1080/10361140601158542.

Campbell, David E., and Christina Wolbrecht. 2006. "See Jane Run: Women Politicians as Role Models for Adolescents." *Journal of Politics* 68(2): 233–47. https://doi.org/10.1111/j.1468-2508.2006.00402.x.

Candelario, Ginetta E.B. 2007. *Black behind the Ears: Dominican Racial Identity from Museums to Beauty Shops*. Durham: Duke University Press.

Carew, Jessica D. Johnson. 2016. "How Do You See Me?: Stereotyping of Black Women and How It Affects Them in an Electoral Context." In *Distinct Identities: Minority Women in U.S. Politics*, edited by Nadia E. Brown, 111–31. New York: Routledge.

Carroll, Susan J., and Kira Sanbonmatsu. 2013. *More Women Can Run: Gender and Pathways to the State Legislatures*. New York: Oxford University Press.

Cassese, Erin C. 2019. "Intersectional Stereotyping in Political Decision Making." In *Oxford Research Encyclopedia of Politics*. March 26. https://doi.org/10.1093/acrefore/9780190228637.013.773.

Cassese, Erin C., and Mirya R. Holman. 2018. "Party and Gender Stereotypes in Campaign Attacks." *Political Behavior* 40(3): 785–807. https://doi.org/10.1007/s11109-017-9423-7.

Catalano, Ana. 2009. "Women Acting for Women? An Analysis of Gender and Debate Participation in the British House of Commons 2005–2007." *Politics & Gender* 5(1): 45–68. https://doi.org/10.1017/s1743923x09000038.

Celis, Karen, Sarah Childs, Johanna Kantola, and Mona Lena Krook. 2008. "Rethinking Women's Substantive Representation." *Representation* 44(2): 99–110. https://doi.org/10.1080/00344890802079573.

Celis, Karen, and Silva Erzeel. 2013. "Gender and Ethnicity: Intersectionality and the Politics of Group Representation in the Low Countries." *Representation* 49(4): 487–99. https://doi.org/10.1080/00344893.2013.850780.

Center for American Women and Politics. 2018. "2018 Summary of Women Candidates." https://cawp.rutgers.edu/candidate-summary-2018.

Chaney, P. 2006. "Critical Mass, Deliberation and the Substantive Representation of Women: Evidence from the UK's Devolution Programme." *Political Studies* 54: 691–714.

– 2008. "Devolved Governance and the Substantive Representation of Women: The Second Term of the National Assembly for Wales, 2003–2007." *Parliamentary Affairs* 61(2): 272–90. https://doi.org/10.1093/pa/gsm063.

– 2012. "Critical Actors vs. Critical Mass: The Substantive Representation of Women in the Scottish Parliament." *British Journal of Politics and International Relations* 14: 441–57. https://doi.org/10.1111/j.1467-856X.2011.00467.x.

Change.org. 2019. "Stop the Nastiness in Politics: MPs Need a New Code of Conduct." Online petition.

Chappell, Louise. 2002. *Gendering Government: Feminist Engagement with the State in Australia and Canada.* Seattle: University of Washington Press.

Chartrand, Fred. 2015. "Trudeau's 'Because It's 2015' Retort Draws International Attention." *Globe and Mail*, 5 November.

Chattopadhyay, Raghabendra, and Esther Duflo. 2004. "Women as Policy Makers: Evidence from a Randomized Policy Experiment in India." *Econometrica* 72(5): 1409–43. https://doi.org/10.1111/j.1468-0262.2004.00539.x.

Cheng, Christine, and Margit Tavits. 2011. "Informal Influences in Selecting Female Political Candidates." *Political Research Quarterly* 64(2): 460–71. https://doi.org/10.1177/1065912909349631.

Childs, Sarah, and Mona Lena Krook. 2006. "Should Feminists Give Up on Critical Mass? A Contingent Yes." *Politics & Gender* 2(4): 522–30. https://doi.org/10.1017/s1743923x06251146.

– 2008. "Critical Mass Theory and Women's Political Representation." *Political Studies* 56(3): 725–36. https://doi.org/10.1111%2Fj.1467-9248.2007.00712.x.

– 2009. "Analysing Women's Substantive Representation: From Critical Mass to Critical Actors." *Government and Opposition* 44(2): 125–45. https://doi.org/10.1111/j.1477-7053.2009.01279.x.

Claveria, Silvia. 2014. "Still a 'Male' Business? Explaining Women's Presence in Executive Office." *West European Politics* 37(5): 1156–76. https://doi.org/10.1080/01402382.2014.911479.

Clayton, Amanda, Cecilia Josefsson, and Vibeke Wang. 2017. "Quotas and Women's Substantive Representation: Evidence from a Content Analysis of Ugandan Plenary Debates." *Politics & Gender* 13(2): 276–304. https://doi.org/10.1017/s1743923x16000453.

Clayton, Amanda, Diana Z. O'Brien, and Jennifer M. Piscopo. 2018. "All Male Panels? Representation and Democratic Legitimacy." *American Journal of Political Science* 63(1): 113–29. https://doi.org/10.1111/ajps.12391.

Clayton, Amanda, and Pär Zetterberg. 2019. "Quota Shocks: The Budgetary Implications of Electoral Gender Quotas Worldwide." *Journal of Politics* 72(4): 849–62.

Collier, Cheryl N., and Tracey Raney. 2018a. "Canada's Member-to-Member Code of Conduct on Sexual Harassment in the House of Commons: Progress or Regress." *Canadian Journal of Political Science* 51(4): 795–815. https://doi.org/10.1017/s000842391800032x.

– 2018b. "Understanding Sexism and Sexual Harassment in Politics: A Comparison of Westminster Parliaments in Australia, the United Kingdom and Canada." *Social Politics: International Studies in Gender, State & Society* 25(3): 432–55. https://doi.org/10.1093/sp/jxy024.

Conover, Pamela Johnston. 1988. "Feminists and the Gender Gap." *Journal of Politics* 50(4): 985–1010. https://doi.org/10.2307/2131388.

Conseil du Statut de la femme. 2015. *Les femmes en politique: En route vers la parité.* https://www.csf.gouv.qc.ca/wp-content/uploads/resume_femmes _politique_version_web.pdf.

Cooper, Brittany. 2017. *Beyond Respectability: The Intersectional Thought of Race Women.* Urbana: University of Illinois Press.

Costantini, Edmond. 1990. "Political Women and Political Ambition: Closing the Gender Gap." *American Journal of Political Science* 34(3): 741–70. https:// doi.org/10.2307/2111397.

Cox, Dame Laura. 2018. *The Bullying and Harassment of House of Commons Staff – Independent Inquiry Report.* https://www.parliament.uk/globalassets /documents/conduct-in-parliament/dame-laura-cox-independent-inquiry -report.pdf.

Crawley, Mike. 2017. "Premier Kathleen Wynne Bombarded on Social Media by Homophobic, Sexist Abuse." *CBC News,* 25 January.

Crenshaw, Kimberlé Williams. 1989. "Demarginalizing the Intersection of Race and Sex: A Black Feminist Critique of Antidiscrimination Doctrine, Feminist Theory, and Anti-Racist Politics." In *Feminist Legal Theory: Readings in Law and Gender,* edited by R. Kennedy and K.T. Bartlett, 57–80. San Francisco: West View.

Crowder-Meyer, Melody. 2013. "Gendered Recruitment without Trying: How Local Party Recruiters Affect Women's Representation." *Politics & Gender* 9(4): 390–413. https://doi.org/10.1017/s1743923x13000391.

Culhane, Dara. 1998. *Pleasure of the Crown: Anthropology, Law, and First Nations.* Vancouver: Talon Books.

Culhane, Leah. 2017. "Local Heroes and 'Cute Hoors': Informal Institutions, Male Over-representation and Candidate Selection in the Republic of

Ireland." In *Gender and Informal Institutions*, edited by Georgina Waylen, 45–66. London: Rowman & Littlefield.

Cummins, Deborah. 2011. "The Problem of Gender Quotas: Women's Representatives on Timor-Leste's Suku Councils." *Development in Practice* 21(1): 85–95. https://doi.org/10.1080/09614524.2011.530246.

Cutts, David, Sarah Childs, and Edward Fieldhouse. 2008. "This Is What Happens When You Don't Listen: All-Women Shortlists at the 2005 General Election." *Party Politics* 14(5): 575–95.

Cutts, David, and Paul Widdop. 2013. "Was Labour Penalised Where It Stood All Women Shortlist Candidates?" *British Journal of Politics and International Relations* 15(3): 435–55. https://doi.org/10.1111/j.1467-856x.2011.00494.x.

Dahlerup, Drude. 1988. "From a Small to a Large Minority: Women in Scandinavian Politics." *Scandinavian Political Studies* 11(4): 275–98. https://doi.org/10.1111/j.1467-9477.1988.tb00372.x.

– 2006. "The Story of the Theory of Critical Mass." *Politics & Gender* 2(4): 511–22. https://doi.org/10.1017/s1743923x0624114x.

– 2009. "Is Parliament Open to Women? Quotas in Global Perspective." In *Is Parliament Open to Women? An Appraisal*, 22–5. Geneva: Inter-Parliamentary Union.

– 2013. *Women, Quotas and Politics*. London: Routledge.

Dahlerup, Drude, Zeina Hilal, Nana Kalandadze, and Rumbidzai Kandawasvika-Nhundu. 2014. *Atlas of Electoral Gender Quotas*. Stockholm, Sweden: Inter-Parliamentary Union. https://www.idea.int/publications/catalogue/atlas-electoral-gender-quotas?lang=en.

Dassonneville, Ruth, and Ian McAllister. 2018. "Gender, Political Knowledge, and Descriptive Representation: The Impact of Long-Term Socialization." *American Journal of Political Science* 62(2): 249–65. https://doi.org/10.1111/ajps.12353.

David-Barrett, Elizabeth. 2015. "Nolan's Legacy: Regulating Parliamentary Conduct in Democratising Europe." *Parliamentary Affairs* 68(3): 514–32. https://doi.org/10.1093/pa/gst049.

Davis, Angela. 1981. *Women, Race and Class*. New York: Vintage.

Dawson, Tyler. 2017. "Threats against Wynne Range from the Bizarre to the Serious, Documents Reveal," *Ottawa Citizen*, 21 June.

Denemark, David, Ian Ward, and Clive Bean. 2012. "Gender and Leader Effects in the 2010 Australian Election." *Australian Journal of Political Science* 47(4): 563–78. https://doi.org/10.1080/10361146.2012.731485.

Derichs, Claudia, and Mark R. Thompson. 2013. *Dynasties and Female Political Leaders in Asia: Gender, Power and Pedigree*. Berlin: LIT Verlag Münster.

Desserud, Don, and Robin Sutherland. 2019. "Striking a Balance: Catherine Callbeck as Premier of Prince Edward Island." In Bashevkin 2019b, 111–31.

Dietrich, Bryce J., Matthew Hayes, and Diana Z. O'Brien. 2019. "Pitch Perfect: Vocal Pitch and the Emotional Intensity of Congressional Speech on Women." *American Political Science Review* 113(4): 941–62. https://doi .org/10.1017/s0003055419000467.

Dittmar, Kelly. 2018. "Invisible Forces: Gender, Race, and Congressional Staff." Paper presented at the annual meeting of the American Political Science Association, Boston, MA, 30 August–2 September.

– 2020. "Urgency and Ambition: The Influence of Political Environment and Emotion in Spurring US Women's Candidacies in 2018." *European Journal of Politics and Gender* 3(1): 143–60.

Dittmar, Kelly, Kira Sanbonmatsu, and Susan J. Carroll. 2018. *A Seat at the Table: Congresswomen's Perspectives on Why Their Presence Matters*. New York: Oxford University Press.

Doan, Alesha E., and Donald P. Haider-Markel. 2010 "The Role of Intersectional Stereotypes on Evaluations of Gay and Lesbian Political Candidates." *Politics & Gender* 6(1): 63–91. https://doi.org/10.1017 /s1743923x09990511.

Dolan, Kathleen. 1998. "Voting for Women in the Year of the Women." *American Journal of Political Science* 42(1): 272–93. https://doi.org /10.2307/2991756.

– 2005. "Do Women Candidates Play to Gender Stereotypes? Do Men Candidates Play to Women? Candidate Sex and Issues Priorities on Campaign Websites." *Political Research Quarterly* 58(1): 31–44.

– 2014. "Gender Stereotypes, Candidate Evaluations, and Voting for Women Candidates: What Really Matters?" *Political Research Quarterly* 67(1): 96–107.

Dworkin, Andrea. 1974. *Woman Hating: A Radical Look at Sexuality*. New York: Penguin Books.

Economist Intelligence Unit. 2019. "Democracy Index 2018: Me Too? Political Participation, Protest and Democracy." *The Economist*. https://www.eiu .com/public/topical_report.aspx?campaignid=Democracy2018.

Edwards, Kyle. 2019. "Jody Wilson-Raybould's Father: 'I Think She Was Kicked in the Teeth.'" *Maclean's*, 8 February.

Edwards, Louise, and Mina Roces. 2006. *Women's Suffrage in Asia: Gender, Nationalism and Democracy*. London: Routledge.

Erickson, Linda. 1993. "Making Her Way In: Women, Parties, and Candidacies in Canada." In *Gender and Party Politics*, edited by Joni Lovenduski and Pippa Norris, 60–85. Thousand Oaks: Sage.

Esping-Andersen, Gøsta. 1990. *The Three Worlds of Welfare Capitalism*. Cambridge: Polity.

Everitt, Joanna. 2015. "Gender and Sexual Diversity in Provincial Election Campaigns." *Canadian Political Science Review* 9(1): 177–92.

Everitt, Joanna, and Michael Camp. 2009. "One Is Not Like the Others: Allison Brewer's Leadership of the New Brunswick NDP." In *Opening Doors Wider: Women's Political Engagement in Canada*, edited by Sylvia Bashevkin, 127–144. Vancouver: UBC Press.

– 2014. "In Versus Out: LGB Politicians in Canada." *Journal of Canadian Studies* 48(1): 226–51. https://doi.org/10.3138/jcs.48.1.226.

Everitt, Joanna, Manon Tremblay, and Angelia Wagner. 2019. "Pathway to Office: The Eligibility, Recruitment, Selection, and Election of LGBT Candidates." In *Queering Representation: LGBTQ People and Electoral Politics in Canada*, edited by Manon Tremblay, 240–58. Vancouver: UBC Press.

Falk, Erica. 2010. *Women for President: Media Bias in Nine Campaigns*. Urbana: University of Illinois Press.

"Federal Election: 'Might End Up with More Women in Cabinet': Scheer." 2019. *Global News*, 17 October. https://globalnews.ca/video/6044509 /federal-election-might-end-up-with-more-women-in-cabinet-scheer.

Fernandez, Lynn, and Jim Silver. 2017. *Indigenous People, Wage Labour and Trade Unions: The Historical Experience in Canada*. Winnipeg: Canadian Centre for Policy Alternatives.

Finzsch, Norbert. 2008. "'[…] Extirpate or Remove that Vermine': Genocide, Biological Warfare, and Settler Imperialism in the Eighteenth and Early Nineteenth Century." *Journal of Genocide Research* 10(2): 215–32. https://doi .org/10.1080/14623520802065446.

Fleschenberg, A., and C. Derichs. 2011. *Women and Politics in Asia: A Springboard for Democracy?* Münster: LIT Verlag.

Ford, Tanisha. 2015. *Liberated Threads: Black Women, Style, and the Global Politics of Soul*. Durham: University of North Carolina Press.

Fox, Richard L., and Jennifer L. Lawless. 2004. "Entering the Arena? Gender and the Decision to Run for Office." *American Journal of Political Science* 48(2): 264–80. https://doi.org/10.1111/j.0092-5853.2004.00069.x.

Franceschet, Susan. 2005. *Women and Politics in Chile*. Boulder: Lynne Rienner.

Franceschet, Susan, Claire Annesley, and Karen Beckwith. 2017. "What Do Women Symbolize? Symbolic Representation and Cabinet Appointments." *Politics, Groups, and Identities* 5(3): 488–93. https://doi.org/10.1080 /21565503.2017.1321997.

Franceschet, Susan, Karen Beckwith, and Claire Annesley. 2015. "Why Are We Still Debating Diversity versus Merit in 2015?" Federation for the Humanities and Social Sciences. https://www.ideas-idees.ca/blog/why -are-we-still-debating-diversity-versus-merit-2015.

Franceschet, Susan, and Jennifer M. Piscopo. 2008. "Gender Quotas and Women's Substantive Representation: Lessons from Argentina." *Politics & Gender* 4(3): 393–425. https://doi.org/10.1017/s1743923x08000342.

– 2012. "Gender and Political Backgrounds in Argentina." In *The Impact of Gender Quotas*, edited by Susan Franceschet, Mona Lena Krook, and Jennifer M. Piscopo, 43–56. New York: Oxford University Press.

– 2014. "Power, Parties, and Elite Political Networks in Argentina." *Comparative Political Studies* 47(1): 85–110. https://doi.org/10.1177/0010414013489379.

Friesen, John W. 1999. "The Function of Legends as a Teaching Tool in Pre-colonial First Nations' Societies." *Interchange* 30(3): 305–22. https://doi.org/10.1023/a:1007601310865.

Fulton, Sarah A. 2012. "Running Backwards and in High Heels: The Gendered Quality Gap and Incumbent Electoral Studies." *Political Research Quarterly* 65(2): 303–14. https://doi.org/10.1177/1065912911401419.

– 2014. "When Gender Matters: Macro-dynamics and Micro-mechanisms." *Political Behavior* 36(3): 605–30. https://doi.org/10.1007/s11109-013-9245-1.

Funk, Kendall D., Magda Hinojosa, and Jennifer M. Piscopo. 2017. "Still Left Behind: Gender, Political Parties, and Latin America's Pink Tide." *Social Politics: International Studies in Gender, State & Society* 24(4): 399–424. https://doi.org/10.1093/sp/jxx012.

– 2019. "Women to the Rescue: The Gendered Effects of Public Discontent on Legislative Nominations in Latin America." *Party Politics*, 21 June, 1–13 (online). https://doi.org/10.1177/1354068819856614.

Funk, Kendall D., and Andrew Q. Philips. 2019. "Representative Budgeting: Women Mayors and the Composition of Spending in Local Governments." *Political Research Quarterly* 72(1): 19–33. https://doi.org/10.1177/1065912918775237.

Gallagher, Michael, and Michael Marsh. 1988. *The Secret Garden: Candidate Selection in Comparative Perspective*. London: Sage.

Garrett, Rachel, and Dominik Stecula. 2018 "Subtle Sexism in Political Coverage Can Have a Real Impact on Candidates." *Columbia Journalism Review*, 4 September (online). https://www.cjr.org/analysis/pink-wave-candidates.php.

Gerrits, Bailey, Linda Trimble, Daisy Raphael, Angelia Wagner, and Shannon Sampert. 2017. "Political Battlefield: Aggressive Metaphors, Gender, and Power in News Coverage of Canadian Party Leadership Contests." *Feminist Media Studies* 17(6): 1088–1103. https://doi.org/10.1080/14680777.2017.1315734.

Gershon, Sarah. 2012. "When Race, Gender, and the Media Intersect: Campaign News Coverage of Minority Congresswomen." *Journal of Women, Politics & Policy* 33(2): 105–25. https://doi.org/10.1080/1554477x.2012.667743.

Gidengil, Elisabeth, and Joanna Everitt. 2000. "Filtering the Female: Television News Coverage of the 1993 Canadian Leaders' Debates." *Women & Politics* 21(4): 105–31. https://doi.org/10.1300/j014v21n04_04.

– 2003. "Conventional Coverage/Unconventional Politicians: Gender and Media Coverage of Canadian Leaders' Debates, 1993, 1997, 2000." *Canadian Journal of Political Science* 36(3): 559–77. https://doi.org/10.1017/s0008423903778767.

Gidengil, Elisabeth, Joanna Everitt, and Susan Banducci. 2009. "Do Voters Stereotype Female Party Leaders? Evidence from Canada and New Zealand." In *Opening Doors Wider: Women's Political Engagement in Canada*, edited by Sylvia B. Bashevkin, 167–93. Vancouver: UBC Press.

Gill, Tiffany. 2010. *Beauty Shop Politics*. Urbana-Champaign: University of Illinois Press.

Goodyear-Grant, Elizabeth. 2013. *Gendered News: Media Coverage and Electoral Politics in Canada*. Vancouver: UBC Press.

Gordon, Ann, and Jerry Miller. 2005. *When Stereotypes Collide: Race/Ethnicity, Gender, and Videostyle in Congressional Campaigns*. New York: Peter Lang.

Gouws, Amanda. 1996. "The Rise of the Femocrat?" *Agenda: A Journal about Women and Culture* 12(30): 31–43. https://doi.org/10.1080/10130950.1996.9675543.

Green, Joyce, Gina Starblanket, Heidi Kiiwetnepinesik Stark, Renae Watchman, Sarah Hunt, Lianne Marie Leda Charlie, Christin O'Bonsawin, waaseyyaan'sin Christine Sy, Jeff Corntassel, Patricia M. Barkaskas, and Dallas Hunt. 2019. "Indigenous Scholars Decry 'Character Assassination' of Jody Wilson-Raybould." *The Tyee*, 13 February.

Greene, Zachary, and Maarja Lühiste. 2018. "Symbols of Priority? How the Media Selectively Report on Parties' Election Campaigns." *European Journal of Political Research* 57(3): 717–39. https://doi.org/10.1111/1475-6765.12247.

Greene, Zachary, and Diana Z. O'Brien. 2016. "Diverse Parties, Diverse Agendas? Female Politicians and the Parliamentary Party's Role in Platform Formation." *European Journal of Political Research* 55(3): 435–53. https://doi.org/10.1111/1475-6765.12141.

Grey, Sandra. 2006. "Numbers and Beyond: The Relevance of Critical Mass in Gender Research." *Politics & Gender* 2(4): 492–502. https://doi.org/10.1017/S1743923X06221147.

Groupe femmes, politique et démocratie. 2019. *Manifeste en faveur de la représentation paritaire des femmes et des hommes dans la réforme du mode de scrutin au Québec*. Quebec City: Groupe femmes, politique et démocratie.

Haider-Markel, Donald, Patrick Miller, Andrew Flores, Daniel C. Lewis, Barry Tadlock, and Jami Taylor. 2017. "Bringing 'T' to the Table: Understanding Individual Support of Transgender Candidates for Public Office." *Politics, Groups, and Identities* 5(3): 399–417. https://doi.org/10.1080/21565503.2016.1272472.

Hart, Cherie. 2012. "UNDP Offers Six-Point Plan to Fast-Track Women in Politics in Asia Pacific." United Nations Development Programme. 20 September.

Haudenosaunee Confederacy. 2019. *Influence on Democracy*. https://www .haudenosauneeconfederacy.com/influence-on-democracy/.

Hawkesworth, Mary. 2003. "Congressional Enactments of Race-Gender: Toward a Theory of Race-Gendered Institutions." *American Political Science Review* 97(4): 529–50.

Heath, Roseanna, Leslie A. Schwindt-Bayer, and Michelle M. Taylor-Robinson. 2005. "Women on the Sidelines: Women's Representation on Committees in Latin American Legislatures." *American Journal of Political Science* 49(2): 420–36. https://doi.org/10.2307/3647686.

Heldman, Caroline, and Lisa Wade. 2011. "Sexualizing Sarah Palin." *Sex Roles* 65(3–4): 156–64. https://doi.org/10.1007/s11199-011-9984-6.

Herrnson, Paul S., J. Celeste Lay, and Atiya Kai Stokes. 2003. "Women Running 'as Women': Candidate Gender, Campaign Issues, and Voter -Targeting Strategies." *Journal of Politics* 65(1): 244–55. https://doi.org /10.1111/1468-2508.t01-1-00013.

Hertzog, Mark. 1996. *The Lavender Vote: Lesbians, Gay Men, and Bisexuals in American Electoral Politics*. New York: New York University Press.

Higginbotham, Evelyn. 1993. *Righteous Discontent: The Women's Movement in the Black Baptist Church 1180–1920*. Cambridge, MA: Harvard University Press.

Hill, Rick. 2013. *Talking Points on History and Meaning of Two Row Wampum Belt*. Ohsweken: Deyohahá:ge.

Hill Collins, Patricia. 1990. *Black Feminist Thought: Knowledge, Consciousness, and the Politics of Empowerment*. Boston: Unwin Hyman.

Hinojosa, Magda. 2012a. "¿Más Mujeres?: Mexico's Mixed Member System." In *Women and Legislative Representation: Electoral Systems, Political Parties, and Sex Quotas*, edited by Manon Tremblay, 183–96. New York: Palgrave Macmillan.

– 2012b. *Selecting Women, Electing Women: Political Representation and Candidate Selection in Latin America*. Philadelphia: Temple University Press.

– 2017. "An 'Alternate' Story of Formal Rules and Informal Institutions: Quota Laws and Candidate Selection in Latin America." In *Gender and Informal Institutions*, edited by Georgina Waylen, 183–202. Lanham: Rowman and Littlefield.

Hinojosa, Magda, and Susan Franceschet. 2012. "Separate but Not Equal: The Effects of Municipal Electoral Reform on Female Representation in Chile." *Political Research Quarterly* 65(4): 758–70. https://doi.org /10.1177/1065912911427449.

Hinojosa, Magda, and Ana Vijil Gurdián. 2012. "Alternate Paths to Power? Women's Political Representation in Nicaragua." *Latin American Politics & Society* 54(4): 61–88. https://doi.org/10.1111/j.1548-2456.2012.00173.x.

Hinojosa, Magda, and Jennifer M. Piscopo. 2013. "Promoting Women's Right to Be Elected: Twenty-Five Years of Quotas in Latin America." In *Cuotas de género: vision comparada,* edited by Luna Ramos and José Alejandro, 55–107. Mexico City: Electoral Tribunal of the Federal Judicial Power of Mexico.

– 2018. "Women Won Big in Mexico's Elections, Taking Nearly Half the Legislature's Seats – Here's Why." *Washington Post,* 11 July.

Hirdman, Anja, Madeleine Kleberg, and Kristina Widestedt. 2005. "The Intimization of Journalism: Transformations of Mediatized Public Spheres from the 1980s to Current Times." *Nordicom Review* 26(2): 109–17. https://doi.org/10.1515/nor-2017-0262.

Holman, Mirya R., and Anna Mahoney. 2018. "Stop, Collaborate, and Listen: Women's Collaboration in US State Legislatures." *Legislative Studies Quarterly* 43(2): 179–206. https://doi.org/10.1111/lsq.12199.

Holman, Mirya R., Jennifer Merolla, and Elizabeth Zechmeister. 2011. "Sex, Stereotypes, and Security: An Experimental Study of the Effect of Crises on Assessments of Gender and Leadership." *Journal of Women, Politics, and Policy* 32(3): 173–92. https://doi.org/10.1080/1554477x.2011.589283.

Holman, Mirya R., and Monica C. Schneider. 2018. "Gender, Race, and Political Ambition: How Intersectionality and Frames Influence Interest in Political Office." *Politics, Groups, and Identities* 6(2): 264–80. https://doi.org/10.1080/21565503.2016.1208105.

Horowitz, Donald L. 1985. *Ethnic Groups in Conflict.* Berkeley: University of California Press.

House of Commons, Canada. 2019. "Elect Her: A Roadmap for Improving the Representation of Women in Canadian Politics." Report of the Standing Committee on the Status of Women. Ottawa: House of Commons.

Htun, Mala. 2005. "Case Study: Latin America. Women, Political Parties, and Electoral Systems in Latin America." In *Women in Parliament: Beyond Numbers,* edited by Julie Ballington and Azza Karam, 112–21. Stockholm: International IDEA.

Htun, Mala, and Mark P. Jones. 2002. "Engendering the Right to Participate in Decision Making: Electoral Quotas and Women's Leadership in Latin America." In *Gender and the Politics of Rights and Democracy in Latin America,* edited by Nikki Craske and Maxine Molyneux, 32–56. London: Palgrave.

Huang, Chang-Ling. 2016. "Reserved for Whom? The Electoral Impact of Gender Quotas in Taiwan." *Pacific Affairs* 89(2): 325–43. https://doi.org/10.5509/2016892325.

Huber, Jessica. 2017. "Why an Intersectional Approach to Gender Quotas Is a Must: An Example from Nepal." International Foundation for Electoral Systems. 16 May. https://www.ifes.org/news/why-intersectional-approach-gender-quotas-must-example-nepal-0.

Hughes, Melanie M. 2011. "Intersectionality, Quotas, and Minority Women's Political Representation Worldwide." *American Political Science Review* 105(3): 604–20. https://doi.org/10.1017/s0003055411000293.

Hughes, Melanie M., Pamela Paxton, Amanda B. Clayton, and Pär Zetterberg. 2016. "Global Gender Quota Adoption, Implementation, and Reform." *Comparative Politics* 51(2): 219–38. https://doi.org/10.2307/26563456.

Hutt, David. 2016. "The Trouble with Timor-Leste's Gender Quotas." *The Diplomat*, 17 December.

Inglehart, Ronald, and Pippa Norris. 2003. *Rising Tide: Gender Equality and Cultural Change*. New York: Cambridge University Press.

Ingraham, Chrys. 1994. "The Heterosexual Imaginary: Feminist Sociology and Theories of Gender." *Sociological Theory* 12(2): 203 19. https://doi.org/10.2307/201865.

Innes, Robert Alexander, and Kim Anderson. 2015. "Introduction: Who's Walking with Our Brothers." In *Indigenous Men and Masculinities: Legacies, Identities, Regeneration*, edited by Robert Alexander Innes and Kim Anderson. Winnipeg: University of Manitoba Press.

Institut NéoQuébec. 2018. "Scope Diversité: Les député.e.s néoquébécois.es de l'Assemblée nationale sortante." https://neoquebec.com/c-e/scope-diversite-les-depute-e-s-neoquebecois-es-de-lassemblee-nationale-sortante/.

International IDEA (Institute for Democracy and Electoral Assistance). 2019. "Electoral System Design Database." https://www.idea.int/data-tools/data/electoral-system-design.

Inter-Parliamentary Union. 1999. "Women in National Parliament: World Average." January. http://archive.ipu.org/wmn-e/arc/world010199.htm.

– 2016. *Sexism, Harassment and Violence against Women in Parliaments*. October. https://www.ipu.org/resources/publications/issue-briefs/2016-10/sexism-harassment-and-violence-against-women-parliamentarians.

– 2019a. *Women in National Parliament. World Average*. February. http://archive.ipu.org/wmn-e/arc/world010219.htm.

– 2019b. "Women in Parliament in 2018: The Year in Review." https://www.ipu.org/resources/publications/reports/2019-03/women-in-parliament-in-2018-year-in-review.

Invert Media. 2015. *Four Directions Teachings*. http://www.fourdirectionsteachings.com/.

Jackson, Stevie. 2006. "Gender, Sexuality and Heterosexuality: The Complexity (and Limits) of Heteronormativity." *Feminist Theory* 7(1): 105 21. https://doi.org/10.1177/1464700106061462.

Jalalzai, Farida. 2013. *Shattered, Cracked, or Firmly Intact? Women and the Executive Glass Ceiling Worldwide*. New York: Oxford University Press.

Johnson Carew, Jessica D. 2012. *"Lifting as We Climb?" The Role of Stereotypes in the Evaluations of Political Candidates at the Intersection of Race and Gender.* Durham: Duke University.

Jones, Mark P. 2004. "Quota Legislation and the Election of Women: Learning from the Costa Rican Experience." *Journal of Politics* 66(4): 1203–23. https://doi.org/10.1111/j.0022-3816.2004.00296.x.

– 2005. "The Desirability of Gender Quotas: Considering Context and Design." *Politics & Gender* 1(4): 645–52. https://doi.org/10.1017/s1743923x05240199.

– 2009. "Gender Quotas, Electoral Laws, and the Election of Women: Evidence from the Latin American Vanguard." *Comparative Political Studies* 42(1): 56–81. https://doi.org/10.1177/0010414008324993.

Joshi, Devin K., and Rakkee Thimothy. 2018. "Long-Term Impacts of Parliamentary Gender Quotas in a Single-Party System: Symbolic Co-Option or Delayed Integration?" *International Political Science Review* 40(4): 591–606. https://doi.org/10.1177/0192512118772852.

Kanter, Rosabeth Moss. 1977. "Some Effects of Proportions on Group Life: Skewed Sex Ratios and Responses to Token Women." *American Journal of Sociology* 82(5): 965–90. https://doi.org/10.1086/226425.

Karp, Jeffrey A., and Susan A. Banducci. 2008. "When Politics Is Not Just a Man's Game: Women's Representation and Political Engagement." *Electoral Studies* 27(1): 105–15. https://doi.org/10.1016/j.electstud.2007.11.009.

Karpowitz, Christopher F., and Tali Mendelberg. 2014. *The Silent Sex: Gender, Deliberation, and Institutions.* Princeton: Princeton University Press.

Kenny, Meryl, and Fiona Mackay. 2013. "When Is Contagion Not Very Contagious? Dynamics of Women's Political Representation in Scotland." *Parliamentary Affairs* 67(4): 866–86. https://doi.org/10.1093/pa/gss109

Kerevel, Yann P. 2019. "Empowering Women? Gender Quotas and Women's Political Careers." *Journal of Politics* 81(4): 1167–80. https://doi.org/10.1086/704434.

Kerevel, Yann P., and Lonna Rae Atkeson. 2013. "Explaining the Marginalization of Women in Legislative Institutions." *Journal of Politics* 75(4): 980–92. https://doi.org/10.1017/s0022381613000960.

Kim, Chong Lim. 1970. "Political Attitudes of Defeated Candidates in an American State Election." *American Political Science Review* 64(3): 879–87. https://doi.org/10.2307/1953469.

Kittilson, Miki Caul. 2005. "In Support of Gender Quotas: Setting New Standards, Bringing Visible Gains." *Politics & Gender* 1(4): 638–45. https://doi.org/10.1017/s1743923x05230192.

– 2006. *Challenging Parties, Changing Parliaments: Women and Elected Office in Contemporary Western Europe.* Columbus: Ohio State University Press.

– 2011. "Women, Parties and Platforms in Post-Industrial Democracies." *Party Politics* 17(1): 66–92. https://doi.org/10.1177/1354068809361012.

Kosiara-Pedersen, Karina, and Kasper M. Hansen. 2015. "Gender Differences in Assessments of Party Leaders." *Scandinavian Political Studies* 38(1): 26–48. https://doi.org/10.1111/1467-9477.12033.

Krook, Mona Lena. 2009. *Quotas for Women in Politics: Gender and Candidate Selection Reform Worldwide*. New York: Oxford University Press.

– 2019. "New Horizons in Women's Political Rights." In *The Palgrave Handbook of Women's Political Rights*, edited by Susan Franceschet, Mona Lena Krook, and Netina Tan, 73–81. New York: Palgrave Macmillan.

Krook, Mona Lena, Joni Lovenduski, and Judith Squires. 2006. "Western Europe, North America, Australia and New Zealand Gender Quotas in the Context of Citizenship Models." In *Women, Quotas and Politics*, edited by Drude Dahlerup, 194–221. New York: Routledge.

Krook, Mona Lena, and Pippa Norris. 2014. "Beyond Quotas: Strategies to Promote Gender Equality in Elected Office." *Political Studies* 62(1): 2–20. https://doi.org/10.1111/1467-9248.12116.

Krook, Mona Lena, and Mary K. Nugent. 2016. "Intersectional Institutions: Representing Women and Ethnic Minorities in the British Labour Party." *Party Politics* 22(5): 620–30. https://doi.org/10.1177/1354068816655564.

Krook, Mona Lena, and Diana Z. O'Brien. 2012. "All the President's Men? The Appointment of Female Cabinet Ministers Worldwide." *Journal of Politics* 74(3): 840–55. https://doi.org/10.1017/s0022381612000382.

Krook, Mona Lena, and Pär Zetterberg. 2014. "Introduction: Gender Quotas and Women's Representation – New Directions in Research." *Representation* 50(3): 287–94.

Lang, Sabine. 2009. "Assessing Advocacy: European Transnational Women's Networks and Gender Mainstreaming." *Social Politics: International Studies in Gender, State & Society* 16(3): 327–57. https://doi.org/10.1093/sp/jxp016.

– 2014. "Women's Advocacy Networks: The European Union, Women's NGOs, and the Velvet Triangle." In *Theorizing NGOs: States, Feminisms, and Neoliberalism*, edited by Victoria Bernal and Inderpal Grewal, 266–84. Durham: Duke University Press.

Langer, Ana Ines. 2010. "The Politicization of Private Persona: Exceptional Leaders or the New Rule?" *International Journal of Press/Politics* 15(1): 60–76. https://doi.org/10.1177/1940161209351003.

Lawless, Jennifer L. 2004. "Politics of Presence? Congresswomen and Symbolic Representation." *Political Research Quarterly* 57(1): 81–99. https://doi.org/10.1177/106591290405700107.

Lawless, Jennifer L., and Richard L. Fox. 2010. *It Still Takes a Candidate: Why Women Don't Run for Office*. New York: Cambridge University Press.

– 2012. *Men Rule: The Continued Underrepresentation of Women in Politics*. Washington, DC: American University, Women and Politics Institute.

Lawless, Jennifer L., and Richard L. Fox. 2015. *Running from Office: Why Young Americans Are Turned Off to Politics*. New York: Oxford University Press.

Lawrence, Bonita. 2002. "Rewriting Histories of the Land: Colonization and Indigenous Resistance in Eastern Canada." In *Race, Space and the Law: Unmapping a White Settler Society*, edited by Sherene H. Razack, 21–46. Toronto: Between the Lines.

Lazarus, Jeffrey, and Amy Steigerwalt. 2018. *Gendered Vulnerability: How Women Work Harder to Stay in Office*. Ann Arbor: University of Michigan Press.

Lépinard, Éléonore. 2016. "From Breaking the Rule to Making the Rules: The Adoption, Entrenchment, and Diffusion of Gender Quotas in France." *Politics, Groups, and Identities* 4(2): 231–45.

Leversridge, Amy. 2019. "Parliament Must Act Now on Bullying and Harassment." *The House*, 1 March.

Lindsey, Treva B. 2017. *Colored No More: Reinventing Black Womanhood in Washington, D.C.* Champaign: University of Illinois Press.

Liu, Shan-Jan Sarah. 2018. "Are Female Political Leaders Role Models? Lessons from Asia." *Political Research Quarterly* 71(2): 255–69. https://doi.org/10.1177/1065912917745162.

– 2019. "Cracking Gender Stereotypes? Challenges Women Political Leaders Face." *Political Insight* 10(1): 12–15. https://doi.org/10.1177/2041905819838147.

Liu, Shan-Jan Sarah, and Lee Ann Banaszak. 2017. "Do Government Positions Held by Women Matter? A Cross-National Examination of Female Ministers' Impact on Women's Participation." *Politics & Gender* 13(1): 132–62. https://doi.org/10.1017/S1743923X16000490.

Lott, John R., and Lawrence W. Kenny. 1999. "Did Women's Suffrage Change the Size and Scope of Government?" *Journal of Political Economy* 107(6): 1163–98. https://doi.org/10.1086/250093.

Lovenduski, Joni. 1986. *Women and European Politics*. Amherst: University of Massachusetts Press.

– 2014. "The Institutionalisation of Sexism in Politics." *Political Insight* 16(9): 16–19. https://doi.org/10.1111/2041-9066.12056.

Lowande, Kenneth, Melinda Ritchie, and Erinn Lauterbach. 2019. "Descriptive and Substantive Representation in Congress: Evidence from 80,000 Congressional Inquiries." *American Journal of Political Science* 63(3): 644–59. https://doi.org/10.1111/ajps.12443.

Lowe, Will, Kenneth Benoit, Slava Mikhaylov, and Michael Laver. 2011. "Scaling Policy Preferences from Coded Political Texts." *Legislative Studies Quarterly* 36(1): 123–55. https://doi.org/10.1111/j.1939-9162.2010.00006.x.

Ludwig, Gundula. 2011. "From the 'Heterosexual Matrix' to a 'Heteronormative Hegemony': Initiating a Dialogue between Judith Butler and Antonio Gramsci about Queer Theory and Politics." In *Hegemony and Heteronormativity: Revisiting "The Political" in Queer Politics*, edited by María do Mar Castro Varela, Nikita Dhawan, and Antke Engel, 43 61. Farnham: Ashgate.

Lussier, Judith. 2012. "Manon Massé: Par-delà la moustache." *Urbania*, 7 August.

MacKinnon, Catherine.1989. *Towards a Feminist Theory of the State*. Cambridge: Harvard University Press.

Maillé, Chantal. 2015. "Feminist Interventions in Political Representation in the United States and Canada: Training Programs and Legal Quotas." *European Journal of American Studies* 10(2): 1–20. https://doi.org/10.4000/ejas.10502.

Major, Lesa Hatley, and Renita Coleman. 2008. "The Intersection of Race and Gender in Election Coverage: What Happens When the Candidates Don't Fit the Stereotypes?" *Howard Journal of Communications* 19(4): 315–33. https://doi.org/10.1080/10646170802391722.

Malbin, Michael. 1980. *Unelected Representatives: Congressional Staff and the Future of Representative Government*. New York: Basic Books.

Mandel, Ruth B. 1981. *In the Running: The New Woman Candidate*. New Haven: Ticknor & Fields.

Mansbridge, Jane. 1999. "Should Blacks Represent Blacks and Women Represent Women? A Contingent 'Yes.'" *Journal of Politics* 61(3): 628–57. https://doi.org/10.2307/2647821.

Markussof, Jason. 2015. "An Alberta MLA on Battling Gender Identity." *Maclean's*, 1 December.

Martin, Lanny, and Georg Vanberg. 2008. "Coalition Government and Political Communication." *Political Research Quarterly* 61(3): 502–16. https://doi.org/10.1177/1065912907308348.

Marx, Susan. 2012. "Can Timor-Leste's Gender Quota System Ensure Women's Participation in Politics?" Asia Foundation, 7 March. https://asiafoundation.org/2012/03/07/can-timor-lestes-gender-quota-system-ensure-womens-participation-in-politics/.

Matland, Richard E. 2002. "Enhancing Women's Political Participation: Legislative Recruitment and Electoral Systems." In *Women in Parliament: Beyond Numbers*, edited by Julie Ballington and Azza Karam. Stockhom: IDEA.

May, K. 2016. "Canadians Open to Quotas to Boost Indigenous Representation in Government." *Ottawa Citizen*, 9 September.

Mazur, Amy G. 2002. *Theorizing Feminist Policy*. Oxford: Oxford University Press.

McAndrews, John R., Jonah I. Goldberg, Peter John Loewen, Daniel Rubenson, and Benjamin Allen Stevens. 2020. "Nonelectoral Motivations to Represent Marginalized Groups in a Democracy: Evidence from an

Unelected Legislature." *Legislative Studies Quarterly*. https://doi.org/10.1111/lsq.12310.

McDermott, Monika L. 1998. "Race and Gender Cues in Low-Information Elections." *Political Research Quarterly* 51(4): 895–918. https://doi.org/10.1177/106591299805100403.

Medeiros, Mike, Benjamin Forest, and Chris Erl. 2019. "Where Women Stand: Parliamentary Candidate Selection in Canada." *Politics, Groups, and Identities* 7(2): 389–400. https://doi.org/10.1080/21565503.2018.1557056.

Meeks, Linsey. 2012. "Is She 'Man Enough?' Women Candidates, Executive Political Offices, and News Coverage." *Journal of Communication* 62(1): 175–93. https://doi.org/10.1111/j.1460-2466.2011.01621.x.

Mendelberg, Tali, Christopher F. Karpowitz, and Nicholas Goedert. 2014. "Does Descriptive Representation Facilitate Women's Distinctive Voice? How Gender Composition and Decision Rules Affect Deliberation." *American Journal of Political Science* 58(2): 291–306. https://doi.org/10.1111/ajps.12077.

Menzel, Donald C. 2009. *Ethics Moments in Government: Cases and Controversies*. Florida: CRC.

Mercer, Kobena. 2005. "Black Hair/Style Politics." In *The Subcultures Reader*, edited by Ken Gelder, 420–35. London: Routledge.

Morgan, Jana, and Magda Hinojosa. 2018. "Women in Political Parties: Seen but Not Heard." In *Gender and Representation in Latin America*, edited by Leslie Schwindt-Bayer, 74–98. New York: Oxford University Press.

Moyser, Melissa, and Amanda Burlock. 2018. "Time Use: Total Work Burden, Unpaid Work and Leisure." Statistics Canada Report, 30 July. https://www150.statcan.gc.ca/n1/pub/89-503-x/2015001/article/54931-eng.htm.

Müller-Rommel, Ferdinand, and Michelangelo Vercesi. 2017. "Prime Ministerial Careers in the European Union: Does Gender Make a Difference?" *European Politics and Society* 18(2): 245–62. https://doi.org/10.1080/23745118.2016.1225655.

Murray, Rainbow. 2007. "How Parties Evaluate Compulsory Quotas: A Study of the Implementation of the Parity Law in France." *Parliamentary Affairs* 60(4): 568–84. https://doi.org/10.1093/pa/gsm039.

– 2010. "Second among Equals? A Study of Whether France's 'Quota Women' Are Up to the Job." *Politics & Gender* 6(1): 93–118.

– 2012. "French Lesson: What the United Kingdom Can Learn from the French Experiment with Gender Parity." *Political Quarterly* 83(4): 735–41. https://doi.org/10.1111/j.1467-923x.2012.02366.x.

– 2014. "Quotas for Men: Reframing Gender Quotas as a Means of Improving Represesentation for All." *American Political Science Review* 108(3): 520–32.

Nash, J.C. 2008. "Re-thinking Intersectionality." *Feminist Review* 89(1): 1–15. https://doi.org/10.1057%2Ffr.2008.4.

National Democratic Institute. 2019. *Reporting Violence against Women*. https://www.ndi.org/reporting-violence-against-women.

National Inquiry into Missing and Murdered Indigenous Women, Girls, and 2SLGBTQQIA People. 2019. *Reclaiming Power and Place: The Final Report of the National Inquiry into Missing and Murdered Indigenous Women, Girls, and 2SLGBTQQIA People*. Vol. 1a. Ottawa: National Inquiry into Missing and Murdered Indigenous Women, Girls, and 2SLGBTQQIA People.

Navarro, P. 2015. *Femmes et pouvoir: Les changements nécessaires, Plaidoyer pour la parité*. Montreal: Leméac.

Neeganagwedgin, Erica. 2012. "'Chattling the Indigenous Other': A Historical Examination of the Enslavement of Aboriginal Peoples in Canada." *Alternative* 8(1): 15–26. https://doi.org/10.1177/117718011200800102.

New Democratic Party. 2016. "Resolutions passed at Convention 2016."

Ng, Eddy. 2016. "Why Do Individuals Oppose Affirmative Action?" *Psychology Today*. https://www.psychologytoday.com/gb/blog/diverse-and-competitive/201606/why-do-individuals-oppose-affirmative-action.

Norris, Pippa. 1985. "Women's Legislative Participation in Western Europe." *Western European Politics* 8(4): 90–101. https://doi.org/10.1080/01402388508424556.

– 2012. "Gender Equality in Elected Office in Asia Pacific: Six Actions to Expand Women's Empowerment." United Nations Development Programme. Bangkok: Asia Pacific Regional Centre.

Norris, Pippa, and Joni Lovenduski. 1989. "Pathways to Parliament." *Talking Politics* 1(3): 90–4.

Nugent, Mary, and Mona Lena Krook. 2016. "All Women Shortlists: Myths and Realities." Parliamentary Affairs 69: 115–35. https://doi.org/10.1093/pa/gsv015.

Nussbaum, Martha C. 1999. *Sex and Social Justice*. New York: Oxford University Press.

O'Brien, Diana Z. 2015. "Rising to the Top: Gender, Political Performance, and Party Leadership in Parliamentary Democracies." *American Journal of Political Science* 59(4): 1022–39. https://doi.org/10.1111/ajps.12173.

– 2018. "Righting Conventional Wisdom: Women and Right Parties in Established Democracies." *Politics & Gender* 14(1): 27–55. https://doi.org/10.1017/s1743923x17000514.

– 2019. "Female Leaders and Citizens' Perceptions of Political Parties." *Journal of Elections, Public Opinion and Parties* 29(4): 465–89. https://doi.org/10.1080/17457289.2019.1669612.

O'Brien, Diana Z., and Catherine Reyes-Housholder. 2020. "Women and Executive Politics." In *Oxford Handbook of Political Executives*, edited by Rudy

Andeweg, Robert Elgie, Ludger Helms, and Juliet Kaarbo, 251–73. Oxford: Oxford University Press.

O'Brien, Diana Z., and Johanna Rickne. 2016. "Gender Quotas and Women's Access to Leadership Posts." *American Political Science Review* 110(1): 112–26. https://doi.org/10.1017/s0003055415000611.

Och, Malliga. 2015. "Conservative Feminists? Feminist Policy Adoption under Merkel's Leadership." Paper presented at the Annual Meeting of the American Political Science Association, San Francisco, 2–6 September.

– 2018. "Conservative Feminists? An Exploration of Feminist Arguments in Parliamentary Debates of the Bundestag." *Parliamentary Affairs* 72(2): 353–78. https://doi.org/10.1093/pa/gsy016.

O'Neill, Brenda, and David K, Stewart. 2009. "Gender and Political Party Leadership in Canada." *Party Politics* 15(6): 737–57. https://doi.org/10.1177/1354068809342526.

Osborn, Tracy. 2012. *How Women Represent Women: Political Parties, Gender, and Representation in the State Legislatures.* New York: Oxford University Press.

Osborn, Tracy, and Jeanette Mendez. 2010. "Speaking as Women: Women and Floor Speeches in the Senate." *Journal of Women, Politics & Policy* 31(1): 1–21. https://doi.org/10.1080/15544770903501384.

Ouellet, Valérie, and Näel Shiab. 2019. "Men Won Almost Twice as Often as Women this Federal Election, CBC Analysis Shows." *CBC News.* 22 November.

Palmer, Barbara, and Dennis Michael Simon. 2012. *Women and Congressional Elections: A Century of Change.* Boulder: Lynne Rienner.

Parmenter, Jon. 2013. "The Meaning of Kaswentha and the Two Row Wampum Belt in Haudenosaunee (Iroquois) History: Can Oral Tradition Be Reconciled with the Documentary Record?" *Journal of Early American History* 3(1): 82–109. https://doi.org/10.1163/18770703-00301005.

Paxton, Pamela, and Melanie M. Hughes. 2015. "The Increasing Effectiveness of National Gender Quotas, 1990–2010." *Legislative Studies Quarterly* 40(3): 331–62. https://doi.org/10.1111/lsq.12079.

Pearson, Kathryn, and Logan Dancey. 2011. "Speaking for the Underrepresented in the House of Representatives: Voicing Women's Interests in a Partisan Era." *Politics & Gender* 7(4): 493–519. https://doi.org/10.1017/s1743923x1100033x.

Pearson, Kathryn, and Eric McGhee. 2013. "What It Takes to Win: Questioning 'Gender Neutral' Outcomes in U.S. House Elections." *Politics & Gender* 9(4): 439–62. https://doi.org/10.1017/s1743923x13000433.

Perrigo, Sarah. 1996. "Women and Change in the Labour Party, 1979–1995." *Parliamentary Affairs* 49(1): 116–30. https://doi.org/10.1093/oxfordjournals.pa.a028662.

Phillips, Anne. 1998. "Democracy and Representation: Or, Why Should It Matter Who Our Representatives Are?" In *Feminism and Politics*, edited by Anne Phillips, 224–41. Oxford: Oxford University Press.

Pierre, M. 2017. "L'atteinte de la parité sans diversité serait un objectif inachevé." *Le Devoir*, 5 January. https://www.ledevoir.com/opinion/libre-opinion/488409/l-atteinte-de-la-parite-en-l-absence-de-diversite-serait-un-objectif-inacheve.

Pires, Milena. 2002. "Imposing Quotas from Above: The Case of East Timor." Chapter 3 of *The Implementation of Quotas: Asian Experiences*. Quota Workshop Report Series, IDEA. https://www.idea.int/publications/catalogue/implementation-quotas-asian-experiences.

Piscopo, Jennifer M. 2011. "Rethinking Descriptive Representation: Rendering Women in Legislative Debates." *Parliamentary Affairs* 64(3): 448–72. https://doi.org/10.1093/pa/gsq061.

– 2016. "Quota Laws and Gender Equality." In *Democracy and Its Discontents in Latin America*, edited by Joe Foweraker and Dolores Trevizo, 149–69. Boulder: Lynne Rienner.

– 2017. "Leveraging Informality, Rewriting Formal Rules: The Implementation of Gender Parity in Mexico." In *Gender and Informal Institutions*, edited by Georgina Waylen, 137–60. Lanham: Rowman and Littlefield.

Pitkin, Hanna Fenichel. 1967. *The Concept of Representation*. Berkeley: University of California Press.

Plutzer, Eric, and John Zipp. 1996. "Identity Politics, Partisanship and Voting for Women Candidates." *Public Opinion Quarterly* 60(1): 30–57. https://doi.org/10.1086/297738.

Prihatini, Ella S. 2019. "Women's Representation in Asian Parliaments: A QCA Approach." *Contemporary Politics* 25(2): 213–35. https://doi.org/10.1080/13569775.2018.1520057.

Proksch, Sven-Oliver, and Jonathan B. Slapin. 2015. *The Politics of Parliamentary Debate*. Cambridge: Cambridge University Press.

Pruysers, Scott, and Bill Cross. 2016. "Candidate Selection in Canada: Local Autonomy, Centralization, and Competing Democratic Norms." *American Behavioral Scientist* 60(7): 781–98. https://doi.org/10.1177/0002764216632820.

Putnam, Robert. 1976. *The Comparative Study of Political Elites*. Englewood Cliffs: Prentice-Hall.

Rai, Shirin, Rarzaba Bari, Nazmunessa Mahtab, and Bidyut Mohanty. 2013. "South Asia: Gender Quotas and the Politcs of Empowerment – A Comparative Study." In *Women, Quotas and Politics*, edited by Drude Dahlerup, 222–46. New York: Routledge.

Razack, Sherene H. 2002. "Introduction: When Race Becomes Space." In *Race, Space & the Law: Unmapping White Settler Society*, edited by Sherene H. Razack, 1–20. Toronto: Between the Lines.

– 2016. "Gendering Disposability." *Canadian Journal of Women and the Law* 28(2): 285–307. https://doi.org/10.3138/cjwl.28.2.285.

Reher, Stefanie. 2021. "How Do Voters Perceive Disabled Candidates?" *Frontiers in Political Science* 2: 23. https://doi.org/10.3389/fpos.2020.634432.

Reilly, Benjamin, and Andrew Reynolds. 1999. *Electoral Systems and Conflict in Divided Societies*. Washington, DC: National Academic Press.

Reingold, Beth. 2008. "Women as Officeholders: Linking Descriptive and Substantive Representation." In *Political Women and American Democracy*, edited by Christina Wolbrecht, Karen Beckwith, and Lisa Baldez, 128–47. Cambridge: Cambridge University Press.

Reingold, Beth, and Jessica Harrell. 2010. "The Impact of Descriptive Representation on Women's Political Engagement: Does Party Matter?" *Political Research Quarterly* 63(2): 280–94. https://doi.org/10.1177/1065912908330346.

Reyes-Housholder, Catherine. 2019. "A Constituency Theory for the Conditional Impact of Female Presidents." *Comparative Politics* 51(3): 429–49. http://www.jstor.org/stable/26663938.

Reynolds, Andrew. 2006. *Electoral Systems and the Protection and Participation of Minorities*. London: Minority Rights Groups International.

Rheault, Ludovic, Erica Rayment, and Andreea Musulan. 2019. "Politicians in the Line of Fire: Incivility and the Treatment of Women on Social Media." *Research and Politics* 6(1) (online). https://doi.org/10.1177/%2F2053168018816228.

Rich, Adrienne. 1981. "La contrainte à l'hétérosexualité et l'existence lesbienne." *Nouvelles questions féministes* 1 (March): 15 43.

Richter, Linda. 1990. "Exploring Theories of Female Leadership in South and Southeast Asia." *Pacific Affairs* 63(4): 524–40. https://doi.org/10.2307/2759914.

Roberts, Andrew, Jason Seawright, and Jennifer Cyr. 2012. "Do Electoral Laws Affect Women's Representation?" *Comparative Political Studies*, 46(12): 1555–81. https://doi.org/10.1177/0010414012463906.

Roesch Wagner, Sally. 2001. *Sisters in Spirit: Haudenosaunee (Iroquois) Influence on Early American Feminists*. Summertown: Native Voices.

Rosenthal, Cindy. 1998. *When Women Lead*. New York: Oxford University Press.

Roza, Vivian. 2010. "Gatekeepers to Power: Party-Level Influences on Women's Political Participation in Latin America." PhD diss., Georgetown University.

Rule, Wilma. 1994. "Women's Underrepresentation and Electoral Systems." *PS: Political Science and Politics* 27(4): 689–92. https://doi.org/10.1017/s1049096500041731.

Saint-Martin, Denis. 2003. "Should the Federal Ethics Counsellor Become an Independent Officer of Parliament?" *Canadian Public Policy* 28(2): 197–212. https://doi.org/10.2307/3552455.

Salmond, Rob. 2006. "Proportional Representation and Female Parliamentarians." *Legislative Studies Quarterly* 31(2): 175–204. https://doi.org/10.3162/036298006x201779.

Sampert, Shannon, Linda Trimble, Angelia Wagner, and Bailey Gerrits. 2014. "Jumping the Shark: Mediatization of Canadian Party Leadership Contests, 1975–2012." *Journalism Practice* 8(3): 279–94. https://doi.org/10.1080/17512786.2014.889444.

Sawer, M. 2012. "What Makes the Substantive Representation of Women Possible in a Westminster Parliament? The Story of RU486 in Australia." *International Political Science Review* 33(3): 320–35. https://doi.org/10.1177/0192512111435369.

Schmidt, Gregory D., and Kyle L. Saunders. 2004. "Effective Quotas, Relative Party Magnitude, and the Success of Female Candidates: Peruvian Municipal Elections in Comparative Perspective." *Comparative Political Studies* 37(6): 704–24. https://doi.org/10.1177/0010414004265884.

Schwarz, Daniel, Denise Traber, and Kenneth Benoit. 2015. "Estimating Intra-Party Preferences: Comparing Speeches to Votes." *Political Science Research and Methods* 5(2): 379–96. https://doi.org/10.1017/psrm.2015.77.

Schwindt-Bayer, Leslie A. 2009. "Making Quotas Work: The Effect of Gender Quota Laws on the Election of Women." *Legislative Studies Quarterly* 34(1): 5–28. https://doi.org/10.3162/036298009787500330.

– 2010. *Political Power and Women's Representation in Latin America*. New York: Oxford University Press.

Schwindt-Bayer, Leslie A., and Catherine Reyes-Housholder. 2017. "Citizen Responses to Female Executives: Is It Sex, Novelty, or Both?" *Politics, Groups, and Identities* 5: 373–98. https://doi.org/10.1080/21565503.2017.1283238.

Sevi, Semra. 2021. "Who Runs? Canadian Federal and Ontario Provincial Candidates from 1867 to 2019." *Canadian Journal of Political Science* 1–6. https://doi.org/10.1017/S0008423920001213.

Sevi, Semra, Vincent Arel-Bundock, and André Blais. 2019. "Do Women Get Fewer Votes? No." *Canadian Journal of Political Science* 52(1): 201–10. https://doi.org/10.1017/s0008423918000495.

Shames, Shauna L. 2017. *Out of the Running: Why Millennials Reject Political Careers and Why It Matters*. New York: New York University Press.

Shewell, Hugh. 2004. *"Enough to Keep Them Alive": Indian Social Welfare in Canada, 1873–1965*. Toronto: University of Toronto Press.

Silbermann, Rachel. 2014. "Gender Roles, Work-Life Balance, and Running for Office." *Political Science Quarterly* 10(2): 123–53. https://doi.org/10.1561/100.00014087.

Simpson, Jeffrey. 2006. "Rona Ambrose Has Been Left to Smile Pretty for the Cameras." *Globe and Mail*, 15 December. https://www.theglobeandmail .com/news/politics/rona-ambrose-has-been-left-to-smile-pretty-for-the -cameras/article733387/.

Simpson, Leanne Betasamosake. 2017. *As We Have Always Done: Indigenous Freedom through Radical Resistance*. Minneapolis: University of Minnesota Press.

Sjoberg, Laura. 2014. "Feminism." In *The Oxford Handbook of Political Leadership*, edited by R.A.W. Rhodes and Paul 't Hart, 72–86. Oxford: Oxford University Press.

Smith, Barbara. 1983. *Home Girls: A Black Feminist Anthology*. New York: Kitchen Table: Women of Color Press.

Stivens, Maila, and Krishna Sen. 1998. *Gender and Power in Affluent Asia*. New York: Routledge.

Stockemer, Daniel, and Aksel Sundström. 2018. "Women in Cabinets: The Role of Party Ideology and Government Turnover." *Party Politics* 24(6): 663–73. https://doi.org/10.1177/1354068817689954.

Stoffel, Sophie. 2008. "Rethinking Political Representation: The Case of Institutionalised Feminist Organisations in Chile." *Representation* 44(2): 141–54. https://doi.org/10.1080/00344890802079631.

Studlar, Donley T., and Ian McAllister. 2002. "Does a Critical Mass Exist? A Comparative Analysis of Women's Legislative Representation since 1950." *European Journal of Political Research* 41(2): 233–53.

Sun, T.W. 2005. "Gender Representation in Politics and Public Administration: Taiwan and Asian Countries." *Ya Tai Yan Jiu Lun Tan* 28: 148–69.

Swers, Michele. 2002. *The Difference Women Make: The Policy Impact of Women in Congress*. Chicago: University of Chicago Press.

– 2005. "Connecting Descriptive and Substantive Representation: An Analysis of Sex Differences in Cosponsorship Activity." *Legislative Studies Quarterly* 30(3): 407–33. www.jstor.org/stable/3598642.

Sykes, Patricia Lee. 2014. "Does Gender Matter?" In *The Oxford Handbook of Political Leadership*, edited by R.A.W. Rhodes and Paul 't Hart, 690–704. Oxford: Oxford University.

Tan, Netina. 2016. "Why Are Gender Reforms Adopted in Singapore? Party Pragmatism and Electoral Incentives." *Pacific Affairs* 89(2): 369–93. https:// doi.org/10.5509/2016892369.

Taylor, Stephanie, and Bill Graveland. 2019. "'Back to Zero': Canada's Premiers Gather in Saskatoon, but None Are Women." *CityNews*, 9 July.

Taylor-Robinson, Michelle M., and Roseanna Michelle Heath. 2003. "Do Women Legislators Have Different Policy Priorities than Their Male Colleagues?" *Women & Politics* 24(4): 77–101. https://doi.org/10.1300 /J014v24n04_04.

Thatcher, Richard. 2004. *Fighting Firewater Fictions: Moving Beyond the Disease Model of Alcoholism in First Nations*. Toronto: University of Toronto Press.

Thomas, Melanee. 2018. "In Crisis or Decline? Selecting Women to Lead Provincial Parties in Government." *Canadian Journal of Political Science* 51(2): 379–403. https://doi.org/10.1017/s0008423917001421.

– 2019. "Governing As If Women Mattered: Rachel Notley as Alberta Premier." In Bashevkin 2019b, 250–74.

Thomas, Melanee, and Marc André Bodet. 2013. "Sacrificial Lambs, Women Candidates, and District Competitiveness in Canada." *Electoral Studies* 32(1): 153–66. https://doi.org/10.1016/j.electstud.2012.12.001.

Thomas, Melanee, and Lisa Lambert. 2017. "Private Mom versus Political Dad? Communications of Parental Status in the 41st Canadian Parliament." In *Mothers and Others: The Role of Parenthood in Politics*, edited by Melanee Thomas and Amanda Bittner, 135–54. Vancouver: UBC Press.

Thomas, Melanee, and Lisa Young. 2014. "Women (Not) in Politics." In *Canadian Politics*, 6th ed., edited by James Bickerton and Alain Gagnon, 373–94. Toronto: University of Toronto Press.

Thomas, Sue. 1991. "The Impact of Women on State Legislative Policies." *Journal of Politics* 53(4): 958–76. https://doi.org/10.2307/2131862.

Thompson, Mark. 2002. "Female Leadership of Democratic Transitions in Asia." *Pacific Affairs* 75(4): 535–55. https://doi.org/10.2307/4127345.

Thomson, Robert, Terry Royed, Elin Naurin, Joaquín Artés, Rory Costello, Laurenz Ennser Jedenastik, et al. 2017. "The Fulfillment of Parties' Election Pledges: A Comparative Study on the Impact of Power Sharing." *American Journal of Political Science* 61(3): 527–42. https://doi.org/10.1111/ajps.12313.

Tolley, Erin. 2011. "Do Women 'Do Better' in Municipal Politics? Electoral Representation across Three Levels of Government." *Canadian Journal of Political Science* 44(3): 573–94. https://doi.org/10.1017/s0008423911000503.

– 2016. *Framed: Media and the Coverage of Race in Canadian Politics*. Vancouver: UBC Press.

Tremblay, Manon. 2012. "Women's Access to Cabinets in Canada: Assessing the Role of Some Institutional Variables." *Canadian Political Science Review* 6(2–3): 159–70. https://ojs.unbc.ca/index.php/cpsr/article/view/241.

Trimble, Linda. 2017. *Ms. Prime Minister: Gender, Media and Leadership*. Toronto: University of Toronto Press.

Trimble, Linda, and Jane Arscott. 2003. *Still Counting: Women in Politics across Canada*. Toronto: University of Toronto Press.

Trimble, Linda, Jennifer Curtin, Angelia Wagner, Meagan Auer, V.K.G. Woodman, and Bethan Owens. 2019. "Gender Novelty and Personalized News Coverage in Australia and Canada." *International Political Science Review*, 25 October (online). https://doi.org/10.1177%2F0192512119876083.

Trimble, Linda, Daisy Raphael, Shannon Sampert, Angelia Wagner, and Bailey Gerrits. 2015. "Politicizing Bodies: Hegemonic Masculinity, Heteronormativity, and Racism in News Representations of Canadian Political Party Leadership Contests." *Women's Studies in Communication* 38(3): 314–30. https://doi.org/10.1080/07491409.2015.1062836.

Trimble, Linda, Angelia Wagner, Shannon Sampert, Daisy Raphael, and Bailey Gerrits. 2013. "Is It Personal? Gendered Mediation in Newspaper Coverage of Canadian National Party Leadership Contests, 1975–2012." *International Journal of Press/Politics* 18(4): 462–81. https://doi.org/10.1177/1940161213495455.

Tripp, Aili Mari, and Alica Kang. 2008. "The Global Impact of Quotas: On the Fast Track to Increased Female Legislative Representation." *Comparative Political Studies* 41(3): 338–61. https://doi.org/10.1177/0010414006297342.

True, Jacqui, Nicole George, Sara Niner, and Swati Parashar. 2013. *Women's Political Participation in Asia-Pacific*. New York: SSRC Conflict Prevention and Peace Forum.

True, Jacqui, and Michael Mintrom. 2001. "Transnational Networks and Policy Diffusion: The Case of Gender Mainstreaming." *International Studies Quarterly* 45(1): 27–57. https://doi.org/10.1111/0020-8833.00181.

Truex, Rory. 2016. *Making Autocracy Work: Representation and Responsiveness in Modern China*. New York: Cambridge University Press.

Truth and Reconciliation Commission of Canada. 2015. *Honouring the Truth, Reconciling the Future: Summary of the Final Report of the Truth and Reconciliation Commission of Canada*. Ottawa: Truth and Reconciliation Commission of Canada.

Trynacity, Kim. 2018. "'A Wake-Up Call': Documents Detail Litany of Threats against Premier Rachel Notley." *CBC News*, 4 May.

Tsebelis, George. 1995. "Decision Making in Political Systems: Veto Players in Presidentialism, Parliamentarism, Multicameralism and Multipartyism." *British Journal of Political Science* 25(3): 289–325. https://doi.org/10.1017/s0007123400007225.

– 1999. "Veto Players and Law Production in Parliamentary Democracies: An Empirical Analysis." *American Political Science Review* 93(3): 591–608. https://doi.org/10.2307/2585576.

– 2002. "Veto Players and Institutional Analysis." *Governance: An International Journal of Policy and Administration* 13(4): 441–74.

United Kingdom Parliament. 2018. *Independent Complaints and Grievance Scheme Delivery Report*. July. London: Independent Complaints and Grievance Policy Programme Team.

– 2019. Standing Orders Addendum, S.O. 150 (12). January.

United Nations Development Programme. 2010. *Women's Representation in Local Government in Asia-Pacific: Status Report 2010*. Bangkok: United Nations

Development Programme. https://www.asia-pacific.undp.org/content
/rbap/en/home/library/democratic_governance/women-local-gov-status
-report-2010.html.

– 2012. "Women's Representation in Leadership in Viet Nam." United Nations
Development Programme.

United States Congress. 2017–18. S.3749, Congressional Accountability Act of
1995 Reform Act.

United States Office of Congressional Workplace Rights. 2019. Brown Bag
Lunch Series, CAA Reform Act. Presented 23 January.

Van Hightower, Nikki R. 1977. "The Recruitment of Women for Public
Office." *American Politics Quarterly* 5(3): 301–14. https://doi.org/10.1177
/1532673x7700500304.

Volden, Craig, Alan Wiseman, and Dana Wittmer. 2013. "When Are Women
More Effective Lawmakers than Men?" *American Journal of Political Science*
57(2): 326–41. https://doi.org/10.1111/ajps.12010.

Wagner, Angelia, Linda Trimble, and Shannon Sampert. 2018. "One Smart
Politician: Gendered Media Discourses of Political Leadership in Canada."
Canadian Journal of Political Science, 52(1): 141–62. https://doi.org/10.1017
/s0008423918000471.

Wagner, Angelia, Linda Trimble, Shannon Sampert, and Bailey Gerrits. 2017.
"Gender, Competitiveness and Candidate Visibility in Newspaper Coverage
of Canadian Party Leadership Contests." *International Journal of Press/Politics*
22(4): 471–89. https://doi.org/10.1177/1940161217723150.

Wasserman, Melanie. 2018. *Gender Differences in Politician Persistence*. Rochester:
Social Science Research Network.

Watkins-Hayes, Celeste. 2009. *The New Welfare Bureaucrats: Entanglements of
Race, Class, and Policy Reform*. Chicago: University of Chicago Press.

Weeks, Ana Catalano, and Lisa Baldez. 2014. "Quotas and Qualifications: The
Impact of Gender Quota Laws on the Qualifications of Legislators in the
Italian Parliament." *European Political Science Review* 7(1): 119–44. https://
doi.org/10.1017/s1755773914000095.

Weeks, Jeffrey. 2007. *The World We Have Won*. London: Routledge.

Weldon, Laurel S. 2002. *Protest, Policy and the Problem of Violence against Women:
A Cross-National Comparison*. Pittsburgh: University of Pittsburgh Press.

Wickham, Hadley. 2014. "Rvest: Easy Webscraping with R." https://blog
.rstudio.com/2014/11/24/rvest-easy-web-scraping-with-r/.

Wilson, Clark, and Roberto Felix Carlos. 2014. "Do Women Representatives Re-
gender Legislative Bureaucracy? Assessing the Effect of Representative Sex
on Women's Presence among US Congressional Staff." *Journal of Legislative
Studies* 20(2): 216–35. https://doi.org/10.1080/13572334.2013.833392.

Wilson-Raybould, Jody. 2019. *From Where I Stand: Rebuilding Indigenous Nations
for a Stronger Canada*. Vancouver: Purich.

Witt, Linda, Karen M. Paget, and Glenna Matthews. 1994. *Running as a Woman: Gender and Power in American Politics*. New York: Free Press.

Wittig, Monique. 1980. "The Straight Mind." *Feminist Issues* 1(1): 103 11. https://doi.org/10.1007/bf02685561.

Wolbrecht, Christina, and David E. Campbell. 2007. "Leading by Example: Female Members of Parliament as Political Role Models." *American Journal of Political Science* 51(4): 921–39. https://doi.org/10.1111/j.1540-5907.2007 .00289.x.

Women's Environment and Development Organization. 2007. *Women Candidates and Campaign Finance*. http://wedo.org/wp-content/uploads /women-candidates-and-campaign-finance-report-final.pdf.

Woodward, Allison. 2004. "Building Velvet Triangles: Gender and Informal Governance." In *Informal Governance in the European Union*, edited by Thomas Christiansen and Simon Piattoni, 76–94. Cheltenham: Elgar.

Young, L. 2013. "Slow to Change: Women in the House of Commons." In *Stalled: The Representation of Women in Canadian Governments*, edited by Linda Trimble, Jane Arscott, and Manon Tremblay, 253–71. Vancouver: UBC Press.

Contributors

Vincent Arel-Bundock is an associate professor of political science at the Université de Montréal.

Tiffany D. Barnes is an associate professor in the Department of Political Science at the University of Kentucky.

Sylvia Bashevkin is a professor of political science at the University of Toronto and the author, most recently, of *Women as Foreign Policy Leaders*.

Victoria Beall is a graduate student with the Political Science Department at the University of Kentucky.

André Blais is a professor in the Department of Political Science at the Université de Montréal, where he holds a research chair in electoral studies.

Robyn Bourgeois is a mixed-race Cree woman born and raised in Syilx and Splats'in territories of British Columbia and connected through marriage and her children to the Six Nations of the Grand River. An associate professor in the Centre for Women's and Gender Studies, Dr. Bourgeois currently serves at Brock University's Vice Provost, Indigenous Engagement.

Nadia E. Brown is a professor in the Department of Government at Georgetown University and director of the Women's and Gender Studies program. She is the lead editor of the journal *Politics, Groups, and Identities*.

Cheryl Collier is an associate professor in the Department of Political Science at the University of Windsor.

Kelly Dittmar is an associate professor of political science at Rutgers-Camden and scholar and director of research at the Center for American Women and Politics, a unit of the Eagleton Institute of Politics at Rutgers-New Brunswick.

Julie Dolan is a professor of political science at Macalester College, St. Paul, MN.

Susan Franceschet is a professor of political science at the University of Calgary and co-editor of *Politics & Gender*.

Roosmarijn de Geus is a postdoctoral researcher with the Nuffield Politics Research Centre at Nuffield College, the University of Oxford.

Elizabeth Goodyear-Grant is an associate professor in the Department of Political Studies and director of the Canadian Opinion Research Archive at Queen's University.

Magda Hinojosa is a professor in the School of Politics and Global Studies at Arizona State University.

Miki Caul Kittilson is a professor in the School of Politics and Global Studies at Arizona State University.

Shan-Jan Sarah Liu is a lecturer in gender and politics in the School of Social and Political Science at the University of Edinburgh.

Peter John Loewen is a professor at the Department of Political Science and the Munk School of Global Affairs & Public Policy at the University of Toronto. He is also a senior fellow at Massey College and a fellow with the Public Policy Forum.

Chantal Maillé is a professor of women's studies at the Simone de Beauvoir Institute, Concordia University.

Diana Z. O'Brien is the Albert Thomas Associate Professor of Political Science at Rice University.

Malliga Och is an assistant professor of global studies at Idaho State University.

Tracey Raney is an associate professor in the Department of Politics and Public Administration at Ryerson University in Toronto.

Semra Sevi is a PhD candidate in the Department of Political Science at the Université de Montréal.

Paru Shah is an associate professor of political science at the University of Wisconsin–Milwaukee.

Semilla Stripp graduated from Macalester College in 2019, and is currently a research assistant with the Associated Press-NORC Center for Public Affairs Research at NORC at the University of Chicago.

Netina Tan is an associate professor in the Department of Political Science at McMaster University.

Erin Tolley is the Canada Research Chair in Gender, Race, and Inclusive Politics and an associate professor of political science at Carleton University.

Manon Tremblay is a professor of political science at the University of Ottawa.

Linda Trimble is a professor in the Department of Political Science at the University of Alberta, Edmonton.

Alexandra M. Williams is a PhD student at the School of Politics and Global Studies, Arizona State University.